Revolution from Within

STUDIES OF COMMUNISM IN TRANSITION

General Editor: Ronald J. Hill
Professor of Comparative Government
and Fellow of Trinity College
Dublin, Ireland

Studies of Communism in Transition is an important series which applies academic analysis and clarity of thought to the recent traumatic events in Eastern and Central Europe. As many of the preconceptions of the past half century are cast aside, newly independent and autonomous sovereign states are being forced to address long-term, organic problems which had been suppressed by, or appeased within, the Communist system of rule.

The series is edited under the sponsorship of Lorton House, an independent charitable association which exists to promote the academic study of communism and related concepts.

Revolution from Within

The Hungarian Socialist Workers' Party and the Collapse of Communism

---

Patrick H. O'Neil

Assistant Professor of Politics and Government, University of Puget Sound, Tacoma, United States

STUDIES OF COMMUNISM IN TRANSITION

Edward Elgar

Cheltenham, UK • Northampton, MA, USA

Published by
Edward Elgar Publishing Limited
8 Lansdown Place
Cheltenham
Glos GL50 2HU
UK

Edward Elgar Publishing, Inc.
6 Market Street
Northampton
Massachusetts 01060
USA

A catalogue record for this book
is available from the British Library

Library of Congress Cataloguing in Publication Data

O'Neil, Patrick H., 1966–
Revolution from within: the Hungarian Socialist Workers' Party and the collapse of communism / Patrick H. O'Neil.
(Studies of communism in transition series)
Includes bibliographical references.
1. Magyar Szocialista Munkáspárt—History. 2. Hungary—Politics and government—1945–1989. I. Title. II. Series: Studies of communism in transition.
JN2191.S920646 1998
324.2439'074'09048—dc21 97–35438
CIP

ISBN 1 85898 766 0

Electronic typesetting by Lorton Hall
Printed and bound in Great Britain by Bookcraft (Bath) Ltd

For Jayne

Contents

Acknowledgements ix
Introduction xi

PART I THEORETICAL APPROACHES

1 Transitions, Institutions and State Socialism 3

PART II THE HUNGARIAN CASE

2 State Socialism and the Intelligentsia in Eastern Europe: Hungary in Comparative Institutional Perspective, 1948–1988 27
3 The Rise of the Reform Circles 71
4 The Organization of the Reform Circle Movement and the Party in Disorder 115
5 The Final Party Congress and the Reform Alliance: Victory or Defeat? 158

PART III CONCLUSIONS

6 Institutional Order and the Path of Political Change: Hungary and Eastern Europe 201

Appendix 1 A Note on Primary Sources 221
Appendix 2 List of Abbreviations 223
Select Bibliography 225
Index 245

Acknowledgements

This work would not have been possible without the assistance of the following individuals, whose comments and criticism on earlier variants of this manuscript were of inestimable value: Professors Jack Bielasiak, James Christoph, Jeffrey Hart and Paul Marer, of Indiana University. As committee chair and general mentor during my doctoral studies, Professor Bielasiak helped guide me through the travails of graduate school, providing support and encouragement for my work. I appreciate his support. Indeed, all members of the committee have had an important impact on my intellectual development during the course of my graduate studies at Indiana.

Initial investigation of this topic began with the help of a grant provided by the Indiana Center on Global Change and World Peace, which allowed the author to spend two months in Hungary during the summer of 1991. During the period 1992–93 research for this study was supported in part by a Fulbright–Hays Grant from the Center for International Education of the US Department of Education, as well as a grant from the International Research and Exchanges Board (IREX), with funds provided by the United States Department of State. Assistance was also provided by the Woodrow Wilson International Center for Scholars by means of a short-term research grant, as well as through participation in the Training Seminar for Junior Scholars, held jointly by the Wilson Center and the Joint Committee on Eastern Europe of the American Council of Learned Societies. None of these organizations is responsible for the views herein expressed.

Research affiliation during the course of my stay in Hungary was graciously provided by the Department of Political Science at the Budapest University of Economic Sciences. I would like to thank all of those in the department – in particular László Vass, András Lánczi and László Szarvas – for their support of my work, assistance in times of frustration, and limitless hospitality. Finally, I would like to thank

Attila Ágh, head of that programme, for making my affiliation with the department possible and for helping me through the labyrinth of the socialist past.

Patrick O'Neil
September 1997

Introduction

Communism begets and nurtures its own dissidents. (György Konrád)

If one were to define the central moment of the post-war era so far it would likely be the collapse of state socialism in Eastern Europe and the Soviet Union. Across the region and within a relatively short period, once seemingly indestructible systems vanished within a matter of months, weeks, days. While social scientists were left scrambling for responses for this unanticipated event, much of the complex dynamics of the collapse were lost amid the din of sweeping generalizations regarding the 'death' of communism. Hope that distance could provide perspective has also meant a decline in interest in the actual transition process itself. Since initial events, much research in the area has moved on to the study of political consolidation and other related topics, foused upon how post-socialist Eastern Europe may integrate into the world capitalist economy and achieve the distinction of liberal democratic nation-states.

But the questions of the transition remain. The most basic concerns the very catalyst of these events: why did socialism in the region collapse? Answers to this puzzle tend to cluster around the bankruptcy of the Soviet system as a whole, the retention of Eastern Europe as a military buffer becoming an expensive and increasingly outdated concept, and the rise of a new generation of modernizers within the Soviet Union who chose to tinker with forces they could not control. Equally intriguing is the question of why such a system should have disintegrated so thoroughly in such a short period of time. The unexpected manner of socialism's decline in the area is truly extraordinary, and suggests larger processes at work which may illuminate our study of transitions as a whole. Finally, an important question that has been neglected in this debate, one which will be central to this study, is that of modality, that is, investigating the particular and differing trajectories that these transition events have taken.

Transition processes in Eastern Europe have been characterized by diversity in their timing, unfolding and central characteristics: the negotiated developments in Poland and Hungary, which had already begun in 1988 if not earlier, as opposed to the rapid collapse of regimes in East Germany and Czechoslovakia, the ambiguous 'revolution' of Romania, or the palace coup in Bulgaria. Such factors point to fundamental differences in state socialism within the region and contradict the external appearance of uniformity among these political structures as replicated from one East European country to the next. That these systems looked virtually identical from a superficial organizational standpoint, but behaved in radically different ways, is puzzling - what are we to make of this? The transition from socialism in Hungary provides a good case study in this regard, in that developments there point to the extent to which our current theoretical understanding of events cannot wholly capture and explain the actual unraveling of state socialism in the region.

OVERVIEW: THE HUNGARIAN TRANSITION AND THE ROLE OF THE 'REFORM CIRCLES'

The central factor that sets the collapse of the ruling Hungarian Socialist Workers' Party (*Magyar Szocialista Munkáspárt*, or MSZMP) apart from other cases of transition in Eastern Europe is both the extent to which the regime was the initiator of its own transition as well as the degree to which the party acted as its own greatest enemy. The unusual manner of the collapse of socialism in Hungary as an internally-driven process, and the effect which this had on the transition to democracy leads one to rethink dominant analytical concepts regarding state socialism in particular as well as political transitions in general.

By mid-1988, with the removal of János Kádár (head of the party since 1956) from the position of general secretary along with many of his hardline supporters from the Politburo, the neo-conservative élite of the party, led by the new general secretary and former prime minister, Károly Grósz, were in ascension. Many in and outside the party were hopeful that the MSZMP was about to embark on a new period of limited political and economic reform, which would modernize existing institutions, creating greater flexibility in many spheres of decision-making and a more rational - although still authoritarian and state socialist - political system. Despite such hopes, however, over the course of the next six months political activity stagnated. The new general secretary, it appeared, was unable to take the necessary steps forward, pragmatic on minor issues and interested in cleaning house but unwilling to confront the deepening national crisis with appropriate action. Opposition forces had begun to coalesce within the country since late 1987, but their impact remained minor and limited to the capital. By all accounts it appeared that Hungary was politically adrift with no clear course set.

Out of this period of stalemate rose a new political force. Whereas traditionally most characterizations of socialist systems centred upon the conflict between 'rulers' and hostile segments of (civil) society or 'dissidents' (this characterization can be extended to analyses of authoritarianism as a whole), by late 1988 there began to develop in Hungary a new mass opposition force *within* the party itself, committed to saving socialism by opposing the Soviet 'bolshevik' system that had clearly gone awry.

This new force was that of the reform circles. They emerged in the southeastern town of Szeged in late 1988, and Rudolf Tőkés has described their initial formation as 'an important day in the history of the old regime's collapse'.[1] Elemér Hankiss similarly notes the democratization of the party itself began to take shape 'only when the first "reform circles" were formed within municipal party organizations; on 15 Apr[il] thirty reform circles held their first national meeting in Kecskemét and adopted a radically reformist platform; by mid-May, the movement had spread to the whole country'.[2] This new movement of reform circles was characterized by the preponderance of party intellectuals within the movement's ranks, their lack of important positions within the party even at the local level, and the origination and development of the movement outside Budapest, the dominant metropolis.

The reform circles increasingly pressured the party leadership for greater reform, arguing that the only way to save socialism was to break fully with the past, develop political institutions that would

1. Rudolf L. Tőkés, *Hungary's Negotiated Revolution: Economic Reform, Social Change, and Political Succession, 1957–1990* (Cambridge: Cambridge University Press, 1996), 296.
2. Elemér Hankiss, *East European Alternatives* (Oxford: Clarendon, 1990), 221, n. 29.

provide basic human rights for all, and end the party's monopoly on power. Functioning contrary to the most basic rules of the party, the reform circles began to link up horizontally, coordinating their actions and exchanging ideas without the benefit of any hierarchical leadership. This attack caught the party as a whole unawares. Indeed, given the historical cleavage between the city and countryside – Budapest with its 20 per cent of the nation's population and its resulting inordinate influence on the rest of the tiny country (this the historical legacy of an imperial capital that has lost its empire) – the activity of the reform circles was initially dismissed by the MSZMP élite as the activity of a group of noisy but unimportant rural party rank and file.

They were mistaken. The reform circles continued to grow in size and power, demanding greater concessions to the population and that the MSZMP negotiate with other nascent political movements on democratization and free elections. Utilizing their unique position within the MSZMP, they brought the very structure of the party to bear against itself. The reform circles' horizontal organization prevented them from being effectively controlled by the rigidly vertical party structure, while their activity below that of the *metropole* gave them the distance necessary to function beyond the effective purview of central power at Budapest. The reform circles' dogged activity pushed the party further and further towards making concessions and helped rend the tightly woven fabric of party discipline, sowing factionalism and confusion within the party ranks at all levels. This in turn only increased the political space in which opposition forces outside the party could organize and strengthen.

By late 1989, tensions within the party had become such that the leadership acceded to reform circle demands that an extraordinary party congress be held to reorientate the party to developments within the country and the socialist camp as a whole. Mobilizing their forces, the reform circles managed to have a significant portion of their members and supporters elected as delegates to the congress, creating the largest single bloc of delegates. With the help of both sympathizers and opportunists who saw the momentum shifting to the reformers within the party, the reform circle delegates and their supporters effectively voted the MSZMP out of existence, ousting Grósz and numerous other hardliners. From the ashes of this congress rose the Hungarian Socialist

Party (MSZP), shorn of its Marxist-Leninist dogmas and committed to free and open elections.

The reform circles had won, but their personal victory seemed pyrrhic. The definite break of the party with the past was tainted by the large number of former conservatives who stayed in the party in the hope of maintaining their old powers and benefits, and this contributed to the MSZP's relatively poor showing in the 1990 elections. However, the reform circles had been in part responsible for something much greater: in the words of Annamária Telekes and János Rechnitzer, alongside the role of the democratic opposition and party reform leadership, 'the MSZMP reform circles' role was definitive in the collapse of the party-state', something with which a number of other Hungarian social scientists and politicians agree.[3]

This particular trajectory of collapse in turn influenced the construction of liberal democracy, shaping the powers and patterns of political and economic life. While largely ignored in the new, competing myths of the Hungarian transition, the reform circles were crucial in dissolving the party from within, leading to an incremental, piecemeal transition quite different from those seen across Eastern Europe.

This case is a puzzle: why did such a movement develop within the communist party of Hungary? Why did it occur in Hungary and not elsewhere? Why did it have an important impact on the party, which let a section of its rank and file 'get away' from them? Although a single case, the investigation of this event serves a comparative heuristic function, in that the exceptional case of Hungary will be used to inform theoretical concepts regarding transition events in Eastern Europe and elsewhere, both in terms of the trajectory of collapse as well as the political systems which emerge from such changes.

3. Annamária Telekes and János Rechnitzner, 'Megmozdult a vidék! [The countryside has stirred!]', in Sándor Kurtán, Péter Sándor and László Vass (eds), *Magyarország politikai évkönyve 1990* (Budapest: AULA-OMIKK, 1990), 152; see also István Stumpf, 'Pártosodás '89 [Party development 1989]', in ibid., 387; Imre Pozsgay, '1989 – sorsdöntő lépés a demokrácia felé [1989: A decisive step toward democracy]', in ibid., 57; László Bruszt, '1989: The Negotiated Revolution in Hungary', in András Bozóki, András Körösényi and George Schöpflin (eds), *Post-Communist Transition: Emerging Pluralism in Hungary* (London: Pinter, 1992), 53–4, 57–8.

OUTLINE OF THE INSTITUTIONAL APPROACH

This study argues that although the development of the reform circle movement in Hungary can be seen as exceptional, diverging from the other patterns of transition in Eastern Europe, the case points out short-comings in existing approaches to the development, replication and decline of state socialist and authoritarian regimes. These problems, however, can be rectified by (rather than replaced with) sociological theories of organizations – notably, those dealing with the process of institutionalization and institutional effects. Institutional theory incorporates a rich literature which has only been glimpsed in the discipline of political science as a whole and state socialist studies within it. The insights provided by this area of research can help pave the way towards general explanations for political activity in the region: explanations that account for the variations within state socialism in practice and in its subsequent collapse.

Earlier (and in many cases still dominant) organizational perspectives have tended to emphasize the internal dynamics of organizations, largely divorced from their broader external context. Organizations are taken to be utilitarian and largely rational constructs, tools in the hands of broader political forces. In contrast, institutional perspectives emphasize the impact of institutions themselves on social interaction, and the critical role of the external environment – its existing forms, patterns, norms and routines – in this process, shaping the structure, procedures and outputs of organizations seated within their matrix.

The emphasis on this interaction between organizations and the environment is a central concept in institutional arguments, and especially relevant for a study of Eastern Europe in particular and political transitions in general. Institutional approaches assert that legitimacy and stability are functions of the interaction between organization and environment, as the organization is influenced by external forces and their attempts to manipulate it to their own advantage. Organizations are consequently shaped by the existing environmental factors as well as by the objectives and resources of the organization itself. This connection to the external environment is thus a central means of organizational replication, forming the mechanism by which organizations become institutionalized.

However, institutionalization carries with it attendant risks, in that this same process can also threaten to subvert existing means–ends relationships within the organization, whereby the means – the institution itself – and its ongoing perpetuation become the key normative values, overshadowing original objectives. Organizational relationships which follow emphasize the maintenance of existing structures rather than their continuing evaluation, reconceptualization and correction in pursuit of external goals. The result is the loss of organizational instrumentality and flexibility. Institutionalization at this level thus shuts out the option for organizational reform, breeding rigidity and unreconcilable inconsistencies between objectives and practice.

Such extreme institutionalization within political organizations can be most clearly seen in the party-states of Eastern Europe. In these cases, autocratic systems were direct institutional replications, subjugating domestic environmental factors to the demands of the Soviet model. But, as a coercively installed external ruling order, the Soviet organizational model in Eastern Europe did not so easily mesh with the domestic social environment in each of these widely different countries, creating pressures to realign these systems with the particular demands or opportunities of each context. Consequently, even with the imposition of the Soviet model, unique patterns of replication – attempts at domestic institutionalization – soon emerged in each country, depending on the social constraints and opportunities confronting the party leadership, the nature of the local environment, the individuals involved and the historical junctures where these patterns were set in motion.

One striking example where this differentiation can be seen is in the reaction of the East European party-states to the process of modernization and the development of an intelligentsia class. All of these systems were by the 1960s faced with the question of how to respond to the creation of this new dynamic within the external environment, which, it was hoped, could address the inefficiencies of state socialism if somehow properly harnessed. At the same time it was feared that their integration could also threaten the stability of the system as a whole, by introducing into the ruling structure a segment of members whose loyalty to state socialism as an *institution* (as opposed to socialism as a concept) was open to question. Consequently, attempts to co-opt this sector led to internal political tensions, eventually resulting in a return to more rigid policies and the marginalization of the intelligentsia.

Only in Hungary was this process of co-optation continued, albeit cautiously. Here it was hoped that, given the disaster of 1956, the participation of the intelligentsia in the party would contribute to institutional legitimacy by generating an image of party rule as one of pragmatism and reform. This pattern served the MSZMP well until the 1980s. However, once Soviet validation for the system eroded, the party faced less an external challenge from society at large than a threat from within – namely, the reform circles.

By seeking to define its relationship to the domestic environment through co-optation and limited technocratic reform rather than through rigid ideological standards and coercion, the Hungarian party in effect created its own internal opposition, a Trojan horse that played a critical role in undermining internal cohesion and authority. This in turn helped pave the way for an incremental, negotiated transition, strongly affecting the manner in which new political parties arose and how post-communist political institutions were constructed.

These arguments have implications for political transitions as a whole. They assert that by incorporating an analysis of institutions and the institutionalization process into our study of authoritarian rule, examining both the source and effect of comparable differences in *degrees* of institutionalization as well as the particular characteristics of *kinds* of institutionalization which result, we shall gain a better sense of the structure of non-democratic orders, the manner of their eventual end, and their influence on new structures that take their place.

In other words, institutional relationships have unforeseen effects on the authoritarian order and its eventual collapse, for they shape the context in which transition events are to occur, the resources open to state and societal actors, and consequently the likely modes of political change which are to follow. The nature of political institutions and the matrix in which they are seated, I argue, do not determine political outcomes but rather create a set of contours which is likely to influence such events. This, in effect, harkens back to what Karl Marx himself pointed out, in his famous statement that 'men make their own history, but they do not make it just as they please; they do not make it under the circumstances chosen by themselves, but under circumstances directly found, given and transmitted from the past'.[4]

4. 'The Eighteenth Brumaire of Louis Bonaparte', in Robert C. Tucker (ed.), *The Marx–Engels Reader* (New York: W.W. Norton, 1972), 437.

PART I

Theoretical Approaches

1. Transitions, Institutions and State Socialism

CURRENT PERSPECTIVES ON AUTHORITARIAN TRANSITION

The events of 1989 in Eastern Europe have been a catalyst for a surge in interest within political science regarding the factors which bring about transitions from authoritarianism and, we hope, towards consolidated democracy - events which do not necessarily follow one another. This is not to say that this area of study is new, as it dates back to the early work of Seymour Martin Lipset, Samuel Huntington and Robert Dahl, and continues to Guillermo O'Donnell, Philippe C. Schmitter and Laurence Whitehead's milestone work *Transitions from Authoritarian Rule* and Juan J. Linz and Alfred Stepan's *Problems of Democratic Transition and Consolidation*, an impressive study of South America, Southern and post-communist Europe.[1] Among much of this diverse

1. The literature on democratic transitions and post-transition consolidation has grown dramatically over the past decade. Notable works include (but are by no means limited to) Guillermo O'Donnell, Philippe C. Schmitter and Laurence Whitehead (eds), *Transitions from Authoritarian Rule*, 4 vols (Baltimore, MD: Johns Hopkins University Press, 1986); Samuel P. Huntington, *The Third Wave* (Norman, OK: University of Oklahoma, 1991); Stephan Haggard and Robert Kaufman, *The Political Economy of Democratic Transitions* (Princeton, NJ: Princeton University Press, 1995): Adam Przeworski, *Democracy and the Market: Political and Economic Reforms in Eastern Europe and Latin America* (Chicago, IL: University of Chicago Press, 1991); Giuseppe DiPalma, *To Craft Democracies: An Essay on Democratic Transitions* (Berkeley: University of California Press, 1990); John Higley and Richard Gunther (eds), *Élites and Democratic Consolidation in Latin America and Southern Europe* (Cambridge: Cambridge University Press, 1992); Richard Gunther (ed.), *The Politics of Democratic Consolidation* (Baltimore, MD: Johns Hopkins University Press, 1995); Nancy Bermeo (ed.), *Liberalization and Democratization: Change in the Soviet Union and Eastern Europe* (Baltimore, MD: Johns Hopkins University Press, 1992); David Held (ed.), *Prospects for Democracy: North, South, East, West* (Stanford, CA: Stanford University Press, 1993); Yossi Shain and Juan J. Linz (eds), *Between States: Interim Governments in Democratic Transitions*

literature a dividing line can be traced, which is commonly set forth as follows: 'structuralist' arguments tend to stress macro-level conditions (typically, economic development and the resulting process of modernization) that are indispensable to the creation of democracy from a non-democratic form of political control. In contrast, 'process' arguments focus to a greater extent on the means and patterns by which actual authoritarian dissolution takes place, concentrating on the interaction of élite political figures in the success or failure of such events to forge a stable democracy.

The two sets of arguments appear to stand in opposition to each other, juxtaposing levels of analysis that seem mutually exclusive. Structuralism, which saw its heyday in the 1960s under the rubric of modernization theory, is often criticized in that economic development and political democratization are taken as largely axiomatic. As states develop economic structures similar to those of the West (this itself is a questionable proposition) their social and political orders will similarly undergo a transformation, shedding their pre-industrial, authoritarian fetters. Within this certainty, the question of the transition event, that is, how a nation-state moves from an authoritarian system to a democratic one, is accorded little consideration; given structuralism's emphasis on broad conditions of development and the seemingly inevitable democratic outcome, the actual process of political change merits little discussion in itself. In a sense, democracy would not be constructed, but rather would come about as a matter of course.[2] For example, while

(Cambridge: Cambridge University Press, 1995); and Juan J. Linz and Alfred Stepan, *Problems of Democratic Transition and Consolidation: Southern Europe, South America, and Post-Communist Europe* (Baltimore, MD: Johns Hopkins University Press, 1996). See also the compilation of important articles in Geoffrey Pridham (ed.), *Transitions to Democracy* (Aldershot: Dartmouth, 1995).

2. Some of the best-known examples in this area include W.W. Rostow, *The Stages of Economic Growth* (Cambridge: Cambridge University Press, 1960); Cyril Black, *Dynamics of Modernization: A Study in Comparative History* (New York: Harper & Row, 1966); Gabriel Almond and James S. Coleman (eds), *The Politics of the Developing Areas* (Princeton, NJ: Princeton University Press, 1960); Seymour Martin Lipset, *Political Man: The Social Bases of Politics* (Garden City, NY: Anchor Books and Doubleday, 1960); for an excellent overview of structuralist modernization literature see Andrew C. Janos, *Politics and Paradigms: Changing Theories of Change in Political Science* (Stanford, CA: Stanford University Press, 1986) and Howard J. Wiarda, 'Comparative Politics Past and Present', in Howard J. Wiarda (ed.), *New Directions in Comparative Politics* (Boulder, CO: Westview Press, 1985), 3–25.

Lipset's milestone piece in this area, 'Some Social Requisites of Democracy', discussed at length the social and economic forces that could promote and sustain democracies, very little attention was paid to how exactly societies moved away from authoritarian systems of government. Democratic change was linked to such variables as higher education, greater per capita wealth, and other factors that would create pressure for democracy once these levels began to approach those of the West. However, the elaboration of *why* did not also create an understanding of *how*, that is to say the mode of transition itself.[3] In other words, in structuralist terms the actual path taken from authoritarianism was less important than the building blocks of modernization that would bring about and sustain such a movement.

While this is not to say that individuals and patterns of indigenous organization were rejected outright, a deterministic view of human development does run through structuralist literature, with progress and modernization viewed as the primary source of an incipient global liberal capitalist culture. Yet overall, this approach does not concern itself with how and in what manner political actors themselves would undertake – or abjure – the dismantling of an authoritarian order. This question would become critical to a later generation of scholars on democratization, particularly as modernization theory began to take a beating in the late 1960s and early 1970s when confronted with the unravelling of many developing states, and worse, the rise of relatively 'modernized' yet still authoritarian political systems. Yet this move away from macro-level analysis has not in fact been absolute, as this perspective continues to be updated and utilized by scholars. Samuel Huntington's recent work on the subject, while stressing the context-specificity of variables that might foster democratization, focuses on macro-level forces such as economic developments, international relations and demonstration effects.[4] Other scholars have argued that the original assumptions of structuralism remain sound and in fact have

3. Although Lipset did note the role of individual actors in shaping 'institutions and events in directions that reduce or increase the chance for the development and survival of democracy': Seymour Martin Lipset, 'Some Social Requisites of Democracy: Economic Development and Political Legitimacy', *American Political Science Review* **53** (March 1959): 103.
4. Samuel P. Huntington, 'Will More Countries Become Democratic?', *Political Science Quarterly* **99** (Summer 1984): 193–218, and idem, *The Third Wave*, esp. 45–6.

been validated by recent developments in Eastern Europe, some linking events in the region primarily to relations in the world economy.[5]

After a number of years during which democracy seemed unlikely to gain further ground, a new wave of political transitions brought scholars back to the same questions that had initially interested modernization theorists some decades before. However, in contrast to structuralism, a new set of process-orientated views began to emerge, concerned specifically with how democracies could be made, by whom, and to what effect. In direct contrast to structuralism, process-based views began to argue that macro-level forces, while present, do not play as vital a role as previously thought in authoritarian collapse or democratic construction; the presence or absence of certain macro-level conditions do not function as necessary or sufficient variables in the collapse of authoritarianism and the creation of democracy. As O'Donnell and Schmitter argue, while 'broad structures filter down to affect the behavior of groups and individuals' at some points in the transition, 'their mediations are looser, and their impacts more indeterminate, than in normal circumstances'. As a result, to focus on such forces in an attempt to understand transition processes would be 'an act of misguided faith'.[6] Transitions are therefore better seen as sudden and unpredictable occurrences which push individual actors on to the centre stage while larger constructs are in a state of flux.

What is thus central to transitions literature are the objectives and calculations of the political élite. These individuals, representative of dominant forces in regime and society, are the relevant actors of the transition. The élite bring about the political 'opening', they interact and interpret each other's positions and objectives, and they negotiate on behalf of their constituents to secure a new political situation that the polity can live with. Following this research, some later contributions have utilized a rational-choice framework to explain the interaction between opposing forces, or investigated the role of institutional 'crafting' in the construction of democratic systems that will succeed.[7]

5. See, for example, Lucian W. Pye, 'Political Science and the Crisis of Authoritarianism', *American Political Science Review* **84** (March 1990): 3–19, and Jadwiga Staniszkis, *The Dynamics of the Breakthrough in Eastern Europe* (Berkeley, CA: University of California Press, 1991).
6. Guillermo O'Donnell and Philippe C. Schmitter, *Transitions from Authoritarian Rule*, vol. 4, *Tentative Conclusions about Uncertain Democracies*: 5.
7. Przeworski, *Democracy and the Market*; DiPalma, *To Craft Democracies.*

Fundamentally, however, this work is bound by the assumption that people – in particular, the political élite – ultimately dominate both process and outcome in the breakdown of authoritarianism and the creation of democracy.

Process-orientated perspectives have provided a needed corrective against the limitations of earlier structuralist theory, returning volition and contingency to the idea of political transition and democratization. Moreover, these views have come to dominate much of our understanding of political transition. However, despite these contributions, process-based analyses themselves suffer from shortcomings which derive from their move away from structuralism and to the other extreme. By centring virtually all attention on the political élite, they provide no context in which events can be placed, relying instead on documenting élite patterns of activity and stressing their resourcefulness as a key variable in the transition – an approach which tends to exclude both state and society as analytical components. The result is thus a list of what appear to be relevant factors affecting political change, and nothing appears more relevant in the actual process than the objectives and activities of the élite.

There can be no doubt that such central figures have a profound influence on the political arena as a whole, wielding the power to mobilize or defuse potential political forces. But there is also an element of research bias in this case, in that the élite are the centre of investigation precisely because they are so obvious and active, and their visual drama is made synonymous with power and influence. As one scholar has noted, the problem lies simply in the fact that 'taking the resourcefulness of political actors as the crucial independent variable does not seem to be a tenable research strategy'.[8] Indeed, such an approach almost inevitably leads into the realm of tautological assertions, given the problems inherent in operationalizing such arguments. As with structuralism, what is missing is any concern for the power or influence of domestic organization and how such configurations may help create distinct modes of transition.

Taking the case of Hungary in particular, the process-based view cannot account for the development of an internal reform movement within the lower ranks of the ruling party which would have such a

8. Metin Heper, 'Transitions to Democracy Reconsidered: A Historical Perspective', in Dankwart Rustow (ed.), *Comparative Political Dynamics: Global Research Perspectives* (New York: HarperCollins, 1991): 194.

dramatic impact, due to the fact that the approach does not allow for non-élite or intermediate forces to play any meaningful role in a transition from authoritarianism. Consequently, the Hungarian transition tends to be misinterpreted so as to fit the model, characterized by the argument that it was the work of the ruling élite, the state and industrial *nomenklatura*, or both, who no longer saw it in their interest to 'prevent' capitalism and multiparty rule, an explanation that lacks both empirical support and a clear causal link.[9]

9. This argument has been raised by a number of authors, notably Iván Szelényi and György Konrád, 'Intellectuals and Domination in Post-Communist Societies', in Iván Szelényi, *A poszt-kommunista átmenet társadalmi konfliktusai* [The social conflicts of the post-communist transition] (Budapest: MTA Politikai Tudományok Intézete, 1992): 59–75; Ákos Róna-Tas, 'The Second Economy in Hungary: The Social Origins of the End of State Socialism' (PhD diss., University of Michigan, 1990); Tamás L. Fellegi, 'Regime Transformation and the Mid-Level Bureaucratic Forces in Hungary', in Peter M.E. Volten (ed.), *Bound to Change: Consolidating Democracy in East Central Europe* (New York: Institute for East–West Studies, 1992): 119–50; Rudolf L. Tőkés, 'Hungary's New Political Élites: Adaptation and Change, 1989–1990', in György Szoboszlai (ed.), *Democracy and Political Transformation: Theories and East–Central European Realities* (Budapest: Hungarian Political Science Association, 1991): 226–86; and Michael Burawoy and János Lukács, *The Radiant Past: Ideology and Reality in Hungary's Road to Capitalism* (Chicago, IL: University of Chicago Press, 1992). The assertion that economic reforms and the potential economic stake of certain actors within the party-state bureaucracy led to their tacit or active support for the transition (the *embourgeoisement* hypothesis) stems from the dubious explanation that these actors suddenly saw their fortunes tied to an emerging market economy, as opposed to their entrenched positions within the party-state apparatus. Indeed, during 1988 and 1989 a new class of party and state bureaucrats did emerge preaching modernization, though their support for democracy is ambiguous at best (marketization and democratization are two different things) and many of their actions in fact came late in the game, in response to the increasing disintegration of the party and the swell of external and internal opposition, rather than before it.

The problem with this argument is that even if we posit that pro-market party leaders were less an obstacle to transition than elsewhere, the casual leap which tends to follow is to assert that these figures in fact *initiated* the transition, which the facts do not bear out. Ironically, the *ad hoc* nature of this contention is underscored by the fact that this same argument was previously used by some of the same scholars to explain why Hungarian state socialism would *persevere*, rather than decline; market reforms would not lead to political change, but rather a form of authoritarian modernization (the Franquist model of Spain): see Iván Szelényi, 'The Prospects and Limits of the East European New Class Project: An Autocritical Reflection on *The Intellectuals on the Road to Class Power*', *Politics and Society* **15** (1986–87): 103–44; also Victor Nee and David Stark, 'Toward an Institutional Analysis of State Socialism', in David Stark and Victor Nee (eds), *Remaking the Economic Institutions of Socialism* (Stanford, CA: Stanford University Press, 1989), esp. 30–31. For a critique of *embourgeoisement* arguments see Jason McDonald, 'Transition to Utopia: A Reinterpretation of Economic Ideas and

It has been clear for some time that within the study of political transitions it is important to establish a link between structure and process, although this has gone largely unheeded. Indeed, one important early contribution in this regard was made by Dankwart Rustow, who argued that given the fact that for the structuralist camp 'the question [was] not how a democratic system comes into existence', macro-level analyses alone would not provide a theory of transitions to democracy; rather, 'any genetic theory of democracy would do well to assume a two-way flow of causality, or some form of circular interaction, between politics on the one hand and economic and social conditions on the other'.[10] In the wake of process-based arguments some work has attempted to follow Rustow's admonition, but these two levels of analysis still remain largely unintegrated. This leaves us with rather incomplete explanations of political events: transitions as the outcome of systemic change, or transitions as the product of bargaining and transaction. Even in Linz and Stepan's magisterial work on political transitions (see footnote 1), while both actors and contexts are investigated in detail, their theoretical interconnection remains unclear.

This lack of integration matters not only in terms of understanding transition events, but in the consolidation of new institutions thereafter; with regard to Eastern Europe in particular, I argue that the current period of political consolidation continues to be strongly influenced by the events which have preceded it, setting a number of constraints and opportunities that will in turn shape the new political order (that is, path dependency). Therefore, research in related topics can be enriched by analyses which provide a framework in which specific issues could be situated.

An integration of structure and process would provide us with a more detailed approach to the study of transitions, but the question remains, how is this to be done? Structuralist arguments provide the broad brushstrokes of a nation-state: levels of social and economic

Politics in Hungary, 1984–1990', *East European Politics and Societies* **7** (Spring 1993): 203–39.

10. Dankwart Rustow, 'Transitions to Democracy: Toward a Dynamic Model', *Comparative Politics* **2** (April 1970): 344, 339–40. Similar arguments were put forth by Juan Linz, who in a study not of democratization but rather of democratic collapse stressed the importance of dynamic and contextual aspects which characterize political transitions as they unfold: Juan J. Linz, *The Breakdown of Democratic Regimes*, vol. 1: *Crisis, Breakdown, and Reequilibration* (Baltimore, MD: Johns Hopkins University Press, 1978).

development, position in the world economy, historical patterns, ethnic or regional identities, and so on. Process arguments provide the fluid dynamic of political actors. Neither approach, however, is directly applicable to the actual political arena in which the transitional battle will be fought, shaped by both macro- and micro-level forces and existing as an intermediate level between the two. Without such a middle course we cannot make any meaningful distinctions between our cases, and our conclusions will remain *post hoc* and non-generalizable.

Political institutions are that bridging mechanism, linking structure and process while they are themselves contingent on the intricacies of macro- and micro-level forces. Institutions represent the coupling of an organization to its environment, a means by which stability and legitimacy may be acquired. We can therefore observe a general set of activities and patterns involved in the institutionalization process, although the particular form of the relationship to the environment is dependent to a large extent on those distinct characteristics that define both the ruling system and the wider environment in which it is seated. These institutional forms shape the roles and actions of individuals within the political process, influencing transition outcomes and the reconstitution of political order. Institutional analysis allows for the particularity of case and the indeterminacy bound up within it, while general conclusions can still be drawn. This gives us a way to bring together our disparate knowledge of autocratic systems, elucidating their variation as well as the paths of their eventual decline. How institutions form and their impact on political activity will be our next consideration.

INSTITUTIONS AS POLITICAL VARIABLES

It is my argument that the shortcomings of both process- and structure-based analyses can be addressed through the use of an institutional approach. The so-called 'new institutionalism', which has enjoyed a good deal of popularity within sociology and political science over the past decade, stresses the impact that these structures may have in the ordering and formation of social and political relations. What are the effects of institutions and institutionalization that make this area of study theoretically valuable? How do these findings apply to analyses of state socialism and authoritarian decline in general? There are no simple answers to these questions, since institutional approaches are characterized by a diversity of views that are not necessarily reconcilable.[11]

However, several central assumptions bind much of this research. To begin with, they take as a starting-point a rejection of the individual-based market analogies of the rational-choice, pluralist or behaviouralist approaches. These approaches typically view institutions as little more than instrumental structures created by actors to serve specific utilitarian functions, 'arenas within which political behavior, driven by more fundamental factors, occurs'.[12] Institutions, as the product of economic or other rational calculations, are for the above perspectives little more than a reflection or aggregation of individual considerations – a contract of interests.

In contrast to such views, institutional perspectives fundamentally rest on the assumption that organizations are often not the transparent, instrumental constructs for which they are commonly taken, but rather are a much more complex and influential part of human behaviour. While these structures derive from human interaction, institutional arguments stress that they do not necessarily follow from purposive human design, often arising instead through unintended actions, replication and default. Although their origins may lie in the quest for rational goal-attainment, their conformity to these expectations can be affected dramatically by the pull of internal and external activity as they strive to maintain and define their own organizational integrity.

Second, institutions, as self-replicating structures, develop a resulting set of particular characteristics: resources, values, norms, routines and patterns, which are in turn passed on to individuals both inside and outside the structure. This tends to bestow on institutions a certain degree of independent power, vesting them with the ability to create and shape the objectives of individual and collective action. In contrast to more atomistic approaches to social choice and behaviour, it is argued that institutions 'establish the very criteria by which people

11. Lynne G. Zucker, 'Introduction: Institutional Theories of Organization – Conceptual Development and Research Agenda', in Lynne G. Zucker (ed.), *Institutional Patterns and Organization* (Cambridge, MA: Ballinger, 1988): xii–xix.
12. James G. March and Johan P. Olsen, 'The New Institutionalism: Organizational Factors in Political Life', *American Political Science Review* **78** (September 1984): 734.

discover their preferences'.[13] Like physical arrangements, institutions can influence our starting perceptions, subsequent goals and the instruments we utilize in their pursuit.

From these assumptions it follows that institutions, as idiosyncratic, intervening variables which affect the palette of political choices, open the door to certain kinds of actions and opportunities while closing the door to others. Theda Skocpol nicely summarizes this point in her observation that 'organizational configurations, along with their overall patterns of activity, affect political culture, encourage some kinds of group formation and collective political actions (but not others), and make possible the raising of certain political issues (but not others)'.[14]

Third, an important corollary to the above arguments is the effect of organizational 'lock in', central to the understanding of institutionalization itself. Institutionalization typically involves the formation of policies and patterns of behaviour in response to social forces in the surrounding environment. Over time these practices tend to harden, becoming themselves an inseparable part of the organization's objectives and blurring relationships between means and ends.[15] Dramatic reorganization is thus relatively rare. In fact, the institutional perspective argues instead that when highly institutionalized systems are confronted with environmental or internal challenges they are more likely to suppress or ignore these contradictions than respond with corrective measures.

This has two implications. First, suboptimal systems can persevere over a long period without major changes; second, if the internal contradictions of the system are such that they foster internal or external pressure, then such institutions are more likely to 'break' rather than 'bend'. That is, an institution will attempt to preserve its status quo, regardless of growing opposition, until the tension is such that the institution is eliminated entirely. To the institutional perspective,

13. Paul J. DiMaggio and Walter W. Powell, 'Introduction', in Walter W. Powell and Paul J. DiMaggio (eds), *The New Institutionalism in Organizational Analysis* (Chicago, IL: University of Chicago Press, 1991): 11.
14. Theda Skocpol, 'Bringing the State Back In: Current Research', in Peter B. Evans, Dietrich Reuschemeyer and Theda Skocpol (eds), *Bringing the State Back In* (Cambridge: Cambridge University Press, 1985): 21.
15. Robert Bierstedt, 'Review of *Exchange and Power in Social Life*', *American Sociological Review* **30** (1965): 790, quoted in Craig Calhoun and W. Richard Scott, 'Introduction', in Craig Calhoun, Marshall W. Meyer and W. Richard Scott (eds), *Structures of Power and Constraint: Papers in Honor of Peter M. Blau* (Cambridge: Cambridge University Press, 1990): 10.

organizational development appears less incremental than tectonic. Such arguments correspond well to our understanding of transitions and revolutions, such as those in Eastern Europe, typically situations which arise without warning, bringing down the authoritarian system within a relatively short period. Thus, organizations may develop a rigidity that has been termed 'over-institutionalization', which makes such structures more vulnerable to environmental shock.[16]

APPLICATION AND MISINTERPRETATION IN INSTITUTIONAL ANALYSIS

There can be no doubt that in social science the institutional perspective has gained a great deal of currency over the past ten years. Many scholars have attempted to use an institutional approach in order to augment or supplant earlier theories of human political activity that stressed individual action without reference to the effect of persistent social constructs. In political science in particular this approach has manifested itself in the investigation of the state as an autonomous political actor,[17] and has influenced rational-choice perspectives as well.[18] Nor has the study of state socialism been immune, where

16. M. Kesselman, 'Overinstitutionalization and Political Constraint: The Case of France', *Comparative Politics* **2** (1970), quoted in Zvi Gitelman, 'The Limits of Organization and Enthusiasm: The Double Failure of the Solidarity Movement and the Polish United Workers' Party', in Kay Lawson and Peter H. Merkl (eds), *When Parties Fail* (Princeton, NJ: Princeton University Press, 1988): 425.
17. 'Statist' writings are now so prevalent that a summary would require an entire chapter of its own. Ground-breaking examples in the area include Stephen D. Krasner, 'Approaches to the State: Alternative Conceptions and Historical Dynamics' *Comparative Politics* **16** (January 1984): 223–46; Theda Skocpol, *States and Social Revolutions* (Cambridge: Cambridge University Press, 1979); and Evans, Reuschemeyer and Skocpol, *Bringing the State Back In*, op. cit. For a critique of statist approaches see Gabriel Almond, 'Return to the State', in *A Discipline Divided: Schools and Sects in Political Science* (Newbury Park, CA: Sage, 1990), 189–218. Studies more explicitly focused on institutional analysis include the central work by March and Olsen, 'The New Institutionalism', and idem, *Rediscovering Institutions: The Organizational Basis of Politics* (New York: The Free Press, 1989); Stephen D. Krasner, 'Sovereignty: An Institutional Perspective', *Comparative Political Studies* **21** (1988): 66–94; John C. Ikenberry, 'Conclusion: An Institutional Approach to American Foreign Economic Policy', in John C. Ikenberry, David A. Lake and Michael Mastanduno (eds), *The State and American Foreign Economic Policy* (Ithaca, NY: Cornell University Press, 1991): 219–43.
18. See, for example, Terry M. Moe, *The Organization of Interests* (Chicago, IL:

institutional analysis in this field has had a noticeable effect.[19] The study of transitions and democratization could use a similar reappraisal, providing a needed corrective to the individualist assumptions dominant in the area, and complementing those structuralist perspectives which ignored meso-level political institutions as a factor in understanding democratization.

Yet while the new wave in institutional analysis is winning a number of converts, the perspective as it is utilized in political science tends to suffer from weaknesses in both definition and theoretical power. One such problem lies in the fact that as viewed in political science, institutions tend to be characterized as little more than self-reproducing constructs, linked to sunk costs and vested interests, rather than as actors in their own right, creating their own organizational culture and resources. This is unfortunate, given that this is one of the earliest and most central concepts derived from such research. As Ronald Jepperson notes, 'institutions are not just constraint structures; all institutions simultaneously empower and control'.[20]

A second problem lies in the overstating of institutional effects. While the institutional perspective has been rightly accorded a role in understanding political order and change, some have chosen to utilize the approach in such a way as to exaggerate the uniqueness of political institutions as clusters of variables. The conclusion drawn from such a view is that political institutions are so context-dependent that they are

University of Chicago Press, 1980); Karen Schweers Cook and Margaret Levi (eds), *The Limits of Rationality* (Chicago, IL: University of Chicago Press, 1990); Kenneth Shepsle, 'The Institutional Foundations of Committee Power', *American Political Science Review* **81** (1987): 85–104; and idem, 'Studying Institutions: Some Lessons from the Rational Choice Approach', *Journal of Theoretical Politics* **1** (1989): 131–47.

19. Within the area of state socialism, notable examples include Ellen Comisso, 'Introduction: State Structures, Political Processes, and Collective Choice in CMEA States', *International Organization* **40** (Spring 1986): 196–238; Ken Jowitt, 'Weber, Trotsky and Holmes on the Study of Leninist Regimes', *Journal of International Affairs* **45** (Summer 1991): 31–48; Nee and Stark, 'Toward an Institutional Analysis of State Socialism': 1–31; Valerie Bunce and Mária Csanádi, 'Uncertainty in the Transition: Post-Communism in Hungary', *East European Politics and Societies* **7** (Spring 1993): 240–75, and Beverly Crawford and Arend Lijphart, 'Explaining Political and Economic Change in Post Communist Eastern Europe: Old Legacies, New Institutions, Hegemonic Norms, and International Pressures', *Comparative Political Studies* **28** (July 1995): 171–99.
20. Ronald L. Jepperson, 'Institutions, Institutional Effects, and Institutionalism', in Powell and DiMaggio, *The New Institutionalism*: 146.

largely non-comparative, downplaying the degree to which institutional effects can be generalized.

This is particularly noticeable in institutional analyses of state socialism.[21] There can be no doubt that the introduction of institutional perspectives into studies of state socialism is to be commended, a welcome change from earlier attempts to force these systems into the rubric of Western political orders. But when this aspect is overemphasized, the term loses its theoretical character, shifting away from a concept stressing *process* towards an ideographic symbol emphasizing *character*, issues of differentiation overshadowing those of causality.

Following this logic, the institutions of state socialism thus become 'novel' because, to use Ken Jowitt's well-worn term, they are 'Leninist', but we fail to grasp the underlying dynamics which have developed and institutionalized Leninism in the first place. A generalizable process of institutionalization is consequently lost. Jowitt rejects even the use of the term 'state socialism', since its use has 'increased the analytic familiarity of Leninist regimes by denying their institutional peculiarity'.[22] As others have noted, such advice does not lend itself well to theory-building or generalization. Nor does it enrich the analytical process by searching for illuminating concepts elsewhere within the social sciences.[23]

In short: institutions are not simple conduits, nor are they notational devices. They are the products of social forces, and while they create unique institutional orders depending on context, they represent a category of broader organizational activity which can itself be generalized to other cases under consideration.

21. See in particular Jowitt, 'Weber, Trotsky, and Holmes on the Study of Leninist Regimes', and Nee and Stark, 'Toward an Institutional Analysis of State Socialism'.
22. Jowitt, 'Weber, Trotsky, and Holmes': 40.
23. See the criticism of Jowitt's approach in Philippe C. Schmitter and Terry Lynn Karl, 'The Types of Democracy Emerging in Southern and Eastern Europe and South and Central America', in Volten, *Bound to Change*: 43–5.

ENRICHING THE 'NEW' INSTITUTIONALISM WITH LESSONS FROM THE 'OLD'

Many of these shortcomings in the so-called 'new institutionalism' appear to stem from the fact that our understanding of the intellectual origins of this field is rather limited. Notable for its absence is any reference to the pioneer of institutional analysis, the sociologist Philip Selznick, whose work on organizational development in the 1940s and 1950s paved the way for later work in the field. This is particularly ironic, given that Selznick's approach is more consistent with institutionalist arguments employed in political science than those found currently in sociology.[24] Given that this study is set firmly within the framework provided by Selznick, it is important that we discuss his main arguments in some detail.

The central institutional arguments of Philip Selznick are scattered among several different works, notably his 1949 study *TVA and the Grass Roots* and his *Leadership in Administration* (1957), in which he emphasized how organizational function may diverge from its ostensible structure and objectives through its relations with the social environment.[25] This argument is brought forth most strongly in his study of the Tennessee Valley Authority. Drawing upon earlier observations by Karl Marx, Gaetano Mosca, Robert Michels and Karl Mannheim, among others, Selznick began with the contention that 'the most important thing about organizations is that, though they are tools, each nevertheless has a life of its own'.[26] While organizations are created with goals in mind and rational instruments to pursue them, Selznick argued that organizations are inevitably confronted with environmental factors, both social and technical in nature: obstacles and challenges to their objectives, demanding the acquisition of information and the neutralization of conflicting external relationships or norms.

24. W. Richard Scott, 'Unpacking Institutional Arguments', in Powell and DiMaggio, *The New Institutionalism*: 179–80.
25. Selznick's early work emphasizes the role of structural-functionalist analysis, although this recedes in his later work. For this earlier emphasis see his 1949 piece 'Foundations of the Theory of Organization', reprinted in Amitai Etzioni (ed.), *Complex Organizations* (New York: Holt, Rinehart & Winston, 1961): 18–31.
26. Philip Selznick, *TVA and the Grass Roots* (Berkeley, CA: University of California Press, 1980 [1949]): 10.

Because of this pressure it is necessary for an organization's leadership to formulate appropriate responses that will both legitimize the organization with regard to the social environment while simultaneously defending the organization from the capitulation of its larger goals.[27] One central method studied by Selznick was *co-optation*, which he defined as 'the process of absorbing new elements into the leadership or policy-determining structure of an organization as a means of averting threats to its stability or existence'.[28] This co-optation, Selznick, argued, could be either formal or informal, depending on the nature of the challenge at hand. Informal co-optation is viewed as a process by which an organization seeks to prevent challenges from specific, organized pressure groups by neutralizing their demands through some arrangement which will ensure the stability of the organization–from either inside or outside. In contrast, formal co-optation is the process which 'involves the establishment of openly avowed and formally ordered relationships', the absorption of new elements into the organization itself. This is likely to occur when the organization (1) seeks to (re)legitimize itself *vis-à-vis* society, or when (2) administrative requirements necessitate the incorporation of external actors to whom certain tasks may be allocated - a technical need. In the end, 'any given act of formal co-optation will tend to fulfill both the political function of defending legitimacy and the administrative function of establishing reliable channels for communication and direction'.[29]

Selznick observes the formal co-optative process in totalitarian 'unity' parties as a clear example of legitimizing co-optation (the shift of communist parties from cadre to mass based), while the second meaning of formal co-optation is similar to the term as understood in the lexicon of state socialist societies (for example, in Hungarian the term *kooptálás*). Corresponding to Selznick's description of co-optation, this action is viewed by communist parties as a process by which individuals are recruited into organizational positions from outside the unit as a reaction to administrative requisites.[30]

Selznick thus viewed co-optation as a basic mechanism of

27. Ibid.: 11–13.
28. Ibid.: 13.
29. Ibid.: 14.
30. Ágnes Dus (ed.), *A Pártélet Kisszótára* [A mini-dictionary of party life] (Budapest: Kossuth, 1984): 15.

organizations. Legitimacy is forged and opposition neutralized through the means of co-optative mechanisms, which couple the organization to its surrounding environment. These actions, linking the organization to various segments of society, contribute to what Selznick understands to be the process of institutionalization, to 'infuse with value beyond the technical requirements of the task at hand'.[31] The organization is no longer simply an instrument of a larger policy goal, but becomes valued for its own sake as an end in itself.

While such activity is a basic tactic for organizational survival, it often generates its own set of dangers. First is that as later institutional research has stressed, the ascription of normative qualities to the institution blurs the distinction between the means and ends of the organization and its goals, making organizational change more difficult to justify. As Selznick notes, institutionalization tends to 'bind the organization to specific aims and procedures, often greatly limiting the freedom of the leadership to deploy its resources, and reducing the capacity of the organization to survive under new conditions'.[32]

A second danger derives from the fact that as organizations seek to stabilize their relationship to the external environment through co-optation, they establish relationships with actors whose overarching commitment to organizational goals may be in question. Particularly in its formal variant, where specific external segments are incorporated into the organization, co-optation raises the possibility that these groups may exploit their position, leading to the complete subversion of the original organizational goals. As Selznick concluded,

> Formal cooptation ostensibly shares authority, but in doing so is involved in a dilemma. The real point is the sharing of the public symbols or administrative burdens of authority, and consequently public responsibility, without

31. Philip Selznick, *Leadership in Administration* (Evanston, IL: Row, Peterson, 1957): 17.
32. This is a point which is unclear to many in regard to Selznick's work, especially as it relates to later institutional research. It is commonly argued that one major difference between earlier institutional approaches and contemporary ones is that the former approach assumes an evolving, flexible, adaptive organizational dynamic, while the latter places a greater emphasis on the stabilization and hardening of such orders. However, while Selznick does indeed see institutionalization as an adaptive process, he also stresses that this process will lead to ossification over time – a viewpoint totally consistent with neo-institutional claims. Selznick in fact links institutionalization with the development of *inflexibility*, a point often misinterpreted by more recent institutional scholars. *Leadership in Administration*: 18.

> the transfer of substantive power; it therefore becomes necessary to insure that the co-opted elements do not get out of hand, do not take advantage of their formal position to encroach upon the actual arena of decision. Consequently, formal co-optation requires informal control over the co-opted elements lest the unity of command and decision be imperiled.[33]

This raises the threat of 'unintended consequences' for the organization, the central conclusion of Selznick's TVA study. At its most extreme, original goals may be sacrificed in order to maintain institutional ties and to appease co-opted elements. His work asserts a kind of paradox: while organizations are responsive to social contexts and can adapt accordingly, this process of adaptation can have the side-effect of limiting the organization's later flexibility. Institutionalization is therefore a reactive process to the environment, which often results in ossification.

While institutionalization generates organizational rigidity, the social context itself remains dynamic. This raises the possibility that succeeding waves of external challenges will develop and that the institution will be less willing or able to respond. One possibility is to continue with the policy of co-optation. However, the more deeply institutionalized the organization, the greater the blurring of the means–ends relationship of the structure, and the more resistant it will be to bringing on board new members whose loyalty to the institution (rather than to its ostensible goals) is in doubt. This is the essence of the struggle within state socialism, described as the battle between the institutional 'red' and the co-opted and independent 'expert' – terms which have become part of our lexicon of organizational behaviour.[34]

INSTITUTIONALIZATION AND THE FORMATION OF STATE SOCIALISM

Armed with the above concepts, we now refocus our attention on the state socialist systems of the USSR and Eastern Europe, clear examples

33. Selznick, *TVA and the Grass Roots*: 261.
34. As Alvin Gouldner argues, this is in fact a basic part of political development in all societies; in the long run, the intellectual 'expert' segment must be 'either coopted into the ruling class or it must be subjected to the repressive control of a burgeoning bureaucracy'. *The Future of the Intellectuals and the Rise of the New Class* (New York: Seabury Press, 1979): 24.

of institutionalization processes in practice. In the Soviet Union, the victory of Lenin's militant vanguard party did not in itself usher in the revolutionary transformation of Russia. The leadership faced the inevitable need to consolidate their fragile gains, shifting from the immediate objective of attaining political power to that of administrative control and social support.

Political consolidation – particularly as decreed by Marxism–Leninism, which saw the expansion of state authority over wide sections of society – would require that the party broaden its base of support and administrative power. There consequently followed a co-optation of 'hostile' class elements, whose technical knowledge was critical to the rebuilding of a national administration. This occurred alongside the incorporation of a new bureaucratic class within the communist apparatus, an immense stratum of new members rapidly promoted from among the proletariat.[35] Through this latter policy in particular, the party created a powerful force whose new-found status was dependent on the current order and the expansion of state power.

Of course, such forms of co-optation are a common facet of political institutionalization, a period of Thermidor in which for the sake of stability formal arrangements are built, social sectors and organizations are incorporated into a system of control. In the Soviet case these developments evoke what Weber referred to as the routinization of charismatic orders.[36] Yet for a revolutionary organization institutionalization also raises the fear that consolidation is tantamount to capitulation. In China, Mao's response to this dilemma was the Cultural Revolution, an attempt to prevent institutionalization (and maintain his own personal power) by unleashing anarchic revolutionary forces against it. Despite similar qualms, however, communism in the Soviet Union took the opposite course, aided in large part by the actions of Stalin.

As a party figure whose power was fundamentally organizational (rather than intellectual or charismatic), Stalin utilized his administrative talents to gain control over the expanding party and state apparatus. Stalin was subsequently able to wield these tools against other party

35. Alf Adeen, 'The Soviet Civil Service: Its Composition and Status', in Cyril E. Black (ed.), *The Transformation of Russian Society: Aspects of Social Change Since 1861* (Cambridge, MA: Harvard University Press, 1960), reprinted in Jack A. Goldstone (ed.), *Revolutions: Theoretical, Comparative and Historical Studies* (New York: Harcourt Brace Jovanovich, 1986): 238–47.
36. Max Weber, *The Theory of Social and Economic Organization*, ed. and trans. by A.M. Henderson and Talcott Parsons (New York: The Free Press, 1947): 363–85.

leaders in his struggle for power. From there on he increasingly attempted to augment this organizational power by emphasizing the concept of the party organization as the embodiment of knowledge and utopia – the fusion of means and ends. Stalin based his authority not on his role as revolutionary, but as the leader of a set of institutions which were defined as the embodiment of the revolution itself. Fallibility thus became impossible.

This combination of utopian ideology (claiming competence over all sectors of the environment) with a leadership whose claim to authority rested on the omnipotence of its organization rapidly formed the Soviet Union's totalitarian character. The tactical forms of Marxism–Leninism took on religious qualities, such that state planning, democratic centralism, and party organization were no longer simply methods, but *values* – part and parcel of the communist future, to be revered accordingly. In sociological terms, the institution developed myths of organizational practice that conferred legitimacy on the structure as a whole – and by way of extension, its membership and leaders.[37]

Those within the party-state were now defined purely by their loyalty to the institution. Since the revolution and the institutions of rule were one and the same, one could not question, oppose or function independently of these institutions without in effect challenging the legitimacy of the revolution itself. This was reinforced by the absorption of existing environmental patterns and organizations into the institutional order (church, cultural myths, history) or, where this was not possible, their eradication.

Also in accordance with this extreme institutionalization, the party took on an anti-intelligentsia quality, something particularly noteworthy given the purely intellectual origins of the communist party. Anti-intelligentsia views within Soviet communism emerge with Stalin and his purges, and although cloaked in the argument that intellectuals represent the defeated bourgeois class, in reality this hostility is based on the fear of intellectual power as a means of autonomous (noninstitutional) knowledge, what Alvin Gouldner calls the 'culture of critical discourse'.[38] Party leaders from the period prior to institutionalization were thus quickly exterminated, as well as many

37. For more on this see John W. Meyer and Brian Rowan, 'Institutionalized Organizations: Formal Structure as Myth and Ceremony', in Powell and DiMaggio, *The New Institutionalism*: 41–62.
38. *The Future of the Intellectuals*: 28–44.

of the pre-revolutionary intellectuals within state and society. This finalizes the institutionalization of the party, with its original objectives lost in the worship of institutional form as the revolution incarnate.

Consequently, even with the death of Stalin and the end of the widespread application of terror, the party-state remained *institutionally* totalitarian, with virtually no change in organizational characteristics. This is not surprising. First, those who comprised the party-state were defined by their institutional loyalty to it; they represented Milovan Djilas's hated 'new class', who justified their power and actions by reference to the infallibility of the party.[39] Second, even if radical changes in the structure of rule had been desired, given the depth to which the system had become institutionalized the modification of organizational tenets would have belied their sacrosanct nature, threatening the rapid unravelling of the whole order. Thus, de-Stalinization became a risky and limited course of action.

The formation of Eastern European state socialism represents an interesting variant of Stalinist institutionalization. In that region we do not see the domestic creation of a set of organizations which become institutionalized over time, in interaction with and in response to the constraints of the domestic environment. Rather, Eastern Europe experiences the simultaneous and wholesale replication of the Soviet set of institutions, from party structure to economy, education to culture. These represent clear cases of what is called institutional isomorphism, where organizations incorporate external institutional rules because of uncertainty in action, coercion and/or the presumed normative values inherent in the forms adapted (the coercive and normative aspects are particularly relevant for the East European cases).[40]

What is important in this regard is that because of their origin as externally installed orders, the primary environment to which they reacted and sought legitimation was not domestic, but rather international: Moscow. All states must seek some recognition and legitimacy from the international environment in order to facilitate needed relationships (for example, conforming to and participating in international regimes and organizations). But in the East European case

39. Milovan Djilas, *The New Class: An Analysis of the Communist System* (New York: Praeger, 1957).
40. Paul J. DiMaggio and Walter W. Powell, 'The Iron Cage Revisited: Institutional Isomorphism and Collective Rationality in Organizational Fields', in Powell and DiMaggio, *The New Institutionalism*: 63–82.

the international (Soviet) level dominated any domestic concerns – a basic structure of most empires, where home institutions are imposed on conquered territory.

Local co-optation consequently took on limited and formal qualities, creating a cadre class of reliable individuals within a much larger mass of members whose support was contingent on largely opportunistic considerations. A policy of broader domestic institutionalization, however, adapting the party-state to the local environment in order to generate legitimacy, was incompatible with the institutional demands of Stalinism and thus rejected. This left coercion and opportunism as the primary means of rule. The social system became penetrated by the party-state not as a means of legitimation but as a means of control. The party itself, contingent on Moscow for its validation, remained quite isolated from and antagonistic to its external environment, and thus quite unstable. By way of illustration, those perceived as hostile to the Stalinist externally-legitimated institutional forms during the period of the purges in the 1950s were primarily native communists, whose conversion had not been through inculcation in Moscow but rather through personal conviction and revolutionary activity. One can see the institutional antagonisms in the expression 'national communism', both as a term of slander against nativists by Muscovites and as a legitimate aspiration. At its most fundamental level, national communism held the view that state socialism must be institutionalized not simply at the international level, conforming to the rigid demands of Stalinism, but also at the domestic level, incorporating local environmental forms – perhaps even at the expense of Soviet party-state institutions.[41] Such concepts indicated that national communists still distinguished between theory and practice, in contrast to the Soviet case, where the two had become completely fused. This made national communism dangerous to the institutional order, and its presumed supporters soon found themselves to be the first purge victims of their Muscovite comrades.

With the death of Stalin, however, the party-states of Eastern Europe and the USSR faced the challenge of how to continue. Stalin had succeeded in the consolidation of institutional power to his own benefit, but the sacrifices made in this quest were all too evident. Ritual or coercion alone would not generate the kinds of technical outputs

41. For a discussion of national communism see H. Gordon Skilling, 'National Communism in Eastern Europe', in Andrew Gyorgy (ed.), *Issues of World Communism* (Princeton, NJ: Van Nostrand, 1966): 108–26.

needed for the development of economy and society. Moreover, in Eastern Europe the tenuous level of party-state integration into the domestic environment meant that uncertain developments in the Soviet Union threatened to undermine this source of control. Socialism in the region could perhaps seek greater domestic legitimacy, still by and large conforming to Soviet norms while also creating a less coercive linkage to the local environment. Technical development was seen as one way to compensate for the deficiencies of the political system. Thus, by the early 1960s state socialism had begun to exhibit what Selznick calls the 'retreat to technology', described as the belief 'that the solution of technical problems will solve institutional problems'.[42] This was no simple task, for it involved a set of compromises in socialist institutions which were hard to swallow. This included the increased formal co-optation of the burgeoning intelligentsia class for their functional skills, as well as so that they could grace the party with an image of an organization less tyrannical and more managerial in nature.

Alongside this new policy of co-optation, the communist parties also began to place a greater emphasis on the development of objective knowledge – something threatening to institutional forms and thus condemned under Stalinism as bourgeois – to yield advances in technology and the economy. This, it was hoped, would in turn compensate for the deficiencies of Stalinist institutions, propping up external legitimacy with domestic support as well. The risk, of course, was that domestic and Soviet legitimation would eventually come into conflict, which it did, bringing an end to such policies everywhere in Eastern Europe – with the exception of Hungary

Hungary is therefore a particularly intriguing case in this regard, for here we see the best example of this balance between domestic and external institutionalization emerging from a set of developments which we might not expect to lead in this direction. A highly repressive regime is destroyed by popular revolt, restored by force, but then pursues a policy of conciliation and co-optation which continues long after this has been rejected as a dangerous policy elsewhere in the region. Selznick's approach provides an explanatory construct from which the following case can be understood, and forewarns – as we shall see in the Hungarian case – that such policies are likely to lead to consequences unforeseen and unintended by those who initiate them.

42. Selznick, *Leadership in Administration*: 148.

PART II

The Hungarian Case

2. State Socialism and the Intelligentsia in Eastern Europe: Hungary in Comparative Institutional Perspective, 1948–1988

Following our arguments regarding the organizational development of state socialism as laid out in the previous chapter, we now turn to the Hungarian case in particular. As we have noted, the institutionalization of state socialism under Josef Stalin created a set of political structures whose instrumental utility was replaced by an emphasis on the organizational form as the source of legitimacy. With the communist takeover in Eastern Europe, an extreme isomorphism to the Soviet order followed. These new party-states, however, while committed to Stalinist institutions, were forced to replicate this alien system within new, quite differing environments, eventually raising concerns as to the domestic stability of these structures outside of the support provided by the Soviet Union.

This was made evident following the death of Stalin and the tentative moves towards de-Stalinization. While in the Soviet Union the institutional sanctity of the revolution could still be upheld as Stalin's own 'personal' crimes were denounced, in Eastern Europe de-Stalinization quickly gained its own momentum as a source of de-institutionalization, calling into question why the Soviet model had to be slavishly adhered to, if it were in fact the product of one ruler's despotism. In the Hungarian case in particular, the social turmoil which these revelations fostered climaxed in revolution and the system's overthrow in 1956. This had the effect not only of eradicating much of the institutional base of the party-state, but following the revolution's crushing it also created a new historical juncture from which General

Secretary János Kádár could attempt to rebuild party rule. The Kádárist policy of co-optation and pragmatic reform which followed in effect built a distinct, almost dualistic institutional order, whereby the sacrosanct organizational forms remained necessarily intact but supplemented by a secondary group of institutions designed to garner legitimacy from a hostile populace.

STALINISM AND REVOLUTION

The establishment of state socialism in Hungary following World War Two does not to a great extent differ from other cases in the region. With the assistance of Soviet forces present in the country, the communist party leadership obtained enough power through various tactics to eventually eliminate other political challengers. By 1950, the party embarked on a programme of widespread nationalization, crash industrialization and the consequent urbanization and mobilization of the populace based on the promise of socialist equality and backed by increasing amounts of coercion.[1] The ranks of the *nomenklatura* swelled as the party created its own 'red directors', manual labourers who despite their lack of education were sent off to university for minimal training, then installed as managers of the economy and state.[2] Intellectuals, in contrast, were stigmatized as 'second-class citizens' and punished with wage and mobility limitations that alienated them from

1. There are a number of good studies of Hungarian political history under state socialism, among them Bennett Kovrig, *Communism in Hungary: From Kun to Kádár* (Stanford, CA: Hoover Institution Press, 1979); Miklós Molnár, *From Béla Kun to János Kádár: Seventy Years of Hungarian Communism* (New York: Berg and St. Martin's Press, 1990); and Tőkés, *Hungary's Negotiated Revolution*. On the 1956 revolution in particular see György Litván (ed.), *The Hungarian Revolution of 1956: Reform, Revolt, and Repression 1953–1963* (London: Longman, 1996), and Bill Lomax, *Hungary 1956* (London: Allison & Busby, 1976).
2. Antal Örkény, 'Social Mobility and the New Elite in Hungary', in Rudolph Andorka and Miklós Hadas (eds), *Social Structure, Stratification, and Mobility in Central and Eastern Europe* (papers presented at the Inter-University Center of Postgraduate Studies, Dubrovnik, Yugoslavia, 14-17 April 1989) (Budapest: Budapest University of Economic Sciences, n.d.): 255–68; also Mária M. Kovács and Antal Örkény, *Káderek* [Cadres] (Budapest: ELTE Szociológiai és Szociálpolitikai Intézet és Továbbképző Központ, 1991).

the new ruling order.[3] Within the party (which as a result of its 1948 forced merger with the Social Democrats had become the *Magyar Dolgozók Pártja* – Hungarian Workers' Party, or MDP) the means of terror were soon turned upon the organization itself, a practice learned well by those party members who had spent the 1930s and 1940s in Moscow, watching many of their compatriots fall victim to Stalin's purges.[4] In keeping with the institutional demands of Stalinism, nativists were a particular target of these purges, notably those who had pursued attempts to create stronger connections between the party and society and adapt the Stalinist order to domestic factors. One example was Politburo member Imre Nagy, who was purged from the party leadership for his attempts to temper collectivization with the more populist idea of supporting small landholders. Another Politburo figure whose purge resulted in more severe punishment was László Rajk, prominent for his attempts to link the party more closely to domestic social movements and organizations, such as the populist-orientated 'peoples' colleges' which involved thousands of young students. When Rajk was tried and arrested in 1949, these connections became one of the major charges levelled against him, for which he was to pay with his life.[5] Thousands of other party figures suspected of ideas incompatible to Stalinism were purged, imprisoned or executed.

Spurred on by the megalomaniacal tendencies of Party Secretary Mátyás Rákosi and fuelled by the Tito–Stalin split (which created along Hungary's southern border a dangerous 'enemy on the left', a challenge more worrisome to institutionalized Stalinism than capitalism), Hungary underwent a period of totalitarian rule not exceeded in its repressiveness elsewhere in Eastern Europe. With the death of Stalin in 1953 and the subsequent moves by Nikita Khrushchev towards de-Stalinization, however, this system of political control quickly began to unravel. Unwilling to accept responsibility for the excesses of Stalinism that had occurred, Rákosi continued to cling to his traditional Stalinist methods, planning widespread arrests in the party and a crackdown against increasing public opposition to the regime, halted only by Soviet veto.[6] His replacement by another Stalinist, Ernő Gerő,

3. György Borsányi and János Kende, *The History of the Working Class Movement in Hungary* (Budapest: Corvina, 1988): 135.
4. Kovrig, *Communism in Hungary*: 125–7.
5. Ibid.: 240–44.
6. Ibid.: 294; Litván, *The Hungarian Revolution*: 47.

underscored the party's inability to make a clear break with the past. Minor concessions towards the population only fomented greater mass opposition, and the proper reburial of Rajk, organized outside of the party and attended by thousands, terrified the regime. Public dissent was increasingly channelled by members of the intelligentsia, who demanded increased democracy both within the party and for society as a whole, and the creation or restoration of truly domestic political institutions. The party feebly attempted to woo the intelligentsia back into their fold so as to better silence them, but their actions came too late.

Under such circumstances it is not surprising that violence should break out against party rule, but the degree to which this snowballed into a fully-fledged revolution was unprecedented in the region and remained so until 1989. When armed conflict broke out on 23 October 1956 at the headquarters of Hungarian Radio over their refusal to broadcast student demands, the party-state began to dissolve almost immediately. The installation of Imre Nagy, the highly respected reform communist as prime minister, and former purge victim János Kádár as first secretary did little to stop the inertia of political decompression, and both found themselves powerless against rising demands for an end to Soviet occupation and the restoration of multiparty democracy - which in fact was re-established on 30 October with the formation of a governmental cabinet comprising many non-communist political leaders from the early post-war period.

At the local and workplace level, revolutionary councils and committees quickly sprang up, appropriating political control from the party-state. Simultaneously, the organizational infrastructure of the party dissipated, along with the vast majority of its members. The party had no links to society, other than opportunism or coercion, and with the loss of both of these powers the system vanished with the membership. Political rule was being rebuilt from the ground up. György Lukács, the well-known Marxist philosopher and member of the multiparty cabinet, gloomily surmised the party's prospects at that time:

> Communism in Hungary has been totally disgraced. Collected around the party will probably be small groups of progressive intellectuals, writers and a few young people. The working class will prefer to follow the social democrats. In free elections the communists will obtain five percent of the

vote, ten percent at the most. It is possible that they won't be in the government, that they will go into opposition.[7]

Faced with the growing prospect that Hungary would reject communist rule in any form and leave the Soviet orbit altogether, Khrushchev, after having earlier promised to withdraw units from Budapest, agreed to an all-out attack, which took place on 4 November 1956. Kádár, who shortly before the intervention had disappeared, resurfaced with several other party leaders in the Soviet Union, and returned to Hungary after the crushing of the revolution on 7 November.[8] The communist leadership now faced the daunting task of re-establishing rule over a population held in check only through the open use of force.

THE RESTORATION OF COMMUNIST RULE

With the imposition of Soviet military rule in Hungary the revolution was effectively brought to an end. But the death of a revolution did not spell victory either for Moscow or for the remaining communists in Hungary, now known as the Hungarian Socialist Workers' Party (MSZMP) - the party having in fact been renamed during the revolution. Kádár, picked by the Soviet leadership to head the new party, was charged not only with restoring order but also with re-establishing some sort of stable authority under which this new party could function, as currently it rested only on Soviet-enforced martial law. One method could have been to re-establish control through the continued threat of force, although this would in no way ensure that the system would become any more stable. Moreover, Rákosi's own use of terror had contributed to the outbreak of the revolution, indicating that such tactics tended to backfire when used against the Hungarian populace. Kádár himself had been imprisoned and tortured under the Rákosi regime, and undoubtedly this contributed towards disabusing him of this particular option.

Rather, early on Kádár apparently realized that security for the party would require some form of legitimacy from the people themselves, and that this in turn would require the party to adapt better to the

7. Kovrig, *Communism in Hungary*: 307.
8. For details see Litván, *The Hungarian Revolution*, chapter 4.

society it ruled. These considerations led Kádár towards a policy of reconciliation, or broad formal co-optation, which originally appears to have envisaged a limited pluralism that would create a role for other political parties as well as for the autonomous workers' councils that had sprung up in the factories. Kádár similarly hoped to garner popular support for the new party leadership by adopting some of the domestic reforms used by both the Poles and the Yugoslavs during their recent political struggles.[9]

However, this policy was apparently thwarted by domestic conservative pressure and even more so by other East European states and the Soviet Union, all of whom were demanding retribution against the revolutionaries. At home, the meagre party ranks (in early December 1957 the party counted fewer than 38,000 members compared to more than 800,000 three months earlier) were dominated by conservative forces, who mistrusted Kádár because of his initial support for the Nagy government.[10] This finally culminated in a dogmatic counter-offensive against Kádár in January 1957, which attacked his moderate policies, praised the Stalinist past and called for widespread domestic reprisals.[11] Within the bloc as a whole, similar demands mounted as Khrushchev's position weakened as a result of events in Hungary. The East German leadership, for example, apparently argued that a minimum of 20,000 Hungarians should be executed to ensure social order.[12]

9. Mária Ormos, 'A konszolidáció problémai (1956–57) [The Problems of Consolidation, 1956–57]', *Társadalmi Szemle* **XLIV**, nos 8–9 (1989): 48–65; György Földes, 'Többpártrendszer (1956–1957) [Multiparty Democracy, 1956–1957], in ibid.: 66–71. Litván's edited volume views these actions as tactical manoeuvres in a prelude to repression, and argues that it was Kádár who held back external calls for repression in early 1957 so as to outflank his Stalinist critics, only to carry out mass retaliation independently once this threat had ended: see *The Hungarian Revolution*: 135.
10. In the words of one Hungarian scholar and former dissident, 'in the eyes of the believers of the *ancien régime* Kádár was the greatest traitor, for along with Imre Nagy he had recognized multiparty democracy and the Workers' Councils, shaken hands with the revolutionaries, and voted to withdraw from the Warsaw Pact and declare political neutrality': see János Kis, 'Az 1956-57-es restauráció [The 1956–57 restoration]', *Medvetánc* nos 2–3 (1988): 235.
11. This was personally led by József Révai, who fled to the Soviet Union during the revolution and returned in January 1957: see Kovrig, *Communism in Hungary*: 329–31; Kis, 'Az 1956–57-es restauráció': 255.
12. Ormos, 'A konszolidáció problémai': 55. It has also been asserted that the Soviet leaders had demanded mass deportations of revolutionaries to the USSR, which

Pressure was compounded by both the recalcitrance of Nagy, who despite his arrest would neither yield nor recant his earlier actions, and the threat of a new rebellion in the spring.

The outcome of these developments was Kádár's eventual shift towards a policy of coercion by the spring of 1957. Those political parties and organizations which had (re-)emerged during the revolution were finally suppressed, mass arrests stepped up, and preparations for Nagy's trial begun. This was complemented by the formation of a paramilitary force, the Workers' Guard, subordinated directly to the party. According to György Litván, between 1957 and 1959 some 26,000 individuals were tried by the regime, and 22,000 were sentenced to various terms of imprisonment. By late 1961 approximately 350 had been executed.[13] Nagy himself, defiant to the end and faithful to his communist beliefs, was executed in June 1958.[14]

As a class the intelligentsia were perhaps hardest hit by the reconsolidation of power during 1957–62. Soon after the revolution's collapse, initial attempts were made by the party to seek greater cooperation with the intelligentsia, who were being blamed by many hardliners for the uprising. In early February 1957 in a public address, Kádár himself argued that 'it is said that the bulk of the intelligentsia supported the counterrevolution. This is not the truth. The intelligentsia is fundamentally not counterrevolutionary. Given that we share a common future, we must naturally work together'.[15]

Kádár blocked: Ferenc Fehér, 'Kádárism as applied Khrushchevism', in Robert F. Miller and Ferenc Fehér (eds), *Khrushchev and the Communist World* (London: Croom Helm, 1984): 221–9.

13. Litván, *The Hungarian Revolution*, 143–4. See also Ormos, 'A konszolidáció problémai': 55; and Éva Kapitány (ed.), *301* (n.p.: Aura, n.d).
14. The degree to which the regime was prepared to forgo capital punishment in the case of Imre Nagy can be found in Politburo and Central Committee documents from February 1958, which discussed the possibility of amnesty for Nagy in keeping with Khrushchev's attempt to better relations with the West and Yugoslavia at that time. However, the subsequent deterioration of relations between the Soviet Union and Yugoslavia soon thereafter apparently increased pressure for retribution against 'revisionism', thereby sealing Nagy's fate. These documents have been reprinted by József Kiss and Zoltán Ripp, '"Mi inkább az elnapolás mellett vagyunk, minthogy enyhe ítéletet hozzunk most": három dokumentum a Nagy Imre-per 1958. februári elhalasztásáról ['We prefer adjournment as we are to pass a lenient sentence at this time': three documents concerning the delay of Imre Nagy's trial in February 1958]', *Társadalmi Szemle* **XLVIII**, no. 4 (1993): 82–95.
15. *Népszabadság*, 8 February 1957; cited in József Németh, *Értelmiség és konszoli-*

Others in the party, however, were not convinced. They viewed the intelligentsia as the spearhead of the uprising, demanding changes in socialism which were taken up by the population as a whole.[16] Khrushchev himself reportedly stated that the entire revolution could have been avoided if some ten writers had been taken out and shot.[17] Party dogmatists, defined by their strong institutional loyalty, correctly viewed the intelligentsia as dangerous precisely because their knowledge did not stem from party doctrine; thus they constituted a tool which could be wielded against the party to devastating effect. A committee set up by the party in December 1956 was charged with the task of addressing the grievances of Hungarian intellectuals, but by spring of the following year it had been made anachronistic by the new policy of repression. The party leadership and base were subjected to a policy of conscious 'proletarianization', which contributed to the further marginalization of intellectuals within the party.[18] The party branded the intelligentsia as 'traditional allies of reactionary dominant classes', and centred much of their crackdown on institutions of learning, the Academy of Science and the Union of Writers.[19]

dáció, 1956–1962 [Intelligentsia and consolidation, 1956–1962] (Budapest: Kossuth, 1988): 71.

16. The party's view of the intelligentsia as the *agents provocateurs* of the revolution and as obstacles to the restoration of communist power eventually abated, but remained a latent force; see, for example, the attack on the role of the intelligentsia organizations during 1956 in Sándor Geréb and Pál Hajdu, *Az ellenforradalom utóvédharca* [The rear-guard battle of the counterrevolution] (Budapest: Kossuth, 1986). This view is, of course, perfectly consistent with communist ideology; an argument that the revolution was initiated or led by the working class would by definition call into question the legitimacy of the party as the true representative of their interests.
17. Kovrig, *Communism in Hungary*, 294.
18 By 1959 the intelligentsia made up only 7 per cent of the party membership, and less than a quarter of the party leadership at the central and local level possessed higher education. Tibor Huszár, *Mit ér a szellem, ha …* [What is the value of the mind, if …] (Budapest: Szabad Tér Kiadó, 1990): 39. See also the excerpts from activities of the MSZMP Intelligentsia Committee in 1957, reprinted in ibid.: 154–8.
19. For details, see ibid.: 12–39.

FROM CONSOLIDATION TO CO-OPTATION: THE ALLIANCE POLICY

However, the period of forced consolidation did not become a permanent fixture of party control. The initial shift from reconciliation towards coercion eventually began to move back towards a more centrist approach, engineered by Kádár. Already from the June 1957 party conference onwards Kádár had begun to outflank the more conservative elements in the party, replacing them with individuals more amenable to efforts towards social accommodation. Simultaneously, those tainted by association with Nagy were purged. Kádár thus pursued an effective two-front policy, eliminating both factions of the party that might challenge his leadership – particularly the dogmatic Rákosiites, whose restoration to power was feared by the population and whose opposition by Kádár won him some popular support.[20]

While these actions can be attributed to the tactical skills of Kádár, an important contributing factor was the state of the party itself. Shattered by the revolution, shorn of members, its heroic myths and much of its leadership, the chaos within the institution gave Kádár the opportunity to incorporate within the structure a new set of administrative ideologies which recognized the need to build stronger institutional ties at the national level. As a consequence, the party turned sharply away from its earlier course, forging a new policy of formal and informal societal co-optation.

With the elimination of party dogmatists and revolutionaries, Kádár began to move once again in favour of a more conciliatory approach to the population as a whole, bolstered by the revival of de-Stalinization in the Soviet Union in 1961. This has been best summed up in his oft-cited quotation in 1962 that 'whereas the Rákosiites used to say that those who are not with us are against us, we say those who are not

20. For an excellent discussion of the early post-revolutionary period and the uncertain position of Kádár against Stalinist forces within the new MSZMP, see Kis, 'Az 1956–1957-es restauráció'. For the party perspective see Iván Szenes, *A Kommunista Párt Újjászervezése Magyarországon 1956–57* [The Reorganization of the Communist Party in Hungary, 1956–57] (Budapest: Kossuth, 1976), and Tibor Erényi and Sándor Rákosi (eds), *Legyőzhetetlen erő: a magyar kommunista mozgalom szervezeti fejlődésének 50 éve* [Undefeatable strength: Fifty years in the development of the Hungarian communist movement] (Budapest: Kossuth, 1974).

against us are with us'.[21] A general amnesty for prisoners of the revolution had already been announced that same year, and between 1962 and 1965 Kádár was able to remove his remaining conservative enemies within the MSZMP, ending the uneasy *primus inter pares* relationship with them that had existed in the post-1956 period.[22]

Equally important, this period set the stage for what was to be known as the 'alliance policy', an expression of informal co-optation. This social contract, described by Ferenc Fehér as 'predicated on the systematic depoliticization of everyday political life', provided greater personal freedom and material comfort in exchange for social peace and the acceptance of the institutional status quo.[23] Despite the removal of Khrushchev in 1964, which some expected to be followed by that of Kádár,[24] the latter managed to win the backing of the new Soviet leadership for himself and his reform policies. Given the level of incompatibility between Soviet institutions and the Hungarian domestic environment, it was grudgingly accepted by Moscow that accommodations should be tolerated in order to create stability that did not stem only from the barrel of a gun. Kádár was able to press forward with his policies with increasing success. As Hankiss summarizes,

> the growing economic prosperity created for the majority of the population the opportunity to raise their standard of living; to build their homes, to eat and dress better, to buy cars and to travel. This trend was reinforced when, in the late 1960s and early 1970s, the outlines of an informal, tacit compromise began to emerge. An unofficial and unsigned deal between the ruling elite and the majority of the population was made: people renounced their rights to power and participation and, in exchange, they got (by East

21. Kovrig, *Communism in Hungary*: 350.
22. Péter Benkő, 'Hatalmi viszonyok a "legvidámabb barakkban"' [Power struggles in the 'happiest of barracks'], *Magyar Nemzet*, 21 January 1991: 8; see also Tőkés, *Hungary's Negotiated Revolution*: 44–6.
23. Fehér sees Kádárism as a form of Khrushchevism which managed to survive his overthrow, if only narrowly: 'Kádárism as applied Khrushchevism': 218–25.
24. Secret correspondence from Kádár to the Politburo indicates clearly that Kádár strongly opposed the removal of Khrushchev and the methods employed in his overthrow, fearing that the new Soviet party leadership would dredge up the circumstances of the 1956 revolution once again in their campaign against Khrushchev, undermining his own position in the process. Kádár's letter on the matter can be found in a collection of documents entitled *El nem égetett dokumentok* [unburned documents] (Budapest: Szabad Tér Kiadó, 1990): 64–8. See also Fehér, 'Kádárism as Applied Khrushchevism': 225, n. 16.

European standards) a relatively tolerant administration, a ceasefire on the ideological front, a consensual rhetoric instead of an aggressive and inquisitive one, a kind of cultural pluralism, and the opportunity to build up for themselves a more and more comfortable, Western-European-style material life.[25]

However, unlike in 1956, or later in Czechoslovakia and Poland, these steps did not represent an attempt to reorganize state socialism so as to better reflect the domestic environment at the expense of Soviet institutional demands. Rather, Kádárism at its essence represented a form of institutional dualism, where a whole array of *ad hoc* organizational forms were created to compensate for, but not replace, the intractable Soviet model.

One of the most important moves in this direction was the initiation of economic reform, beginning in the early 1960s. A working group on the subject, under the direction of Politburo member and Minister of Finance Rezső Nyers, had by 1965 presented a first draft on reform, dealing with industrial reorganization and autonomy and also changes in central planning and the incentive structure embodied within it. The political rationale for such actions was provided by linking the political

25. Hankiss, *East European Alternatives*: 35. This argument has been a basic explanation for much of Hungarian politics by specialists in the area. Some examples include Kovrig, *Communism in Hungary*, and idem, 'Hungary: The Deceptive Hybrid', *East European Politics and Societies* **1** (Winter 1987): 113–34; William F. Robinson, *The Pattern of Reform in Hungary* (New York: Praeger, 1973); William Shawcross, *Crime and Compromise: Janos Kadar and the Politics of Hungary Since Revolution* (New York: Dutton, 1974); Paul Lendvai, *Hungary: The Art of Survival* (London: I.B. Tauris, 1988); Peter Toma, *Socialist Authority: The Hungarian Experience* (New York: Praeger, 1988); Iván Völgyes, *Hungary: A Nation of Contradictions* (Boulder, CO: Westview Press, 1982). With reference to the role of artists and intellectuals in particular, see Miklos Haraszti, *The Velvet Prison* (New York: Basic Books, 1987), as well as the brilliant piece by Timothy Garton Ash, 'A Hungarian Lesson', in his *The Uses of Adversity* (New York: Vintage Books, 1990): 143–56.

Some general retrospectives on the eventual disintegration of this 'Kádárist compact' include László Lengyel, *Végkifejlet* [Final denouement] (Budapest: Közgazdasági és Jogi Könyvkiadó, 1989); Attila Ágh, *A Századvég Gyermekei* [The children of the end of the century] (Budapest: Közgazdasági és Jogi Könyvkiadó, 1990); István Schlett, 'Egy ál(lam)párt tündöklése és bukása [The rise and fall of the (pseudo-) party-state]', *Századvég* nos 3–4 (1990): 50–58; Júlia Szalai, 'A társadalmi integráció és dezintegráció a Kádár-korszakban [Societal integration and disintegration in the Kádár era]', ibid.: 38–49.

crisis in 1956 in part to economic deficiencies under Rákosi, thereby drawing attention to the implicit need for domestic reform as a requisite of political stability.[26] The removal of Khrushchev in 1964 led to a temporary suspension of these plans, but by 1966, with confidence in Kádár reaffirmed by the new Soviet leadership, the Central Committee formally approved the reform package created by Nyers and his advisers.

Implemented in 1968, the New Economic Mechanism (NEM), as it came to be known, represented the first attempt at comprehensive economic reform within the Warsaw Pact, far enough ahead of its time that it became a real source of government interest in the Soviet Union only during the Gorbachev period.[27] Fundamentally, the NEM led to the elimination of most compulsory directives to industries from the centre, a greater role for enterprise autonomy and market forces, and an increase in the role of the private and cooperative sectors, creating a more decentralized and mixed socialist economy which permitted a greater role for entrepreneurial activity.[28] Even where such reforms were eventually scaled back through fear of their undermining socialism, the secondary level of private and semi-legal production remained intact and strongly influenced Hungarian economic life. Parallel with these developments in the economic sphere and the resulting increase in consumer prosperity (the development of what Hungarians called 'frigidaire socialism'), the party initiated a rapid liberalization within society in general. While fundamental issues regarding basic Marxist–Leninist tenets (the organizational core of the party) and the relationship between Hungary and the Soviet Union were not open to discussion, the party slowly withdrew its control in most other areas of debate. This had a profound effect on the ability of society, and particularly the intelligentsia, to acquire and transmit information. The

26. Judy Batt, *Economic Reform and Political Change in Eastern Europe* (New York: St. Martin's Press, 1988): 126.
27. Anders Åslund, *Gorbachev's Struggle for Economic Reform* (Ithaca, NY: Cornell University Press, 1989): 33–4.
28. Paul Marer, 'Economic System', in Klaus-Detlev Grothusen (ed.) *Hungary*, Handbook on South Eastern Europe, vol. V (Göttingen: Vanderhoeck & Ruprecht, 1987): 276-301. For overviews of economic reform during this period see also Robinson, *The Pattern of Reform in Hungary*, esp. chaps 5–6; Batt, *Economic Reform and Political Change*; Iván Berend, *The Hungarian Economic Reforms 1953–1988* (Cambridge: Cambridge University Press, 1990); Nigel Swain, *Hungary: The Rise and Fall of Feasible Socialism* (London: Verso, 1992).

former 'bourgeois' sciences, such as sociology, political science, philosophy, genetics, cybernetics and psychology, were similarly allowed to function as distinct disciplines.[29]

In the media, self-censorship became the primary method of party control, which permitted a greater expression of opinions through the policy of '*támogátott, tűrt, tíltott* [supported, tolerated, and forbidden]'.[30] New journals aimed at the intelligentsia (such as *Új irás*, *Alföld*, *Jelenkor*, *Tiszatáj*, *Valóság*, and later *Mozgó Világ*) became the main arenas for various frank debates. The limit to what could be published was instead replaced by the channelling of radical views into such peripheral journals, which had little impact on society as a whole. Contacts with nations outside the Warsaw Pact were also eased. One study of the rural Hungarian intelligentsia (those outside Budapest) undertaken in 1968 found that some 34 per cent of those surveyed had travelled to the West by that time. This developed simultaneously with increased travel to Yugoslavia and the rapid influx, as well, of millions of Western tourists into Hungary itself.[31] While the core institutions of the party-state remained intact, new routines and practices were forming around the edges of the political system, leading to what a number of Hungarian social scientists came to call the 'dual' or 'second society'.[32]

A formal process of party co-optation also took place, as the MSZMP began to actively court the growing intelligentsia. This was particularly the case with younger members of non-intelligentsia parents, whose rise to this class could be traced directly to the economic progress which had occurred under socialism and were presumably more supportive of socialist institutions as a result.[33] This

29. This is a fascinating topic that requires a study in itself, particularly in the areas of sociology and political science, where, as former prime minister turned radical sociologist András Hegedüs put it, Western concepts and methodology were 'smuggled' into Marxist theory: András Hegedüs, *Élet egy eszme árnyékában* [Life in the shadow of an idea] (Budapest: Bethlen Gábor Könyvkiadó, 1989).

30. For details on self-censorship and the liberal policy towards the Hungarian media see Toma, *Socialist Authority*, chap. 6, and Ash, 'A Hungarian Lesson'.

31. Iván Szelényi, *A vidéki értelmiség helyzete* [The state of the rural intelligentsia], vol. 1 (Budapest: TTI, 1971): 158; Jörg K. Hoensch, *A History of Modern Hungary* (London: Longman, 1988): 262.

32. Hankiss, *East European Alternatives*, chap. 3.

33. For details see Tamás Kolosi and Edward Lipinski, *Equality and Inequality Under Socialism* (Beverly Hills, CA: Sage, 1983). Between 1949 and 1970 the number of

policy underscores Selznick's view of co-optation as a means by which organizational control and legitimacy can be defended by the incorporation of, or through conciliation with, social forces, and also as a means by which administrative functions can be enhanced.

One example of this policy was the creation of the *Társadalomtudományi Intézet* - Social Science Institute, or TTI. This organization was not a subunit under the Ministry of Education, but rather was connected directly to the Central Committee of the MSZMP, and came to involve many of the best-known social scientists in Hungary. Founded in the late 1960s, the TTI served as a kind of exile for more radical thinkers in the party whose activity was seen as potentially dangerous; rather than ejecting them from the party or firing them from the universities they were instead often invited to work at the more insulated TTI. The institute thus served as a kind of 'safety-valve', permitting all kinds of sensitive research within and under the auspices of the party, which hoped to limit the scope of its impact.[34] The author's own perusal of the TTI's former library turned up hundreds of unpublished papers on various social and political topics, as well as numerous Western books and articles dealing with sociology, political science and East European state socialism, all originally provided for the use of the Institute but otherwise under closed access. At the state level, the *Pénzügykutatási Intézet* (Financial Research Institute) served a similar function, bringing together prominent party economists and 'overseeing' their work.[35] Overall, party policies towards the intelligentsia were highly successful. One study showed that by the late 1960s nearly half of the intelligentsia between 30 and 50 belonged to the MSZMP.[36] The Kádárist system, by promoting 'reform' as a new

persons with higher education in Hungary had tripled from approximately 100,000 to more than 300,000: Huszár, *Mit ér a szellem*: 93.

34. Csaba Gombár, personal interview by the author, Budapest, 19 April 1993. Gombár illustrated this point with the fact that although the TTI was ostensibly created to serve the Central Committee as a kind of technocratic 'brains trust', the TTI was never commissioned to conduct work on their behalf. Similarly, Gombár noted that in the early 1970s he was allowed to travel to the US to study at Berkeley, but the party would not grant him permission to travel to the USSR - for fear that his views would horrify their Soviet comrades.

35. See McDonald, 'Transition to Utopia': 227–8; also László Lengyel, interview by Zoltán Ács, in *Kizárt a párt* [Expelled from the party] (n.p.: Primo Kiadó, n.d.), 51–3.

36. Szelényi, *A vidéki értelmiség*, vol. 7 (Budapest: TTI, 1973), 9.

ideology, was consequently able to recast itself completely – from the image of a Soviet puppet regime to that of a pragmatic, paternalistic leadership.

THE INTELLIGENTSIA 'NEW CLASS' IN HUNGARY AND EASTERN EUROPE: LIMITS TO POWER

This general process of liberalization and co-optation of the intelligentsia was, however, not unique to Hungary during this period. This must be set within the context of the time period: by the 1960s, faith in capitalist 'bourgeois democracy' had been called into question by many in the West, contributing to the rise of the New Left movement and its profound impact on politics in all of Europe. In much of Eastern Europe there were attempts at domestic legitimation to various degrees, predicated on both the 'technological fix' of technical reforms and the opening-up of domestic discourse. Neo-Marxism began to strongly influence intellectual thought (particularly in the universities), which ranged from re-examinations of Marx's writings to Maoist and anarchist thought, complemented by theoretical perspectives derived from Western social science. Hungary in particular saw the formation of the so-called 'Budapest School' of critical Marxists, influenced by the work of György Lukács.[37]

As in Western political science, among many of the East European intelligentsia perspectives on technology and ideology began to merge, as there grew a strong belief that the modernization process and the 'technological imperative' involved therein would fundamentally change the nature of state socialism as currently understood. This view

37. Excellent discussions of the Hungarian generational context can be found in Huszár, *Mit ér a szellem*, 46–7; László Kéri, *Politikai folyamatok szocializációs metszetben* [Political processes in segmented socialization] (Budapest: TTI, 1989), esp. 147–209; Iván Völgyes, 'Political Culture', in Grothusen, *Hungary*: 191–212.
There are numerous discussions, both historical and philosophical, of the Budapest School: see, for example, Szelényi, 'The Prospects and Limits of the East European New Class Project'; George Schöpflin, 'Opposition and Para-Opposition: Critical Currents in Hungary, 1968–78', in Rudolf L. Tőkés (ed.), *Opposition in Eastern Europe* (Baltimore, MD: Johns Hopkins University Press, 1979): 142–86; Andrew Arato, 'The Budapest School and Actually Existing Socialism', in *From Neo-Marxism to Democratic Theory*: 122–45.

foresaw the rise of the intelligentsia as the next 'New Class', pushing aside old dogmatists and transforming the party into a rational instrument of socialist progress.

In Eastern Europe this idea was perhaps best articulated by Radovan Richta, whose book *Civilization at the Crossroads* predicted the end of both capitalism and the bureaucratic disorders of socialism, and which Iván Szelényi describes as 'a bible of members of the East European New Class around 1968'.[38] A plethora of studies and arguments within the same vein soon followed, some notable examples being the work of Rudolf Bahro and Robert Havemann in East Germany, Jacek Kuroń, Karol Modzelewski and Leszek Kolakowski in Poland, and Iván Szelényi and György Konrád in Hungary, who expressed perfectly the essence of this 'new New Class' contention in the title of their book, *The Intellectuals on the Road to Class Power*.[39] The idea of rationalization, the interpenetration of Marxism and technological development, was for many of the East European intelligentsia logical and axiomatic, given the definition of Marxism as a scientific theory of human progress rather than an institutional ideology as it had become under Stalin.

As events were to show, however, this perspective proved fatally flawed, and a number of intellectuals were to suffer for it. Interestingly, it was Talcott Parsons who first alluded to this issue, a problem in the Weberian rationalization perspective which he dealt with in his introduction to his edited volume of Weber's writings, *The Theory of Social and Economic Organization*. Parsons argued that Weber had confused two forms of authority, one based on technical expertise and one which derives from a 'legally defined office'. This created the possibility that technical authority might find itself subordinate to organizational authority, for with regard to the latter 'it is not logically essential to it that its exerciser should have either superior knowledge or superior skill as compared to those subject to his orders'.[40]

38. Radovan Richta et al., *Civilization at the Crossroads: Social and Human Implications of the Scientific and Technological Revolution* (New York: International Arts and Sciences Press, 1969); Szelényi, 'The Prospects and Limits of the East European New Class Project': 112.
39. Iván Szelényi and György Konrád, *The Intellectuals on the Road to Class Power* (New York: Harcourt Brace Jovanovich, 1979). Indeed, much of Szelényi's work on this topic was initially sponsored by the TTI: see note 31.
40. Talcott Parsons, introduction to Weber, *The Theory of Social and Economic Organization*: 59. Parsons's observations are critiqued in Charles Perrow, *Complex*

While Parsons did not pursue the logical implications of his statement, others began to argue by way of extension that there was no reason to suppose that 'experts' would overtake 'reds' as a matter of organizational course. This was further developed by a number of sociologists, among them Gouldner, whose empirical studies concentrated on the development of social roles within organizations and reformulated Weberian perspectives of organizational rationalization. The number of 'experts' brought into the hierarchy of the organization, Gouldner concluded, was contingent on the unit's perception of the social environment external to it. As Gouldner noted, 'it cannot be supposed … that a bureaucracy operating in an environment which is dangerous to it or is regarded as such … will give the recruitment of expert personnel a more salient place than the reinforcement of loyalty'.[41]

Drawing upon these conclusions, in later analyses Gouldner specifically dealt with the idea of the new intelligentsia class, touching upon its position under state socialism. Along the lines of institutional arguments and shaped by the work of Weber and Michels, Gouldner stressed that although revolutionary organizations inevitably fall victim to a bureaucratic class engendered by their very success, technological imperatives eventually dictate a need for intelligentsia skills, and as a result some kind of compromise may be forged – as we have mentioned previously.

However, the bureaucracy, fully aware that their power rests fundamentally upon institutional authority as opposed to technical competence, are unlikely to willingly give up power and surrender the institution and its ideology to technological pragmatism. In Eastern Europe, as with the case of the French Jacobins, the intelligentsia thus becomes a 'blocked class', kept down by 'the requirements of ideological certification'.[42] This is reminiscent of Weber's discussion not of

Organizations: A Critical Essay (New York: McGraw-Hill, 1986): 42–6.

41. 'Cosmopolitans and Locals: Toward an Analysis of Latent Social Roles – I', *Administrative Science Quarterly* **2** (December 1957): 465–6. See also idem, *Patterns of Industrial Bureaucracy* (Glencoe, IL: Free Press, 1957).
42. Gouldner, *The Future of the Intellectuals and the Rise of the New Class*: 50–53, 60–63, 91–2. While Gouldner did believe in the inevitable victory of the 'new New Class', he argued that this would occur through conflict; a dialectical, as opposed to evolutionary, process. See also Donald C. Hodges, *The Bureaucratization of Socialism* (Amherst, MA: University of Massachusetts Press, 1981). For the opposite view, see David Lane, *The Socialist Industrial State* (Boulder, CO: Westview Press, 1976), esp. 92–7.

rationalization, but rather of the routinization of charismatic orders, their 'traditionalization' as opposed to 'legalization', such that a patrimonial order will be the end result.[43]

Thus, the likelihood of the gradual overwhelming of state socialism by the intelligentsia was of questionable validity. Anthony Giddens, in his criticism of convergence and evolutionary arguments regarding Eastern Europe and the Soviet Union, concluded that

> a mode of social and economic organization which breeds definite tensions does not on that account necessarily undergo change, and even if such change does take place, the direction which it follows is not inevitably towards 'adaptation', in any simple sense ... the response of the Party organizations, or the state socialist governments generally, might be to retrench the position of the Party more strongly than is the case at the present, and it is not at all obvious that such a path of action is foredoomed to ultimate failure.[44]

State socialist institutions, as hardened organizational forms valued and defended by their own *apparatchiki*, were not likely to give way happily to radical reform.

These arguments were supported by several studies that attempted to test the hypothesis of the growing rationalization of communist parties, as indicated by their increasing co-optation of the intelligentsia. An

43. Weber, *The Theory of Social and Economic Organization*: 363–86.
44. Anthony Giddens, *The Class Structure of Advanced Societies* (New York: Harper & Row, 1975): 247.

This point has been shared by a number of other authors, for example Melvin Croan, who saw that intelligentsia forces are more likely to be shut out of political power specifically because of their inherent danger, since 'revisionist exposition of revolutionary ideology, especially at the hands of critical communist intellectuals ... can readily become a guide not for the institutionalization of one-party rule but rather its dismantlement': see his 'Is Mexico the Future of Eastern Europe?: Institutional Adaptability and Political Change in Comparative Perspective', in Huntington and Moore, *Authoritarian Politics in Modern Society*: 475. In addition, Jowitt's discussion of 'inclusion' as a necessary process in Leninist nation-building also deals directly with the tension created by inclusion processes and their potential for reversal as a result. However, Jowitt stressed that such a conflict within state socialism was not zero-sum, but rather a natural part of nation-building, and that as a result 'unprecedented types of modern systems' may emerge from these systems, an evolutionary 'third road' perspective which he later abandoned: Kenneth Jowitt, *New World Disorder: The Leninist Extinction* (Berkeley, CA: University of California Press, 1992), esp. chaps 3–4.

early study by Frederic Fleron on the Soviet leadership found that specialized intelligentsia were in fact being co-opted into lower party bodies; for example, since the 1950s this group showed strong gains in representation at party congresses. Yet this did not translate into significant gains within higher political structures. In the Central Committee representation hovered at about 15–17 per cent, while within the Politburo intelligentsia representation dropped dramatically between 1952 and 1961 - from 25 per cent to zero. Fleron concluded that while the incorporation of the intelligentsia was part of socialist rule, there was no correspondence of this activity to the actual sharing of political power.[45]

A later study by Jack Bielasiak concerning the same question but with regard to Eastern Europe also showed that 'communist leaders have responded by recruiting better trained specialists, while at the same time compensating for the lack of political socialization among the experts by restricting their areas of authority'. In fact, in a number of cases, Bielasiak found that the co-optation of intellectuals was offset by a simultaneous increase in the predominance of party *apparatchiki* at higher levels.[46] The new intelligentsia were being checked by the party bureaucracy, leading to the utilization of intelligentsia skills without allowing them control over spheres of central decision-making.

Thus, the main flaw of many neo-Marxist perspectives stemmed from the fact that they perceived state socialism as an evolutionary organism or administrative tool rather than as an institution concerned fundamentally with its own survival over the achievement of any concrete notions of socialist progress - for the party élite the two were one and the same. Consequently, as reformist views became more prominent and radical in intellectual circles in Eastern Europe during the late 1960s the more the party feared for its own stability, resisting intelligentsia notions of the party as an instrument to be reformed or dispensed with, rather than as a structure to be revered in and of itself.

With the rise in new modes of critical socialist thought, the East European communist parties eventually sought to defend themselves through a return to anti-reform rhetoric and actions, in order to preserve

45. Frederic J. Fleron, 'Cooptation as a Mechanism of Adaption to Change', *Polity* **2** (Winter 1969): 177–201.
46. Jack Bielasiak, 'Lateral and Vertical Elite Differentiation in European Communist States', *Studies in Comparative Communism* **11** (Spring/Summer 1978): 141.

themselves and the institutional status quo. Reform Marxists had not understood the institutionalized nature of their own parties: Szelényi, in a later self-critique of *The Intellectuals on the Road to Class Power*, confessed that

> although we noted the uneasiness of the Stalinist bureaucracy with the increasing ascendancy of the intellectuals to positions of domination and we carefully analyzed their 'counteroffensive', we believed that the bureaucratic estate would be rational enough to give up its hegemony and make a deal with the technocracy, a deal that might save state socialism and the bureaucracy. We were wrong. The bureaucracy proved to be stubborn and less willing to share power and to compromise than we anticipated.[47]

From 1968, the intelligentsia class of Eastern Europe (as well as that of the Soviet Union) came under increasing attack by the party, resulting in widespread purges, intelligentsia alienation and the reassertion of more hardline, anti-reformist attitudes.[48] Where domestic institutionalization was still pursued, its predication on increased intellectual autonomy was discarded in favour of appealing either to narrow technocratic claims, rationalizing (but not liberalizing) the centralized economy, or to traditional legitimizing forms, defining and justifying the party-state with the same myths used by their ruling predecessors.

In Czechoslovakia, where dramatic reform unfolded within a process of late de-Stalinization, the country was finally invaded for this heresy. Massive purges of close to one-third of the membership followed, hitting the party intelligentsia - who had spearheaded the Prague Spring - particularly hard. After 1968 the party returned to a highly centralized form, legitimized primarily by its conformity to Soviet strictures, and institutionalizing what has been called 'the framework for a permanent purge'.[49] Unlike the Hungarian case, attempts to institutionalize the political order at the domestic level were

47. Szelényi, 'The Prospects and Limits of the East European New Class Project': 116.
48. See Michael Shafir, 'Political Stagnation and Marxist Critique: 1968 and Beyond in Comparative East European Perspective', *British Journal of Political Science* **14** (1984): 435–59.
49. Jacques Rupnik, 'The Restoration of the Party-State in Czechoslovakia since 1968', in Leslie Holmes (ed.), *The Withering Away of the State?* (London: Sage, 1981): 110. On the effect of purges on the membership and its demographics, see Gordon Wightman, 'Membership of the Communist Party of Czechoslovakia in the 1970s', *Soviet Studies* **XXXV** (April 1983): 208–22.

rejected completely, driving intellectuals and much of the population away from the party.

East Germany also soon launched its own offensive against the intelligentsia; Havemann and Bahro came under attack by the party, and that nation 'descended rapidly into the shadows of cultural retrenchment if not outright repression'.[50] However, the party-state continued to emphasize the need for technocratic reform and economic rationalization, co-opting technical specialists while marginalizing non-technical intellectuals, and overall maintaining its hardline institutional stance – a policy, not coincidentally, reminiscent of German fascism.[51] Legitimacy, to the extent that it was generated, derived from the high standard of living attributed to this narrow emphasis on economic rationality, creating a form of institutionalization that dissident Wolfgang Biermann called 'computer Stalinism'.[52]

Other conflicts over domestic legitimation were evident elsewhere in the region. In Poland, the party had long struggled with reform as a means of coaxing support from an overtly hostile society, first attempting political reforms (such as in 1956) and then technocratic ones. Internal party opposition and tensions bred by these policies, however, inevitably followed, leading the party time and again to retrench. In 1968, increasing intellectual ferment eventually led to student riots, which provided the justification for an anti-intellectual, anti-Semitic purge of thousands from the party.[53] Under the leadership of Edward Gierek in the early 1970s, the party attempted instead to emphasize the

50. Henry Krisch, 'Political Legitimation in the German Democratic Republic', in T.H. Rigby and Ferenc Fehér (eds), *Political Legitimation in Communist States* (London: Macmillan, 1982): 119; see also David Childs, 'The SED Faces the Challenges of Ostpolitik and Glasnost', in David Childs, Thomas A. Baylis and Marlyn Reuschemeyer (eds), *East Germany in Comparative Perspective* (New York: Routledge, 1989): 3–14.

51. On the question of technical cooptation Thomas A. Baylis, in his important study on East Germany, noted that the increased emphasis on technical expertise did not translate into greater intelligentsia influence within the party, who remained locked out of the Central Committee and government; the absence of the cultural intelligentsia in particular from the party higher ranks, Baylis observed, was 'glaring': see his *The Technical Intelligentsia and the East German Elite* (Berkeley, CA: University of California Press, 1974), esp. 271–4.

52. Leslie Holmes, 'The GDR: "Real Socialism" or "Computer Stalinism"?', in Holmes, *The Withering Away of the State?*: 125–50.

53. Jan B. de Weydenthal, *The Communists of Poland* (Stanford, CA: Hoover Institution Press, 1986): 128–30.

technical rationalization of the party-state, but the results were so disastrous they eroded any domestic institutional linkages, paving the way for the rise of Solidarity and the party's desperate recourse to coercion through martial law.[54]

Even in Romania and Bulgaria, where liberalization had been modest to begin with, those minor steps forward were quickly reversed. This was most notably capped off in Romania by the initiation of a 'little cultural revolution', directed against the party intelligentsia and apparently inspired by Nicolae Ceauşescu's visit to North Korea.[55] Instead, domestic institutionalization was sought through traditional, 'Balkan' institutional forms, such as the development of sultanistic and dynastic party apparatuses, as well as the resurrection of nationalism and pre-communist history which placed the party as the expression of national destiny.[56]

The dismal setback of the party intelligentsia across the bloc by the early 1970s led to a gloomy reappraisal of the earlier hopes for real reform. One critique by expelled Hungarian party members János Kis and György Bence (writing under the pseudonym of Marc Rakovski) argued that the supposed rise of the intelligentsia in Eastern Europe had been in reality the product of their manipulation by the ruling party élite during their post-Stalinist internecine battles. Consequently,

> once the division in the ruling class had been overcome (the definitive date for the East European countries as a whole was the end of the 1960s), it was time for disillusion. The new elite in power will only tolerate autonomy to the extent that the unified hierarchical system of institutions is not threatened with disintegration. It is clear now that we are not headed towards the institutionalization of cultural and scientific freedoms, and that public debates are no longer permitted to continue even at the level which they had reached during the years of destalinization.[57]

54. Michael D. Kennedy, *Professionals, Power, and Solidarity in Poland* (Cambridge: Cambridge University Press, 1991).
55. Daniel Chirot, 'The Corporatist Model and Socialism: Notes on Romanian Development', *Theory and Society* **9** (March 1980): 374; see also Michael Shafir, 'Political Stagnation and Marxist Critique', 456–9.
56. Bogdan Szajkowski, 'Albania, Bulgaria, Romania: Political Innovations and the Party', in Holmes, *The Withering Away of the State?*: 33–50.
57. Marc Rakovski [pseud. of János Kis and György Bence], *Toward an East European Marxism* (London: Allison & Busby, 1978): 53.

Despite the conclusions of Kis and Bence, within all of Eastern Europe the counterattack against reform and the intelligentsia was weakest of all in Hungary. To be sure, dogmatic forces still held power within the MSZMP, who increasingly responded to the successes of the NEM by questioning whether such reform would eventually undermine socialist institutions as a whole.

Seizing upon this threat, by 1972 party conservatives had mustered enough power and apparent support from Moscow (which had grown wary of economic and political pluralization after the Prague Spring) to launch a direct attack against the emboldened reformist intelligentsia, party reform policies, and Kádár himself.[58] The first victims singled out were some of the most prominent members of the party intelligentsia (the Budapest School in particular), whose critical analyses of socialism were not appreciated by the party's higher ranks. A number came under severe criticism by the party, and by 1973 had been expelled from the MSZMP, leaving the country shortly thereafter.[59] The Central Committee declared that the party had assigned 'a more than necessary significance ... to the party's intelligentsia', and returned to the

58. Hoensch, *A History of Modern Hungary*, 241–8. Documents which have recently come to light support the long-standing rumour that a 'palace coup' of sorts had been organized against Kádár in the spring of 1972, led by hardline Politburo members Zoltán Komócsin and Béla Biszku. In response to this challenge, Kádár openly petitioned to retire, and thus brought into the struggle the Central Committee, where he continued to enjoy strong support. In the end his 'request' was denied. Copies of the documents surrounding Kádár's 1972 petition to retire can be found in *El nem égetett*: 75–105; see also András Nyírő (ed.), *Segédkönyv a politikai bizottság tanulmányozásához* [Resource guide to the study of the Politburo] (Budapest: Interart, n.d.): 265, 290; and Tőkés, *Hungary's Negotiated Revolution*: 102–7.

59. Notably Ferenc Fehér, Ágnes Heller, György and Mária Márkus, György Bence, János Kis, Iván Szelényi, András Hegedüs and Mihály Vajda. For the official position taken against the radical intelligentsia, see the March 1973 party proclamation 'Néhány társadalomkutató antimarxista nézetei [The anti-Marxist views of some social researchers]' in *Az MSZMP határozatai és dokumentumai 1971/75* [decisions and documents of the MSZMP, 1971–75] (Budapest: Kossuth, 1976): 456. Some of those sympathetic to the Budapest School were later to become key figures of the urban opposition, eventually embracing liberal views as a response to the encroachments of the party-state. For a more general discussion of these purges and the impact of this period of counter-reform within the party see Imre Pozsgay, 'Az óvatos duhaj [The cautious reveler]', interview by Ervin Csizmadia, *Mozgó Világ* 18 (October 1992): 45–61.

standard call for a greater co-optation of the working class in their stead.[60]

The NEM soon came under fire as well, not only for the 'petit bourgeois' social strata it was seen to foster, but for its presumed role in social pluralization. Hardliners managed to achieve the recentralization of much of industry and scale back the achievements of the NEM. This culminated in the removal of Nyers not only from his position as head of the Central Committee Secretariat for economic reform, but by 1975 from the Politburo as well.[61]

Still, despite these gains, many of those same hardliners were themselves soon isolated from positions of power within the Politburo, reminiscent of Kádár's earlier two-front policy. Equally important, party expulsions or resignations did not go beyond that of the few radical intellectuals who had run foul of the leadership, as opposed to the tens of thousands who were purged or left the party elsewhere in the bloc. Research by several scholars indicates that in Hungary the party continued to actively co-opt the intelligentsia and white-collar workers, further deepening the MSZMP's middle-class character.[62] Economic reform was halted, although moves back in this direction slowly re-emerged by 1978.[63] Limited administrative reform was also initiated, within both the state and party apparatus. Changes in territorial administration attempted to devolve more decision-making power to the local level, while inside the party the *nomenklatura* system of direct party appointments was nearly halved, with this directed particularly towards the lower levels of the state.[64] Finally, at the informal level the policy

60. 'Történelmi utunk [Our historical road]', *Társadalmi Szemle* **XLIV**, special issue (February 1989): 60.
61. Nyírő , *Segédkönyv*: 302–3; Berend, *The Hungarian Economic Reforms*, chap. 20; see also Rezső Nyers, interview by György Baló, in idem, *Kilenc beszélgetés a 80-as évekből* [Nine conversations from the 1980s] (Budapest: Múzsák, 1988): 11–23.
62. Szonja Szelényi, 'Social Inequality and Party Membership: Patterns of Recruitment into the Hungarian Socialist Workers' Party', *American Sociological Review* **52** (October 1987): 559–73; Tamás Kolosi and Ágnes Bokor, 'A párttagság és a társadalmi rétegződés [Party membership and social stratification]', in *A társadalmi struktúra, az életmód és a tudat alakulása Magyarországon* [Social structure and the formation of lifestyle and consciousness in Hungary] (Budapest: TTI, 1985): 77–111.
63. Berend, *The Hungarian Economic Reform*, chap. 23.
64. On the decentralization policy of the MSZMP see Robinson, *The Pattern of Reform in Hungary*: 245–56; with regard to the reduction in the size of the *nomenklatura*,

of social liberalization rebounded by the late 1970s, and the relative freedom of the press continued to develop despite occasional sanctions.[65] In the rest of the region the hope of the intelligentsia for reform was dead. Yet in Hungary it remained the central source of institutionalization and legitimacy, blunted but not so easily discarded. The cultivation of the party's image as the instrument of change and progress remained critical to national stability.

Through the mid-1980s the party was consequently able to achieve a relatively high level of legitimacy, as indicated by public opinion polls which showed that as late as 1985 two-thirds of those surveyed were both content with the party's work and believed that the MSZMP served their interests.[66] This triumph of the party seems almost

see György T. Varga and István Szakadát, 'Íme, a nómenklatúrák! [Behold the *nomenklatura*!]', *Társadalmi Szemle* **XLVII**, no. 3 (1992): 75.

65. The best example here is the firing of Ferenc Kulin from his job as head of *Mozgó Világ* in 1983 for the journal's 'systematic defiance' of party guidelines, to which Kulin's open association with members of the dissident community probably contributed as well. However, Kulin's replacement did not lead to the end of *Mozgó Világ* as a source a nonconformist and critical thought; the first issue under the new editorship included an interview with the outcast Rezső Nyers, who spoke openly of his removal in 1974 as part of a conservative 'counter-reformation'. This action is indicative of the two-steps forward, one-step back policy towards the intelligentsia, Haraszti's 'velvet prison' or Ash's 'hall of mirrors'. For many intellectuals and dissidents it was thus a great source of confusion (and symptomatic of the Kádárist system of social control) that from 1984 on in many ways *Mozgó Világ* continued its critical function that it had prior to its editorial shake-up – according to some even better than before. This confusion is discussed clearly in Sándor Radnóti, 'Mozog-e a világ? [Is the earth moving?]', *Hírmondó*, 1984 no. 5, reprinted in *Szamizdat '81–89: Válogatás a Hírmondó című folyóiratból* [Samizdat 1981–1989: Selections from the periodical *Hírmondó*], edited by Gábor Demszky (Budapest: AB, 1990): 92–5; see also Gáspár Miklós Tamás, roundtable discussion with Iván Vitányi and István Eörsi, 'Egyezzünk ki [We should compromise]', *Mozgó Világ* 18 (June 1992): 32–3.

66. László Bruszt and János Simon, 'Politikai orientációk Magyarországon a rendszerváltás évében [Political orientations in Hungary during the transition]', in *A lecsendesített többség* [The appeased majority] (Budapest: TTI, 1990): 22, table 6. The public opinion studies conducted by Bruszt and Simon led them to the conclusion that although the general public did not believe that they had an effective voice in government or party affairs, they believed that policies carried out for them were in their best interest – what they term a symptom of 'late paternalism'. See also László Bruszt, '"Without Us but For Us?" Political Orientation in Hungary in the Period of Late Paternalism', *Social Research* **55** (Spring/Summer 1988): 43–76. A similar study by Radio Free Europe also acknowledged the success of the

inconceivable in retrospect – how could a counterrevolutionary force, installed by Soviet power, be considered legitimate? As Ágnes Heller, one of the Hungarian party intellectuals purged in the 1970s, explained,

> for what is meant by legitimation is not legitimation of a government but rather a form of domination, and the Hungarian government enjoys a degree of support by the people despite its exercising a form of domination which they reject, precisely because it exercises it in a more bearable manner than do the governments of other similar countries.[67]

CO-OPTATION AND THE SEGREGATION OF THE HUNGARIAN PARTY INTELLIGENTSIA

The party continued to rely on reform and co-optation as the source of domestic institutionalization, purging only those few individuals who were perceived as a potential threat to party sanctity. Hungary remained unique in that the party did not expel or alienate the reformist core of the party intelligentsia, and pressed on with the continued development of liberalization policies, which some went so far as to call a kind of 'controlled pluralism'.[68] Whereas elsewhere the conservative backlash of the late 1960s and 1970s served to destroy the socialist illusions of many intellectuals and pave the way for active or passive dissent, in Hungary a significant section of the Hungarian intelligentsia remained within the party, supporters of the concept of 'reform' socialism. Ironically, however, this same liberalization which helped build institutional support for the MSZMP also fostered the critical discourse of the party intelligentsia segment, who over time separated their support for socialism as a concept from the institutions which supposedly embodied it.

This was compounded by the fact that while there can be no doubt that co-optation policies continued to have a strong impact on the party

'Kádárist compromise' in generating public support; Radio Free Europe Eastern European Area Audience and Opinion Research, 'Political Legitimacy in Eastern Europe: A Comparative Study' (March 1987): 11.

67. Ágnes Heller, 'Phases of Legitimation in Soviet-Type Systems', chap. in Ferenc Fehér, Ágnes Heller and György Márkus, *Dictatorship Over Needs* (New York: St. Martin's Press, 1983): 46.
68. Jeffrey D. Porro, 'Controlled Pluralism: Is Hungary the Future of Eastern Europe?' (Santa Monica: Rand Corporation, 1975): P-5386.

from the late 1960s on, the incorporation of young intellectuals into the party did not inevitably result in the ascension of an intelligentsia new class. Rather, in contrast to elsewhere in the region, where the battle between institutional sanctity and objective reform led to purges and backlash, the Hungarian party combined its co-optative practices with the creation of ideological roadblocks within the party, to serve what Fleron and Bielasiak had earlier described – the simultaneous utilization and segregation of the intelligentsia class. This took the form of the colonization of the 'weak' state organs by the intelligentsia, while the high echelons of the party – the real centre of power – were kept off limits.

The Hungarian sociologist Ferenc Gazsó has provided solid empirical evidence in this regard. In his analysis of some 6,000 high-level members of the *nomenklatura*, Gazsó found that the anticipated 'fusion' of reds and experts in Hungary did not in fact take place; rather, the two remained segregated, with the technical intelligentsia in particular holding sway over the subordinate state apparatus. As Gazsó notes,

> naturally, the party-state badly needed the professional competence of the intelligentsia, but it seems able to make use of the brainwork of the intelligentsia in such a way that the profession would take part in the work of the state machinery only in the role of experts, which meant that they were supposed to serve as an advisory group to the ruling elite.[69]

For example, within the state apparatus more than 90 per cent of the *nomenklatura* held university degrees by 1989, compared with some 57 per cent of cadres working within the party structure – indicating the disproportionate role of the working class within the party structures despite the 'intellectualization' of state organs.[70] While this difference is notable, it hides the even more striking fact that among those cadres with higher education working within the party, the bulk of these

69. Ferenc Gazsó, 'Cadre Bureaucracy and the Intelligentsia', *Journal of Communist Studies* **8** (September 1992): 86–7.

70. This is in keeping with the findings of an internal 1983 demographic study of the MSZMP by the Central Committee Department of Party and Mass Organizations which shows that while former manual labourers made up 58 per cent of the party *apparatus*, within the state organs their representation was only 37 per cent. *Statisztikai adatok a káderállományról* [Statistical data on cadre positions] (Budapest: MSZMP KB Párt- és Tömegszervezetek Osztálya, 1983): 10, 67.

degrees were attained *following* their ascendancy to power, rather than serving as a prerequisite to it. Gazsó states that 'it was mainly the teacher-training institutions and the universities of economics or law that offered them an opportunity to gain the (formal) degrees and diplomas that were required in their new position', degrees whose emphasis was on conferring status rather than on real educational content.[71]

Thus, when this same sample is analysed in terms of their 'convertible' skills, that is, professional training that could provide employment in an open labour market (such as foreign languages, doctoral degrees or specialized intellectual qualifications) the figures change dramatically. Among the state *nomenklatura* 71 per cent possessed such 'convertible' skills, while among cadres only 29 per cent had such qualifications.[72] Higher up the party hierarchy, other studies indicate that among the top 100 party cadres approximately half had no more than a tenth-grade education, while at the top levels of power – the Central Committee and the Politburo – membership and top political posts remained dominated by those of working-class backgrounds, a gerontocracy originating from the early recruitment waves of the 1950s.[73] As Rudolf Tőkés concludes,

> to counter the experts' growing influence, the PB [Politburo] sought to immunize the party *apparat* from ideological contraband brought in by 'the intellectuals' through the accelerated cooptation of blue-collar workers in key party positions. Cadre recruitment policies of deliberately bypassing even *first* generation university graduates (many of them with working-class backgrounds) in favor of quickly retrained manual laborers were desperate and politically self-defeating measures to preserve party control of the commanding heights of power in Hungary. (emphasis in original)[74]

71. Gazsó, 'Cadre Bureaucracy': 82; Örkény, 'Social Mobility': 261–2.
72. Gazsó, 'Cadre Bureaucracy': 87.
73. András Nyírő , 'Miért nem voltak hasznára az ancien regime-nek a diplomás káderek [Why were cadres with university diplomas of no use to the *ancien regime*?]', unpublished manuscript, 1990, cited in Rudolf L. Tőkés, 'Hungary's New Political Elites: Adaptation and Change, 1989–1990': 242–3; Szonja Szelényi, 'Social Inequality and Party Membership': 571. The present author's own analysis of the membership of the Politburo from 1956 to 1985 showed that more than 60 per cent of members were originally manual labourers, while the remaining white-collar members came primarily from pedagogical backgrounds as teachers in elementary or technical schools. The raw data was derived from Nyírő, *Segédkönyv*.
74. Tőkés, 'Hungary's New Political Elites': 248; see also idem, *Hungary's Negotiated*

One can debate the extent to which this specific recruitment policy of the MSZMP was 'desperate', as characterized by Tőkés; within the rubric of co-optation it indicates the degree to which the party was cognizant of the dangers associated with its domestic policies and responded accordingly. What is certain is that this method of recruitment and control limited the skills and flexibility of the party's higher ranks, particularly as they grew older and more insulated from new recruits (the classic Pareto 'circulation of élites', or what was sarcastically referred to as 'bureaucratic centralism') and faced a new crisis of economic decline. Moreover, it created a still-indistinct generation of intellectuals *within the party* who remained loyal to the idea of socialism but were marginalized by the party *apparat*, thus generating their hostility to the institutional forms that had relegated them to a peripheral role. Slowly but surely, the party was creating its own internal opposition.

THE MSZMP IN CRISIS AND THE EROSION OF THE ALLIANCE POLICY

Despite an increase in reform rhetoric (much of it spurred on by economic difficulties) by the early 1980s it became increasingly clear that the social contract of economic well-being in exchange for political passivity was eroding in Hungary. The mushrooming of the 'second economy' had created a large private sector, functioning alongside the traditional state industry, which remained sluggish and uncompetitive. Many Hungarians participated in both spheres, overworking themselves in the second economy where 'real money' could be made while their jobs in the state economy suffered.[75] Sharp class divisions began to reemerge as well, reinforcing among many a sense of a 'dual society' and undermining civic and collective social values (which had already

Revolution: 140–60.

75. For example, by the late 1980s studies indicated that half of all those employed worked more than 60 hours a week in two or more jobs: George Schöpflin, Rudolf L. Tőkés and Iván Völgyes, 'Leadership Change and Crisis in Hungary', *Problems of Communism* **37** (September–October 1988): 25. See also István Kemény, 'The Unregistered Economy in Hungary', *Soviet Studies* **XXXIV** (July 1982): 349–66, and idem, *Szociológiai írások* [Sociological writings] (Szeged: Replika Könyvek, 1992), esp. 219–52.

been eroded by the atomizing tendencies of Kádárist liberalization and the NEM).[76]

Functioning behind much of this were foreign loans, as the government borrowed heavily from the late 1970s on, creating the highest per capita foreign debt among the Warsaw Pact states. The resulting debt service burden, the increasing obsolescence of industry and infrastructure as well as the schizophrenic nature of private versus state enterprises began to take their toll on the economy and society. From the mid-1980s, Hungary exhibited negative growth rates; prices rose by more than 200 per cent from 1978 to 1988, and real wages fell to 1973 levels. By 1988 nearly one-quarter of the population had slipped into poverty, and life expectancy was ranked as the lowest among developed nations.[77] The attempt by the MSZMP to have it both ways, to combine rigid and omnicompetent institutional demands with *ad hoc* and largely incompatible routines and policies was generating dangerous levels of stress on the system as a whole.

But the party leadership, isolated by its own recruitment practices, was unable to respond with the kind of radical economic proposals deemed necessary, or even recognize the warning signs of economic crisis.[78] For example, the 1985 party congress was anticipated by many

76. Hankiss cites particularly striking statistics showing the destruction of a community-based value system in Hungary, based on results from the 1985 European Value Systems Study. *East European Alternatives*: 36.
77. Ágh, *A századvég gyermekei*: 32; see also Schöpflin, Tőkés and Völgyes, 'Leadership Change and Crisis': 23–7. For more on the economic woes of the Hungarian system, see Attila Ágh, 'Az elfáradt permanens forradalom avagy az extenzív politikai rendszer korlátai [The exhausted permanent revolution, or the barriers of the extensive political system]', *Tiszatáj* **XLII** (Fall 1988): 80–92, and László Bogár, *Kitörési kísérleteink* [Our attempts to break out] (Budapest: Közgazdasági és Jogi Könyvkiadó, 1989).
78. Prior to this there had been attempts to warn the party hierarchy of the deepening crisis. For example, in 1984 a conference sponsored jointly by the TTI and the Central Committee Agitation and Propaganda Department addressed specifically the topic of economic development, during which numerous participants warned of a social backlash were the party not to institute needed reforms – albeit to little effect. László Thoma, 'A magyar értelmiség 1970–1985 [The Hungarian intelligentsia, 1970–85]', unpublished paper, TTI collection, Budapest, 1988: 120; the conference is also covered in '"Gazdasági fejlődésünk és a gazdaságirányítás továbbfejlesztése"; országos elméleti tanácskozás Veszprémben ['Our economic development and the continued improvement of the directed economy': National theoretical conference in Veszprém]', *Társadalom-tudományi Közlemények* **XIV**

to be the MSZMP's turning-point, where the party would take advantage of the increasing opportunities provided by the new Gorbachev leadership, acknowledge the seriousness of conditions in Hungary, and take the steps necessary - both in terms of policy and personnel - to address the situation. Instead, while admitting setbacks in the economy, the party leadership spoke with unfounded optimism, capping the congress with the ascension of several younger neo-conservatives into the Politburo and Central Committee Secretariat - among them Károly Grósz, Budapest party secretary since 1984.[79] The lack of a serious response by the congress sent a wave of profound frustration within the party and society as a whole, and observers began to speak of 'leadership drift' and the deepening of a potentially explosive national crisis.[80]

PRESSURE FOR REFORM

In 1987 Grósz became prime minister. Although this position often served as a detour from real party power (and intentionally so), Grósz took advantage of his new office and embarked on a streamlining of the government apparatus, recruiting a new generation of experts and discussing openly the need for changes in the organization and function of

(1984): 408-24.

79. See the excellent analysis of the 1985 party congress in Polgár (pseudonym of Gyula Kozák), 'A pateralizmus vége? [The end of paternalism?]', *Hírmondó*, no. 17 (May-June 1985), reprinted in Demszky, *Szamizdat '81-89*: 308-17; also 'Az első posztkádárista kongresszus [The first post-Kádárist congress]', *Hírmondó*, no. 18 (August-September 1985), reprinted in ibid.: 318-27; László Kéri, 'Hungary from the Single-Party System to Free Elections: The Kádár Regime Falls Apart', in *Between Two Systems: Seven Studies on the Hungarian Political Changes* (Budapest: Institute for Political Science, Hungarian Academy of Sciences, 1992): 19-23.

80. Iván Völgyes, 'Leadership Drift in Hungary: Empirical Observations on a Normative Concept', *Studies in Comparative Communism* **XXII** (Spring 1989): 23-41; see also Attila Ágh, 'A félfordulát év [The year of the half-turn], in Sándor Kurtán, Péter Sándor and László Vass (eds), *Magyarország Politikai Évkönyve 1988* (Political yearbook of Hungary, 1988) (Budapest: Reform, 1989); 24; László Gyurkó, 'A magyar szocializmus válsága [The crisis of Hungarian socialism]', *Valóság*, no. 3 (March 1988): 12-25; and Péter Kende, 'A szocialista államrend válsága Magyarországon [the crisis of the socialist state in Hungary]', *Magyar Füzetek* (Paris), nos 19-20 (1988): 5-29.

the party-state. There could be no doubt that from the traditionally weak position of the government Grósz hoped to consolidate a power base, but there were other motivations at work. Grósz began to show himself as amenable to reforms within the system, if only within the context of a kind of populist 'technocratic reform dictatorship' – a more recent variation on Selznick's concept of the retreat to technology.[81]

Grósz, like many younger conservatives, followed the Gorbachev line, believing that technical changes in the institutional order could bring the system back into economic and political stability. His objectives included a greater separation of the MSZMP and the government, such that would place the party in a more detached guiding role with less direct interference in the formation of state policy, as well as an increase in market forces to stimulate the economy.[82]

The rise of Grósz as prime minister was symptomatic of a new conflict developing within the party. For some time, as the first generation of poorly educated party élite continued their entrenchment against party intellectuals and society as a whole, a new party élite waited in the wings. These party technocrats (the so-called 'little Grószes'[83]) had made their careers in industrial or state institutions, and were characterized by relatively more pragmatic policy orientations. The failure of the Kádár system was perceived as a product of bad policy from an incompetent leadership, but these technocrats found their path blocked by this old guard, for whom they had little respect and with whom their patience was wearing thin. As Gouldner has noted, this 'muffled conflict' of the technocratic segment against old-line bureaucracy is

81. This term is described by László Lengyel in 'Ezerkilencszáznyolcvannyolc [Nineteen hundred and eighty eight]', in Kurtán, Sándor and Vass, *Magyarország Politikai Évkönyve 1988*: 81–2; and in László Lengyel, 'Reformdiktatúra vagy bürokratikus authoritarianizmus [Reform dictatorship or bureaucratic authoritarianism], *Valóság* no. 5 (May 1989): 61–7.

82. Károly Grósz, personal interview by the author, Gödöllő, 2 June 1993; Imre Pozsgay, personal interview by the author, Budapest, 15 February 1993; Tőkés, Schöpflin and Völgyes, 'Leadership change and Crisis': 32; Tamás Kolosi, 'Jegyzetlapok 1989 nyarán [Notes in the summer of 1989]', *Valóság* no. 10 (October 1989): 4.

83. László Lengyel, *Micsoda év!* [What a year!] (Budapest: Szépirodalmi Könyvkiadó, 1991): 19.

often the first shot in the wider battle against an existing power structure.[84]

These developments paralleled more concrete and radical demands for change that began to emanate from elsewhere within the party, notably those social scientists affiliated with the TTI and the Financial Research Institute. Numerous articles, conferences and working papers materialized which openly discussed the possibilities and varieties of integrated political and economic reform, couched within the framework of the leading role of the MSZMP and the inviolability of the basic precepts of state socialism.[85] The most notable proposal put forth, entitled *Fordulat és reform* (*Turnabout and Reform*) called for a 'comprehensive, radical, democratizing and decentralizing market reform' which would be successful only if enacted alongside democratization in the political sphere.[86]

84. Gouldner, *The Future of the Intellectuals*: 52.
85. Excellent overviews of these various studies can be found in McDonald, 'Transition to Utopia': 218–28; Hankiss, *East European Alternatives*: 218, 226–9; Rudolf L. Tőkés, 'The Science of Politics in Hungary in the 1980s: People, Ideas, and Contradictions', *Südosteuropa* **37** (1988): 8–32; Attila Ágh, 'The Emergence of the "Science of Democracy" and its Impact on the Democratic Transition', *Aula* **XIII** (1991): 96–111; István Kemény, 'Programok és ellentmondások [programs and contradictions]', *Magyar Füzetek* (Paris) nos 19–20 (1988): 53–77. The proceedings of two TTI conferences in 1988 and 1989 dealing with the subject of political and economic reform can be found in *A modellváltás anatómiája* [The anatomy of the change of model] (Budapest: TTI, 1989). The best known 'reform documents' outside of those mentioned include Béla Pokol, 'Alternatív utak a politikai rendszer reformjára [Alternative roads to the reform of the political system]', *Valóság* no. 12 (December 1986): 32–45, and István Schlett, 'Közelítések a politikai rendszer reformjához [Approaches to the reform of the political system]', *Társadalmi Szemle* **XLII** (1987): 41–53.

   Within the dissident community the most notable reform document was the samizdat 'Társadalmi szerződés [Social contract]', written by János Kis, Ferenc Kőszeg and Ottilia Solt, which, among other things, called for Kádár's removal: *Beszélő*, special issue (June 1987). See the comparison of this document with *Turnabout and Reform* in Iván Szelényi, 'Eastern Europe in an Epoch of Transition: Toward a Socialist Mixed Economy?', in Stark and Nee (eds), *Remaking the Economic Institutions of Socialism*: 208–32.
86. László Antal, Lajos Bokros, László Lengyel and György Matolcsy, 'Fordulat és reform [Turnabout and reform]', *Medvetánc*, special issue (1987): 5–129. The study's origins stretch as far back as 1981, when an early version was suppressed by the party. It first appeared publicly – in a truncated form – in the June 1987 issue of *Közgazdasági Szemle*, after it was clear that the party would not formally

A companion piece authored by Mihály Bihari, *Reform és demokrácia* (*Reform and Democracy*) envisaged (1) institutional reform which would give greater power to legal/constitutional structures, providing the underpinnings of a *rechtsstaat* while not challenging communist rule itself, and (2) the sanctioning of other political and interest organizations within specific limits. As the study argued, 'the monopolistic (exclusive) possession of power must be transformed into an alliance-based hegemonistic power bloc of the political forces and movements, a bloc in which the communist party wins and maintains its dominant (but not autocratic) role by political means'.[87] While other works emphasized different mechanisms by which state socialism in Hungary could be reformed, all were characterized by their focus on the need to pluralize politics and the economy without threatening the MSZMP itself – in essence, the destruction of the existing system in order to save it. This, of course, ran explicitly counter to institutional dogma, and this pressure for organizational change would inevitably bring the two into conflict.

This 'reform fever' among party intellectuals did not occur without some support. Many of them had by the late 1980s begun to gravitate towards Imre Pozsgay, former minister of culture and a well-known supporter of political reform who had been 'sent down' to head the Patriotic Peoples' Front (*Hazafias Népfront*, or HNF) in 1982 because of his critical views and frequent clashes with the powerful party cultural specialist, György Aczél. As with Grósz, this demtour had unexpected benefits. Pozsgay found a new source of influence through the daily paper of the HNF, *Magyar Nemzet*, while his relative distance from the centre of party power made his reform stance somewhat more palatable to the leadership, expanding the limits of his actions.[88] However, unlike the ascendant technocrats, Pozsgay was distinguished by his higher education in philosophy, his membership of the Hungarian Academy of Sciences and his publications from the 1970s on the subject of democracy. Pozsgay was one of those rare party figures, a

accept the document. László Lengyel interview, *Kizárt a párt*: 52–4; McDonald, 'Transition to Utopia': 225–8.

87. Translated in *JPRS Report: East Europe* (19 January 1989): 58.

88. Although head of the HNF, Pozsgay was not a member of the Politburo as was normally the case with this position, a clear sign of the mistrust which the party leadership felt towards him.

high-ranking party intellectual.[89] During the late 1980s, Pozsgay used the HNF to give its backing to a number of reform-orientated studies by party intellectuals, including support for *Turnabout and Reform* itself.

Outside the party, Pozsgay used his position to cultivate relations with the more conservative, 'populist' intelligentsia. In September 1987 he helped organize a gathering of populist intellectuals in the village of Lakitelek, in which more than two hundred individuals took part. While members of the more radical 'urban' dissident community were not invited, a number of prominent party reform intellectuals, such as Mihály Bihari, Csaba Gombár, László Lengyel and István Schlett took part.[90] Discussions centred upon reform possibilities and the

89. Pozsgay had first made a name for himself as a result of his doctoral dissertation, entitled 'Some Questions of the Further Development of Socialist Democracy and our Political System', which he defended in 1969. Coming on the heels of the invasion of Czechoslovakia he was not allowed to publish it, but the defence itself apparently attracted a great deal of attention among the intelligentsia: Imre Pozsgay, *1989*: 30; see also Tőkés, *Hungary's Negotiated Revolution*: 222–5. A selection of speeches and interviews with Pozsgay from the period 1978–1988 can be found in Andor Kloss and Imre Mónus (eds), *Esélyünk a reform* [Our chance is reform] (Győr: Hazafias Népfront Megyei Bizottsága, 1988); see also Imre Pozsgay, interview by Zoltán Biró, *Októberi kérdések* [October questions] (n.p.: Eötvös Kiadó and Püski Kiadó, 1988).

90. Transcripts of the speeches from this meeting can be found in *Lakitelek 1987: a magyarság esélyei* [Lakitelek 1987: The chances of Hungariandom] (Budapest: Püski Kiadó and Antológia Kiadó, 1991).

The split in the Hungarian intelligentsia between populists and urbanists stretches back to the beginning of the century, a division to some extent reinforced by the period of socialist rule. To use a very general characterization, populist intellectuals concentrated on the idea of the preservation of the Hungarian nation, 'Hungarianness' (*magyarság*) and its presumed values. Their recent critiques often focused on the negative effects of modernization and the plight of Hungarians in Transylvania. The urbanists, in contrast, tended to focus on the idea of modernity, particularly in the form of liberal values and ideas; many urbanists came from the new left of the late 1960s, reborn as radical liberal dissidents and the authors of such samizdat journals as *Beszélő* and *Hírmondó*. The latent anti-Semitism of some within the populist camp (who often link Judaism to communism) combined with the Jewish and ex-communist backgrounds of many within the urbanist camp has exacerbated tensions between the two camps since the mid-1970s. In 1985 populist and urbanist activists met in the village of Monor to try to smooth out some of these differences, but to little effect; during and after 1989 the consolidation of these groups into political parties increased hostility between the two. A short but excellent characterization of this conflict can be found in Ash, 'A Hungarian

pluralization of the political system, and concluded with the call for the formation of a 'Hungarian democratic forum', a non-party organization which could contribute to the creation of a dialogue on reform. Pozsgay saw to it that he was interviewed about the meeting in *Magyar Nemzet*, and that the concluding declaration of Lakitelek was appended to the interview.[91] It appeared that Pozsgay was contemplating a political coalition with populist forces outside the party, to be organized as a satellite of the MSZMP. The populists' 'third road', latent anti-capitalist views complemented MSZMP reformist policy and could provide new legitimacy and stability to a process of limited political pluralization.[92]

Other non-party groups began to coalesce independently as well, emboldened by the apparent paralysis of the MSZMP. More prominent among them were the Alliance of Young Democrats (*Fiatal Demokraták Szövetsége*, or FIDESZ) which rose as a direct challenge to the MSZMP's youth organization, as well as the Network of Independent Initiatives (*Hálozat*), which gathered members of the Budapest dissident movement, eventually to become the Alliance of Free Democrats (*Szabad Demokraták Szövetsége*, or SZDSZ).[93]

None of this, of course, was occurring in a vacuum. Changes in Eastern Europe as a whole were strongly influenced by the rise of Mikhail Gorbachev and his increasing moves towards political and economic reform. While in the Hungarian case tentative steps towards liberalization predated, rather than followed, Soviet policy, Moscow's wide-ranging re-evaluation of socialism and East–West relations seemed to finally vindicate Kádár's longstanding policy of reconciliation and reform, generating enormous public support for the Soviet

Lesson'; see also the dated but still useful discussion of Hungarian populism in Schöpflin, 'Opposition and Para-Opposition': 167–80; a more recent discussion of populism and anti-Semitism in Hungary during the transition and post-communist era can be found in Randolph L. Braham, *The Politics of Genocide*, revised and enlarged edn, vol. II (New York: Columbia University Press, 1994): 1353–65.

91. Alfred Reisch, 'PPF Daily Publishes Statement of Hungarian Democratic Forum', *Radio Free Europe Report* (hereafter *RFER*) (28 November 1987): 13–18.
92. Lengyel, *Micsoda Év!*, esp. 31–4.
93. The rapid development of civil organizations during this period is covered in detail in *Szószék: Alternatív krónika '88* [Pulpit: Alternative chronicle 1988] (n.p.: n.d.), and *Lel-Tár: Új társadalmi szervezetek katalógusa I* [Inventory: Catalogue of new social organizations I] (Budapest: Pszichoteam, 1988).

leader as a symbol of positive change.[94] Yet rather than creating the context in which Hungary could finally engage in fundamental institutional change, Gorbachev's policies actually had the effect of eroding the authority of the MSZMP. No longer could the party claim to be the only reformers within the bloc; no longer could Kádár be praised for his balancing act between domestic concerns and international realities. The locus of reform had now shifted, leaving Hungarian leaders clearly disorientated.

THE FINAL COUNTEROFFENSIVE OF THE OLD GUARD AND THE MAY 1988 PARTY CONFERENCE

Thus, while the rapid development of movements both inside and outside the party-state, combined with developments in the Soviet Union, seemed to signal a new wave of liberalization and change, institutional arguments tell us that even where external validation and legitimacy is waning, ossified structures are unlikely to accept the need for dramatic organizational reform. In keeping with this hypothesis, indications that the party leadership was not amenable to such actions were soon forthcoming, as growing calls for radical change inevitably led to a sharp reaction by party leaders in defence of the existing structure of control.

The Financial Research Institute, source of *Turnabout and Reform*, was closed down shortly after the document's publication. In April 1988, Bihari, Lengyel, Zoltán Biró (one of the main organizers of the Lakitelek meeting) and Zoltán Király (an outspoken parliamentarian from Szeged and also a Lakitelek participant) were expelled from the party, apparently at the direct behest of Kádár. Kádár also personally initiated disciplinary actions against Pozsgay for his role at Lakitelek.[95] A similar threat confronted Rezső Nyers, who despite his long semi-

94. For a good account of relations between Eastern Europe and the Soviet Union during this period see J.F. Brown, *Surge to Freedom* (Durham, NC: Duke University Press, 1991), esp. chap. 4 on Hungary; and Alex Pravda, 'Soviet Policy Towards Eastern Europe in Transition: The Ends Justify the Means', in Alex Pravda (ed.), *The End of the Outer Empire: Soviet–East European Relations in Transition* (London: Sage, 1992): 1–34.
95. Károly Grósz personal interview; Pozsgay, *1989*: 82.

obscurity returned to prominence as an early architect of reform, and who in late 1987 was instrumental in the formation of a new quasi-MSZMP reformist organization, the New March Front. Nyers was warned by the party leadership against the group's open establishment, and its founding statement remained suppressed until the autumn of 1988.[96] Pressure against organizations unconnected to the MSZMP also quickly mounted. A new onslaught of anti-intellectual repression, similar to that in the 1970s, seemed in the offing, much like the wave of neo-Stalinist reaction developing against Gorbachev at the same time.[97] The new cycle of reform in Hungary appeared to have reached its limits, and rather quickly at that.

But these actions were to be the swan song of Kádár and the old guard in general.[98] After much pressure within the Central Committee the general secretary had accepted calls to relinquish his post, which would be given over to Grósz while Kádár would take the newly-created position of party president (and thus maintain partial control). This shift in power, along with a few other minor changes in the party leadership, had been hammered out in advance and were scheduled to take place at an extraordinary party conference in May.[99]

96. The purpose of the New March Front, initially the concept of the editorship at the journal *Valóság* (of which Nyers was a member), was to coalesce intelligentsia forces from within the party in order to press the MSZMP to enact reform. Its membership was therefore not mass based. Many intellectuals who allied themselves with Pozsgay also joined the New March Front, for example Bihari, Lengyel and Király, whose participation in the New March Front apparently contributed to the decision to have them expelled from the party. The founding document of the group, dated March 1988, was not published until September: see Schöpflin, Tőkés and Völgyes, 'Leadership Succession and Crisis in Hungary': 35–6. Interviews and documents detailing the development and activities of the New March Front can be found in *Új Márciusi Front 1988* [New March Front, 1988] (Budapest: Múzsák, 1989).
97. László Kéri calls this 'Hungary's Andreyeva period': see 'Hungary from the Single-Party System': 28–30; see also Lengyel, 'Ezerkilencszáznyolcvannyolc': 83.
98. For details on the events surrounding the party conference see Tőkés, *Hungary's Negotiated Revolution*: 278–85.
99. One clue as to why Kádár, despite his advanced age, was unwilling to relinquish full power stems from a series of conversations held between émigré historian Péter Gosztonyi and Politburo member János Berecz. Berecz indicated to Gosztonyi that with the rise of Gorbachev Kádár feared that his removal from power would initiate a complete evaluation of 1956 and his role within it; only Soviet pressure in the end forced Kádár to relent: Péter Gosztonyi, 'Találkozásaim Bereczczel [My meetings with Berecz]', *Élet és irodalom*, 4 January 1991: 3, 8; see

What the party leadership had not anticipated, however, was the degree to which the party rank and file had itself grown angry over the inability of the leadership to respond to the deepening crisis in Hungary, and the extent to which the delegates were willing to express their displeasure.

This pent-up frustration exploded at the party conference, catching the old leadership off guard. The delegates' ire was captured perfectly in the speech of one delegate, a university student, who flatly blamed the MSZMP alone for the current domestic situation, portraying the leadership as 'erratic, confused and lacking expertise', and asserting that their conduct had discredited the party as a whole.[100] Even more startling was the degree to which party institutions had lost legitimacy even among the faithful. Delegates attacked the general practices of the MSZMP itself, its overcentralization and monopolization of power, and made unprecedented calls for platform freedom within the party (something strictly against Leninist tenets) and greater political pluralism outside it, a clearer separation of party and state, and the decentralization of party power.[101]

Taking advantage of this unexpected mutiny of the normally placid delegates, Grósz and his allies pushed through even more widespread changes in the composition of the Politburo than had been originally anticipated, largely at the expense of the old guard. By the end of the congress some eight of the thirteen members of the Politburo had been removed, and more than one-third of the Central Committee as well, sweeping away many of the most powerful old figures of the party. The victors were overwhelmingly the new young technocrats; industry heads made up half of the new Central Committee members, another 35 per cent came from state and public sectors, while only 15 per cent came from the party apparatus itself.[102]

also Völgyes, 'Leadership Drift': 32–3.

100. Quoted in Ágh, 'A félfordulat év': 26.

101. Iván Berend, 'Magyarország 1988 [Hungary 1988]', in Kurtán, Sándor and Vass, *Magyarország Politikai Évkönyve 1988*: 46–7.

102. This figure is based on calculations of the new Central Committee members by the author, based on raw data from 'A legfőbb hatalmi intézmények és vezetőik [The main institutions of power and their leaders]', in Kurtán, Sándor and Vass, *Magyarország Politikai Évkönyve 1988*: 494–501. See also Erzsébet Szalai, *Gazdasági mechanizmus, reformtörekvések és nagyvállalati érdekek* [Economic mechanism, reform endeavours and the interests of large enterprises] (Budapest: Közgazdasági és Jogi Könyvkiadó, 1989): 199.

One major exception was the election of Pozsgay and Nyers to the Politburo. Shortly thereafter Pozsgay was also elected minister of state, a subordinate position below that of prime minister. The inclusion of these two reformers was an obvious move by Grósz to boost the legitimacy of the party among the membership and society at large (Pozsgay in particular was lionized by many in Hungary), utilizing their skill and popularity to help the image of the Politburo while reining in Pozsgay and Nyers. The two remained in the minority, exceptions to what otherwise had amounted to a power struggle between generations, each loyal to the institution itself.

Indeed, in other aspects the May party conference was as notable for what did not occur as for what did. Despite the radical calls by many delegates, the central party statement approved by the conference made few concrete proposals for political or economic reform, reflecting the institutional loyalty of the new leadership. The 'renewal' or democratization of existing organizations, rather than their transformation, was stressed, although mention was made of the need for constitutional reform as a requisite of 'socialist pluralism', including changes in the electoral system. In addition, greater autonomy for social

An important study by János Simon in 1989 on the party leadership also provides important data in this regard. Based on a questionnaire sample of 113 top members of the MSZMP élite, Simon was shocked to find not only that these individuals were relatively young (75 per cent under 50) and highly educated (all with university diplomas, 80 per cent with technical, agricultural or natural science degrees), but also that their orientation towards the economy was what he called 'conservative-liberal', less supportive of state intervention in the economy, price controls or wage equality than found among the population in much of Western Europe, as well as the Hungarian population itself!

Simon attributes this to proof of the successful cooptation of the intelligentsia into the party leadership over time, but this contradicts the more comprehensive survey by Gazsó. Instead, given the time frame in which Simon's sampling took place (April 1989) what Simon has recorded is in fact the new technical intelligentsia following their ascendancy to power in May 1988. All of the positions that Simon surveyed – primarily ideological, political economy and first secretaries at the capital, regional and Central Committee level – underwent a dramatic turnover in 1988 as the old guard was forced out of power. What is thus provided is a snapshot of this new group at the apex of power, a technocratic class which the survey shows placed its trust in Gorbachev and Grósz more than in Pozsgay – exactly the opposite of the population – and who showed little devotion to Kádár. János Simon, 'Vajúdnak a hegyek [The travails of the mountains]', chap. in Bruszt and Simon, *A lecsendesített többség*: 66, 75–88.

organizations was referred to, as well as the need for market reform. Overall, while it was a distinct shift from previous policy and more in line with developments in the Soviet Union, the new party policy remained quite restricted, more concerned with tinkering with the system and maintaining institutional sanctity than contemplating its overhaul.[103]

THE PARTY LEADERSHIP IN CONFLICT

From that spring to the end of 1988 the MSZMP leadership continued to speak vaguely about reforms, and little concrete policy appeared to be in the offing – much to the frustration of those who had high hopes in the new leadership. Although comprehensive economic reforms existed on paper, the new leadership seemed unwilling to carry them out, despite the new opportunities afforded by changes in the international environment.[104] Trapped by their origins as products of the institution, even the party technocrats could not bring themselves to dismantle the existing totalitarian institutional forms and create a domestic model of state and economy. The sense of stagnation and crisis deepened, and public confidence in Grósz quickly disintegrated.

Organizations outside the party took advantage of this indecision, continuing to develop and take on increasing characteristics of political parties – most notably FIDESZ, SZDSZ and the now fully established Hungarian Democratic Forum (*Magyar Demokrata Fórum*, or MDF) – despite the lack of any new law on association or clear indications that the MSZMP would permit multiparty elections in the near future (or at all). The MSZMP flipped back and forth in its responses to these developments, alternating between expressions of support, a neutral legalistic stance, and outright threats.[105] It remained obvious that the party was prepared to allow a pluralization of views only inasmuch as

103. MTI (Hungarian Telegraph Agency), 22 May 1988; reprinted in *Daily Report: East Europe* (23 May 1988): 36–44.
104. McDonald, 'Transition to Utopia': 218–20.
105. A collection endlessly contradicting quotations by Politburo members on the introduction of a multiparty system can be found in 'A többpártrendszer nincs napirenden [The multiparty system is not on the agenda]', in Kurtán, Sándor and Vass, *Magyarország Politikai Évkönyve 1988*: 570–93.

they remained policy specific, supporting the objectives and general legitimacy of the MSZMP but not challenging party rule itself. For example, a demonstration in May by some 2,000 against a dam project on the Danube was not only permitted, but given extensive and favourable coverage in the press. A similar mass protest of some 25,000 against the Ceauşescu regime was similarly permitted in June. In contrast, a rally that same month to commemorate the execution of Imre Nagy was met with police truncheons, and a number of prominent dissidents were beaten and arrested.[106]

By autumn even the tentative spirit of reform that emerged from the May conference came under outright attack from conservatives (both old and new) within the party's upper ranks. During the Central Committee meeting of 27 September, party leaders recognized the increasing deterioration of the economy as well as the resulting internal and external erosion of party legitimacy, but conservatives took a reactionary stance, blaming the party's troubles on its toleration of increasing opposition within Hungarian society.[107] Already Grósz himself had made a number of public comments that brought his commitment to political reform into question, emboldening more conservative party members. Notably, in an address made before members of the paramilitary Workers' Guard, Grósz referred to social pluralization in terms of 'increasingly open manifestations of enemy and opposition activities', and raised the possibility that the party would have to act accordingly.[108]

The lack of a clear consensus on political change within the Politburo was now manifest, underlined by Grósz's comments in contrast to Pozsgay's continuing support for radical political pluralization outside the party.[109] In early October, Pozsgay and a number of his supporters

106. Judith Pataki, 'Demonstrations for Nagy's Rehabilitation Brutally Halted in Budapest', *RFER* (8 July 1988): 3–7.

107. Alfred Reisch, 'HSWP CC Keeps to Reform Course Amid Conservative Fears and Rumblings', and idem, 'The Polarization in the HSWP over Reform: Conservatives Speak Out', *RFER* (28 October 1988): 41–50.

108. Pataki, 'Demonstration for Nagy's Rehabilitation': 4. This statement echoes one made by Grósz one year before, when he spoke of 'extremist elements' in society, drawing a parallel with events in 1956 and the possibility that force might be necessary in response. Reisch, 'PPF Daily Publishes Statement': 17, n. 4.

109. See, for example, Imre Pozsgay, interview by Zsusza Simonfi, Budapest Domestic Service, 7 October 1988; translated in *Daily Report: East Europe* (24 October 1988): 26.

agreed to convene a 'reform conference' for the following month, which would involve prominent figures from inside and outside the party, including central opposition figures from both the populist and urban camps. A press conference would provide the leaders of these alternative organizations the chance to introduce themselves and their programmes to the public. As one of its planners noted, 'this meeting would have shown that there in fact exists an MSZMP reform wing, that this wing recognizes the possibility of a multiparty system, and that it was amenable to negotiate with alternative organizations and parties'.[110] This would also have coincided with the introduction of comprehensive legislation on democratic reform, authored by Bihari and to be submitted to parliament that same month.[111]

But this conference was not to take place. On 15 November a protest rally commemorating riots in Braşov, Romania, the year before was broken up violently by the police. The order to use force was apparently given by Grósz directly, without any prior consultation of the Politburo. The willingness of Grósz to undertake such an action frightened Pozsgay, who saw it as a direct provocation, and convinced him that not only would the reform conference lead to the immediate expulsion of the participants from the party, but that serious reprisals could follow. The conference was cancelled.[112]

On 23 November Grósz resigned his prime ministerial position, retaining his primary job as general secretary. Many hoped that Pozsgay or Nyers would be promoted to the post, but instead the position went to Miklós Németh, a young and relatively unknown economist regarded by some as an ambitious protégé of Grósz (Németh had previously locked horns with both Nyers and Pozsgay).[113] As a concession, Nyers was made a minister of state alongside Pozsgay. With Németh's appointment, Grósz appeared to ensure his control over

110. Lengyel, *Micsoda év!*: 76, n. 1. An earlier attempt to convene a similar public meeting in August 1988 was scuttled when the Politburo demanded the meeting be held in secret, at which the opposition balked: idem, 'Ezerkilencszáznyolcvannyolc', 87.

111. See Hankiss, *East European Alternatives*: 226; Alfred Reisch, 'National Assembly Approves Radical Political Reform Program', *RFER* (15 December 1988): 15-20; Pozsgay, *1989*: 86-7.

112. Lengyel, *Micsoda Év!*: 76, n. 1.

113. Alfred Reisch, 'Young Proreform Economist Replaces Károly Grósz as Prime Minister', *RFER* (15 December 1988): 9-13; Lengyel, *Micsoda év!*: 76, n. 2.

the state apparatus without running it personally, sidetracking party reformers in the process. Despite intimations towards reform, the nascent MSZMP reform wing remained outnumbered and outflanked. The new conservatives appeared fully in control, just as unwilling or unable as their predecessors to dismantle those structures which defined and legitimized their positions and political views.

3. The Rise of the Reform Circles

In 1980 Daniel Chirot concluded in an article on Romanian corporatism that

> There is no theoretical reason which prevents the intelligentsia from forming an active class in opposition to the old elite; there is, however, a very practical political reality which rules out this possibility. In order to act as a horizontally based class, the intelligentsia would have to create its own party, or take over a section of an existing party … and unite across functional lines. That is permissible in capitalist societies, but anathema in communist polities.[1]

Yet in Hungary this is precisely what occurred. During the summer and autumn of 1988, while the party élite in Budapest struggled over the issue of political reform, a separate movement within the party was beginning to take shape. A product of the institutional characteristics of the Kádárist political system, the *reformkörök*, or reform circles, sprung from rural obscurity within the party to become a major political actor by spring of the following year. What was it about the political system in Hungary that fostered such a development rather than elsewhere in the region? While this chapter will attempt to answer the question in some detail, the explanation lies in that as Selznick and others have warned, co-optation, while an effective tool of institutionalization, runs the risk of incorporating members whose organizational goals may be far different from that of the leadership, and who may as a result of their position be able to turn the routines and structures of the organization against itself.

1. Daniel Chirot, 'The Corporatist Model and Socialism: Notes on Romanian Development', *Theory and Society* **9** (March 1980): 375.

THE SOCIAL ORIGINS OF THE REFORM CIRCLE MOVEMENT

Although the beginnings of the reform circle movement can be traced back to a series of specific events, places and points in time, a deeper explanation lies in the history of Hungarian institutional development and its impact on the social order. As we have discussed at length, Hungarian socialism as institutionalized under the leadership of Kádár created a kind of dual existence, whereby state socialism remained organizationally conformist to the Soviet model while a broad range of secondary practices and policies developed to pacify and co-opt the population through recruitment, limited liberalization and the deideologization of everyday life.

These party policies continued to attract large numbers of younger members into the MSZMP during the course of the 1970s and early 1980s, particularly from the white-collar clerical, technical and managerial sectors, who saw party membership as a means to occupational advancement and a guarantor of middle-class life. These members eventually came to dominate the ranks of the party as the biggest single occupational group, largely disinterested in ideology but supportive of the party and the status quo for the benefits it had provided: 'apartment, weekend home, car, foreign vacations, a little work in the private sector, social peace, little political activity – all of this attracted hundreds of thousands of average people into the Kádárist MSZMP'.[2]

But while this party middle class developed into the effective backbone of the MSZMP, large numbers of the intelligentsia – those with advanced education, rather than the clerical or administrative white-collar stratum – were also swelling the party ranks. In many cases the motivation for membership was little different from that described above. However, there were also many for whom membership took on a more highly-charged political nature, rather than one based merely on economic gain or social security. This was particularly true of many within the immediate post-war generation, what we can call the Hungarian 'baby boomers'.

In his studies of political socialization in Hungary, the sociologist László Kéri has explored the unique social milieu in which the

2. Lengyel, *Micsoda év!*: 21.

intelligentsia born in the years between 1948 and 1955 matured – the period in which the overwhelming majority of prominent reform circle members were born. For this group it was not simply the years of war and extreme deprivation that were unknown, but also the social tension of the Rákosi period and the revolution of 1956. These key political events did not shape their experience of socialism or its distortion under Stalinism. Rather, their early political socialization came during the later years of dramatic reform in Hungary – the apex of 'goulash communism' when Kádár was no longer reviled by the population as a puppet of the Soviets but rather affectionately referred to as '*János bácsi*' – 'uncle János', the wily defender of Hungary against the Russians.[3] This emerged coterminous with the rise of the new left movement, discussed in the last chapter, as well as the development of an anti-establishment youth subculture influenced by the West.

Hungarian post-war youth, particularly university students, thus matured within the spirit of critical thinking, the notion of revolutionary liberation, and the spirit of non-conformism, which Kéri notes is typified by the 'Che Guevarra myth' so prevalent among the young at that time.[4] Among reform circle interview subjects these same themes emerged consistently, important sources of their later political activity: the experiences of rapid social mobility credited to the party, the impact of Western 'alternative' cultural products during their youth, as well as flirtations with leftist radicalism and party membership when they were still teenagers. As one of the founders of the first reform circle described it, the movement was strongly generational in its origins, belonging to the 'jeans-wearing, long-haired generation of the 1960s and 1970s'.[5] When the MSZMP finally backed away from its reform projects and cracked down on active neo-Marxist dissent, it only

3. Kéri, *Politikai folyamatok*: 175-7; see also Iván Völgyes, 'Political Culture', in Grothusen, *Hungary*: 191–212.
4. Kéri, *Politikai folyamatok*: 180. For a general discussion of Hungarian youth during the late 1960s and early 1970s see also Shawcross, *Crime and Compromise*, chap. 11.
5. József Géczi and György Kerényi, 'A tétlenség anarchiája [The anarchy of inaction]', interview by Henrik Havas, *168 óra*, 23 May 1989: 18–19.

One example comes from an interview subject, now a lawyer, who displayed two large posters in his office: one of Che Guevarra, and the other of Jim Morrison. As the subject explained, both were the heroes of his youth: Che Guevarra as the great revolutionary, and Jim Morrison as the great poet.

indirectly affected this generation, whose role in the new left movement was more as observer than participant.[6]

Many from this younger generation subsequently lost faith in the party leadership, turning away from the MSZMP or remaining a member for largely opportunistic reasons. Others, however, remained devoted to their early radical ideals. Party ties were retained, despite the glaring difference between personal views and the reality of party activity, in the hope that change could somehow be effected from within. This can be contrasted with the experiences of the following generations: for those groups the predominant socializing force was the disillusionment and decline of youth and radical movements, accompanied by political retrenchment at home and elsewhere in the bloc. This fostered cynicism towards politics and drove many younger intellectuals towards populist or neo-liberal ideologies and movements (the source of later youth-based opposition groups such as FIDESZ).[7]

Many from the generation of intellectuals born in the first decade after the war consequently became a unique political segment *within* the MSZMP, a large 'party opposition' within the party itself. Such social segments have elsewhere been referred to as 'political generations' or 'cohorts', groups which form the core element of social movements.[8] These dissenters, scattered among the party ranks, displayed political views that leaned towards social democracy and decentralized political power, seeking the realization of a socialism that had been betrayed by the current political order.[9] Having embraced the domestic institutionalization policies of the party as a 'Hungarian road' towards

6. Although the emulation of Western youth culture eventually also came under attack by the party: see Shawcross, *Crime and Compromise*: 221–30.
7. Kéri, *Politikai folyamatok*: 187; Huszár, *Mit ér a szellem*: 70–76.
8. For a discussion of the role of political generations in the creation of movements see Rudolph Heberle, *Social Movements: An Introduction to Political Sociology* (New York: Appleton, 1951).
9. András Körösényi, 'Vázlat a magyar értelmiség szellemi-politikai tagoltságáról [Outline of the intellectual–political articulation of the Hungarian intelligentsia]', *Magyar Politikatudományi Társaság Évkönyv 1987: Válság és reform* [Hungarian Political Science Association Yearbook 1987: Crisis and reform] (Budapest: MPT, 1987): 43–58; and idem, 'Újjaéledő politikai tagoltság [Reemerging political articulation]' in Kurtán, Sándor and Vass, *Magyarország Politikai Évkönyve 1988*: 285–86; András Bozóki, 'Post-Communist Transition: Political Tendencies in Hungary', in Bozóki, Körösényi and Schöpflin, *Post-Communist Transition: Emerging Pluralism in Hungary*: 13–29.

communism, this group was successfully co-opted into the party, but on an institutionally dangerous pretext: loyal to autonomous notions of socialism as embodied in the idea of reform, rather than a loyalty based primarily on organizational sanctity.

As this group grew older and more established within party and society, they grew as a latent, but very real threat to the party order. Their relationship to the MSZMP was not based on a utilitarian demand to promote their own interests (as tends to be the source of power struggles at the top) but rather stemmed from normative considerations, which over time increasingly saw the necessity of a fundamental transformation of the institutional status quo.[10] Lengyel thus describes this cohort as a 'party opposition [that] did not identify with the Rákosi nor the Kádárist model, or the Stalinist or post-Stalinist systems that they had created. "This is not our system, not our socialism. *We joined the party so that we could transform this model*"' (italics added).[11]

As seen in the previous chapter, during the course of the 1970s and 1980s the post-war generation of intelligentsia made little headway in conquering the party's commanding heights, as was the case with their mentors, the older neo-Marxist radicals of the late 1960s. But the Kádárist system of co-optation and control was not simply that of a rudimentary gatekeeper. In order to maintain the continuing incorporation of the intelligentsia, the party had to provide some kind of benefit to garner support – or at least acceptance – just as economic policies had succeeded with the population in general.

Of course, such opportunities existed, particularly for the best and the brightest. For those with technical specialization desired by the party there were jobs to be had in the state sector or industry. The most talented individuals in the social sciences could similarly find positions in the top universities, the Academy of Science, or in different 'think-tanks' associated with the party or various ministries, to name a few. As seen earlier, loose political groupings eventually formed from these co-opted segments; cadre technocrats, chafing under the inept rule of the old guard, became the power base behind Grósz in his struggle

10. For a discussion of this distinction see Cornelius J. Lammers, 'Strikes and Mutinies: A Comparative Study of Organizational Conflicts between Rulers and Ruled', *Administration Science Quarterly* **14** (December 1969): 558–72, and Louis R. Pondy, ' Varieties of Organizational Conflict', *Administrative Science Quarterly* **14** (December 1969): 499–505.

11. Lengyel, *Micsoda év!*: 20.

against Kádár, while many prominent intellectuals drew close to reform politicians such as Pozsgay and Nyers. At the centre of power, the party brought intellectuals into the fold by offering them the opportunity for status and access *within the existing system*, and moreover, a role in the reform project for which Kádárism stood. Szelényi and Konrád capture this effect of the development perfectly:

> Official and private trips to the West became routine, often extending beyond a 2–3 day visit with a delegation to conferences or meetings ... to longer stays as IREX fellows, Fulbright scholars, trade representatives and visiting professors. The cadre elite, and particularly their children, learned languages and began to feel at ease with living in the West and communicating with Western colleagues. The best of them even realized that they have marketable skills on Western markets. If they wish they can find employment either in large corporations or universities. Many of these state-intellectuals, rectors, leading economic bureaucrats, and academicians impressed their Western colleagues. They were so unlike the old cadre-academics they knew from the Soviet Union, East Germany or previously also from Hungary and Poland.[12]

The Kádárist system thus worked well in incorporating much of the intelligentsia by making the party the instrument (instead of the enemy) of intellectual and political pursuits, enervating social critique by appropriating it within the ideology of reform. Yet while Szelényi and Konrád illustrate the results of party policy towards the intelligentsia, this description carries only a limited relevance. At the *metropole* level, where political and economic possibilities were highly concentrated, there were opportunities for party intellectuals to pursue their vocations, enjoy certain privileges, even play a limited part in political developments if they stepped carefully. The intelligentsia were seen by the party as a distinct threat to stability, and so the party made certain it cultivated their support.

Yet this segment represented only part of the party intelligentsia. Outside Budapest it was an entirely different story, where intellectuals were far from the centre of power and thus of much less concern to the MSZMP leadership. For many thousands of party intelligentsia in the

12. Iván Szelényi and György Konrád, 'Intellectuals and Domination in Post-communist Societies', in Iván Szelényi, *A poszt-kommunista átmenet társadalmi konfliktusai* [Societal conflicts of the post-communist transition] (Budapest: MTA Politikai Tudományok Intézete): 65.

countryside the prospects of social or political rewards for their continuing tacit support for the MSZMP were much dimmer, compounded by a number of related factors.

RURAL INTELLIGENTSIA AND OBSTACLES TO POWER

The first was simply that of resource concentration. As a former imperial capital, Budapest overshadows the rest of the nation, holding some 20 per cent of the nation's population. Intellectual, economic and political resources still remain highly centralized at that level, magnifying the difference between centre and periphery and creating at times a palpable antagonism between those who live in Budapest and those who do not.

With the advent of socialism this institutional legacy was reinforced by the particular dynamics of rapid industrialization. As elsewhere in Eastern Europe, the lop-sided nature of Hungarian economic development under socialism led to levels of social investment that failed to keep pace with industrial development.[13] This was further intensified by the disproportionate dispersal of development funds, close to half of which went to Budapest alone.[14] For many skilled workers and peasants the NEM's expansion of the private sector in the 1970s, particularly in agriculture, created compensatory opportunities in what has been called 'socialist entrepreneurialism'; for this segment the result was rising income averages, and the creation of a new class of relatively wealthy peasantry.[15] For members of the intelligentsia, however, the late 1970s brought a decrease in relative incomes, totalling close to 20 per cent within half a decade.[16] Intellectuals in the smaller cities thus saw themselves as particularly disadvantaged, from both an income and a resource standpoint – trapped between capital and village, and unable to exploit the possibilities of either level. These frustrations of

13. See Iván Szelényi, *Urban Inequalities Under State Socialism* (Oxford: Oxford University Press, 1983).
14. Toma, *Socialist Authority*: 233.
15. This point has been raised specifically in Iván Szelényi, *Socialist Entrepreneurs* (Madison, WI: University of Wisconsin Press, 1988).
16. Swain, *Hungary: The Rise and Fall of Feasible Socialism*: 171–5, 192.

countryside intellectuals were intensified by the nature of local politics. The party-state systems of Eastern Europe have never been noted for their attention to local representation. Centralized power has been their hallmark. In Hungary this lack of local political power also has a historical component, existing long before the advent of socialism.[17] Extensive studies carried out by TTI during the 1970s clearly illustrated the lack of local autonomy and decision-making responsibility, the maintenance of paternalistic political attitudes, and the use of regional party and state institutions not as a tool of local representation but rather as a means of control by the central authorities.[18] Ironically, these tendencies were reinforced by the administrative reforms of the early 1970s, which in effect recentralized power at the county level at the expense of town councils, strongly undercutting local self-government.[19]

To make matters worse, the MSZMP policy of blocking party intellectuals from gaining access to important positions of power was also duplicated at the regional administrative level, limiting their role in local party and governmental activity (see Table 3.1). Similar findings were obtained by Gazsó; they show that, using his criteria of convertible qualifications, fewer than a third of county party cadres fell into this category.[20] At the local level of party and state, intelligentsia

17. Csaba Gombár, 'A helyi hatalomról [On local power]', in *Magyar Politikatudományi Társaság Évkönyve 1984: Ideológia és demokrácia* [Hungarian Political Science Association Yearbook 1984: Ideology and democracy] (Budapest: Magyar Politikatudományi Társaság, 1984): 191-4; Antal Bőhm, 'A helyi hatalom és a lakosság részvételi esélyei [Local power and the chances for community participation]', *Tér és társadalom* **1** (1987): 17-30. The discussion of this issue stretches back to the work of Hungarian sociologists beginning in the 1930s, in particular the work of Ferenc Erdei.
18. Antal Bőhm and László Pál (eds), *Helyi Társadalom* [Local society] vols 1-5 (Budapest: TTI, 1983-1987); see also Antal Bőhm, 'A helyi vezetés és az információ néhány kerdése [A few questions concerning local leadership and information]', unpublished paper, TTI collection, Budapest, n.d.
19. Huszár, *Mit ér a szellem*: 42; György Szoboszlai, 'Az önkormányzat társadalompolitikai feltéleiről [On the social-political conditions of local government]', in *Magyar Politikatudományi Társaság Évkönyve 1984*: 194-200; Antal Bőhm and László Pál, 'Helyi társadalom - előtanulmány a helyi társadalom tagoltságának vizsgálatához [Local society: Preliminary study for an examination of the features of local society]', in idem, *Helyi társadalom*, vol.1 (1983):11-30.
20. Gazsó, 'Cadre Bureaucracy': 86; see also Tőkés, *Hungary's Negotiated Revolution*: 140-60.

Table 3.1 Nomenklatura *positions outside Budapest, 1983 (percentages)*

Sector	Original Occupation		
	Worker/Peasant	White collar	Intellectual
State and cooperatives	31	36	31
Party	58	20	22

Source: Statisztikai adatok a káderallományról [Statistical data on Cadre Positions] Budapest: MSZMP KB Párt- és Tömegszervezetek Osztálya, 1983, 22–3, 92–3.

presence within the administrative strata declined rapidly once one moved up the hierarchy to where county-level power was effectively consolidated: the nineteen county party first secretaries who oversaw MSZMP activity outside Budapest.

County party organizations in Hungary were generally regarded as the true conservative bastions of the party, overwhelmingly staffed by older hardliners of proletarian background. Moreover, contrary to expectations these individuals also exhibited a greater demographic consistency with the more repressive East European party-states.[21] As in the case of the Budapest apparatus, conservative county secretaries insulated the party centre against local or sectoral interests and threats

21. Data show that in 1987 some 90 per cent of county first secretaries in Hungary were over 50 years of age; by way of comparison, in Poland the same figure for regional *voivode* party first secretaries was less than 40 per cent. The Hungarian figures match more closely the figures for *kraj* party first secretaries in Czechoslovakia, where one presumes older hardliners were retained to staff regional positions following 1968. One consequently sees the paradox of 'liberal' Hungary, whose cadre policy resembles some of its more Stalinist counterparts. These findings are based on data from *Directory of Hungarian Officials* (Washington, DC: Central Intelligence Agency, 1987); *Directory of Polish Officials* (Washington, DC: Central Intelligence Agency, 1987); *Directory of Czechoslovak Officials* (Washington, DC: Central Intelligence Agency, 1988).

With regard to class background, Hungarian party data from 1983 show that at that time 14 of 19 county first secretaries were of worker or peasant background, while the remaining five were of clerical or other non-intelligentsia occupational origin: see *Statisztikai adatok*: 48.

by means of a peripheral career track for politically loyal but not necessarily talented party cadres. By way of illustration, Budapest city party secretaries could generally be considered a direct path to Politburo membership: from 1961 to 1989 seven of nine men who held this position also became Politburo members (usually holding both positions simultaneously), including Grósz himself. For county party secretaries, however, only 14 per cent ever made their way up into the ranks of the Politburo as full or candidate members, and until 1989 only one county party secretary had ever been co-opted directly from his post.[22] Nearly 40 per cent of party county secretaries never even gained membership into the Central Committee. For the county party secretary this position usually represented the limit to his or her ascendancy, occasionally rotating from county to county but rarely upwards. Long tenure became a defining feature of the county secretary. From 1960 onwards fifteen county party secretaries served in one location for more than ten years, two of those for more than twenty.[23]

While this system served its purpose in segregating regional interests and objectives from that of the party, it had its negative effects. The long periods of tenure for party officials, combined with the increase in county-level power following the administrative reforms of the 1970s, in effect encouraged the creation of party fiefdoms and the spread of corruption within them. Several Hungarian scholars have noted that in many areas county first secretaries and the subordinate administrative county councils developed into monopolistic 'dynastic clans' where personal and family ties, overlapping membership, and patron–client relationships dominated.[24] These practices were further promoted by the standard institutional order of state socialism, where informal channels and clientelistic arrangements dominated decision-making and

22. Based on calculations by the author with raw data derived from Nyírő, *Segédkönyv*, as well as those by István Szakadát and Gábor Kelemen, 'Career Types and Mobilization Channels in the Hungarian Communist Party, 1945–1990', *Journal of Communist Studies* **8** (September 1992): 46–61.
23. Based on data derived from Nyirő, *Segédkönyv*.
24. This is a central theme in András A. Gergely, *A pártállam varázstalanítása* [The disenchantment of the party-state] (Budapest: TTI, 1992). See also the personal account of a former county planner in Borsod county: László Bogár, 'A megye pártszervek szerepe a megyei tanácsi területfejlesztési döntési mechanizmusban [The role of county party organs within the regional development decision-making mechanism of the county council]', unpublished paper, TTI collection, Budapest, 1989.

appointments, hidden behind the formal activities of county or city councils and party committees.[25]

Such corruption and clientelism was of course by no means unique to Hungary. However, at the central party level such activities were more limited and discrete, reflecting Kádár's own puritanical behaviour and his distaste for personal gain – in keeping with the projected image of the party as the judicious manager of the nation-state. In comparison to other East European nations, the benefits of the Hungarian central party élite were relatively few.[26] Yet this made the aggregation and abuse of power at the county level all the more obvious – although the party turned a blind eye towards such practices, perhaps accepting them as an unfortunate byproduct of maintaining rural control. Whatever the reason, it intensified the perception of local leaders as imperious and corrupt.[27] For the rural intelligentsia these practices were particularly pernicious because they were not able to share in the spoils of these ruling clans. Despite their inclination towards political participation, intellectuals were naturally seen by local party cliques as 'suspicious', lacking the necessary occupational pedigree or personal connections.

25. One particularly interesting study of this 'entangled network' in practice has been documented by Mária Csanádi, 'The Diary of Decline: a Case-study of the Disintegration of the Party in One District in Hungary', *Soviet Studies* **43**, no. 6 (1991): 1085–99. Although Csanádi's study is of a Budapest county district, her observations of the structure and function of local government at that level are applicable to the party outside the capital. See also István Balázs, 'The Transformation of Hungarian Public Administration', *Public Administration* **71** (Spring/Summer 1993): 75–7, and the discussion of this topic by Ágnes Horváth and Árpád Szakolczai, *The Dissolution of Communist Power: The Case of Hungary* (London: Routledge, 1992), and Hankiss, *East European Alternatives*.

For similar studies with regard to Poland, see Winicjusz Narojek, 'The Structure of Power in a Local Community', in Jerzy Wiatr (ed.), *Studies in the Polish Political System* (Warsaw: Ossolineum, 1967): 179–200, and Wanda Harz and Aleksandra Jasinka, 'Problems of the Representation of Interest Groups in the Peoples' Council', in ibid.: 210–16.

26. Bennett Kovrig, 'The Hungarian Socialist Workers' Party (MSZMP)', in Grothusen, *Hungary*: 161.

27. One journalist has provided a clever example in his observation that the further one traveled from the capital and out from under the gaze of '*az Öreg*' – 'the old man', meaning Kádár – the more audacious were the party élites, and thus the more sumptuous their food: 'nowhere else could one find a more exceptional kitchen than at the county party committee'. László Hovanyecz, 'Háborús gyerek [Children of wartime]', *Népszabadság*, 15 May 1993: 21.

Rural intellectuals commonly found themselves shut out of these patronage systems.[28]

Given these obstacles, why did rural party intelligentsia stay within the party? One can assume that many did not. However, since other options for political or civic 'self-actualization' were virtually non-existent, in the countryside the party often represented the only real avenue for intellectual and political activity, to carry on the fight from within. This point finds resonance in Albert Hirschman's discussion of 'exit, voice and loyalty', in which he argues that loyalty to the normative objectives of an organization is liable to increase the possibility of individual or collective action (voice), particularly where the cost of exit is high.[29] In the Hungarian countryside the party, although often in direct conflict with the local intelligentsia, was the only political option available.

To summarize, political institutions at the countryside level in Hungary created a situation opposite from that in the capital, the reverse of what we might imagine. Reform and liberalization in Hungary were organized and directed at the centre, leaving the periphery neglected and subject to abuse. Large numbers of rural intellectuals, despite their commitment to political and civic activity, found their options limited by the dearth of resources and their access blocked by hardline political cliques which dominated local party and governmental organs. Here the institutional patterns of Kádárism as they related to the intelligentsia failed – or perhaps more accurately, reached their limits, having committed their resources and attention to the political centre. While the party had succeeded in co-opting intellectuals through the use of its liberalization policies, the secondary mechanism of resources and access was neglected outside of the *metropole*, and made all the more glaring by the conservatism, corruption and sheer incompetence of the rural party apparatus.

Talented yet not a part of the *metropole* élite, these regional 'second-tier' intellectuals knew none of the privileges elaborated by Szelényi and Konrád, and frequently complained about their marginal status '*Isten háta mögött*' – 'behind the back of God', as it was often put.[30]

28. Gergely, *A pártállam varázstalanítása*; Bogár, 'A megye pártszervek szerepe'.
29. Albert O. Hirschman, *Exit, Voice, and Loyalty* (Cambridge, MA: Harvard University Press, 1970).
30. Zsolt Szoboszlai, 'Vázlat a vidéki értelmiségről, [Outline of the rural intelligent

Interestingly, a number of interview subjects used the historical analogy of feudal Hungary, describing themselves as *köznemesek* - literally, 'lesser nobility', far from the distant 'court' at Budapest and thus more connected to the true state of the nation.

Besides the obvious impact on the rural intelligentsia in terms of their alienation from the institutional status quo, another important consequence of this narrow field of movement for the younger rural intelligentsia was that lacking formal horizontal institutions (journals, conferences, societies) and channels for access, members of this second tier used the party to cultivate their own informal networks in order to exchange ideas and transmit information, arrangements obscure and distant from the centre of political power and thus largely ignored by the party élite.[31] In sociological terms, the deprivations of the younger generation of rural party intelligentsia encouraged the formation of 'solidarity groups', bound by common values and interaction. These groups are critical to later developments among the rural intelligentsia, as they typically form a key building block of partisan organization.[32]

CENTRE VERSUS PERIPHERY AND POLITICAL MOBILIZATION

The characterization of the Hungarian county-level party system as the wellspring of conservative activity would initially appear to mesh well

sia]', *Juss* **II/III**, (December 1989/January 1990): 103–12. Endre Bilecz, 'A helyi társadalmak állapota Magyarországon [the state of local societies in Hungary]', in Kurtán, Sándor and Vass, *Magyarország politikai évkönyve 1988*: 134–43; Pál Bánlaky, 'A kisvárosok értelmisége a "helyi társadalom" közéletében [The small-town intelligentsia in the public life of "local society"]', Tibor Huszár (ed.), *A magyar értelmiség a '80-as években* [The Hungarian intelligentsia in the 1980s] (Budapest: Kossuth, 1986): 114–48.

31. See Bánlaky, 'A kisvárosok', on the importance of this information system for the rural intelligentsia, and also Zoltán Varga, 'Politikai vitaklubok Vas megyében [Political debate clubs in Vas county]', *Propagandista* **XIII** (1989): 130–36. It has also been emphasized that this secondary intellectual strata played an important role in creating a support structure for those radicals ostracized by the party, who in turn provided a means to access alternative sources of critical information. Rakovski [Kis and Bence], *Towards an East European Marxism*: 58–62.
32. William Gamson, *Power and Discontent* (Homewood, IL: Dorsey, 1968), esp. 32–7.

with dominant centre–periphery theory, which has tended to characterize the countryside as the source of 'pre-modern' political behaviour, more distant from central values and thus more resistant to change emanating from that direction. This is above all an essentially normative assumption, extolling the superiority of the central values of modernity versus 'provincialism', a term which semantically burdens peripheral values and goals with the presupposition of their obsolescence.[33]

Yet as critics such as Sidney Tarrow point out, this perspective essentially strips the periphery of any real content: 'politics, values, the techniques of rule – all these are properties of the center. The periphery is pictured simply in terms of this proclivity to resist the propagation of modernizing norms', something which 'begs the question of the conditions under which the periphery revolts'.[34] One need only think of regional movements in northern Italy to realize the inapplicability of this approach in such cases. Regional politics is not necessarily the politics of immobility or resistance, although such conditions at the élite regional level can promote the mobilization of local actors below them. Importantly, Tarrow's own study of regional politics in Italy and France concluded that where central political institutions are immobilized and fragmented, and where local political power serves only the local élite, one possible outcome is popular mobilization at the grassroots level which may eventually transform the centre itself.[35]

Such revolts were less likely in Eastern Europe, particularly within the communist party itself. Members were screened for their reliability to the institutional order and often made dependent upon it for the maintenance of their livelihoods. Dissent or independent political

33. See, for example, Edward Shils, *Center and Periphery: Essays in Macrosociology*, selected papers of Edward Shils, vol. 2 (Chicago, IL: University of Chicago Press, 1975); Jean Gottman, *Center and Periphery: Spatial Variation in Politics* (Beverly Hills, CA: Sage, 1980), and Seymour Martin Lipset, 'Revolt against Modernity', in Per Torsvik (ed.), *Mobilization, Center–Periphery Structures and Nation-Building* (Bergen: Universitetsforlaget, 1981): 431–500.
34. Sidney Tarrow, *Between Center and Periphery* (New Haven, CT: Yale University Press, 1977): 20.
35. Ibid.: 253–5; see also the discussion of centre and periphery in John W. Meyer and W. Richard Scott, 'Centralization and the Legitimacy Problems of Local Government', in John W. Meyer and W. Richard Scott (eds), *Organizational Environments: Ritual and Rationality* (Beverly Hills, CA: Sage, 1983): 199–215.

activity was swiftly suppressed, even on the outskirts of power. But where societal co-optation over institutional loyalty becomes an overriding concern, rank-and-file membership can become more heterogeneous, particularly in areas assumed to be peripheral in either a geographic or functional sense. Consequently, crisis situations at the top can sometimes result in peripheral revolts from within. This was, for example, the case in the Polish United Workers' Party (PZPR). During the course of the early 1970s, the PZPR engaged in a major drive for increased party membership which largely discarded ideological certifications in favour of numerical objectives. By 1979 the party ranks had swelled by almost a third, to more than three million members.[36] But this sudden increase in membership brought attendant dangers, as the PZPR brought into the organization large numbers of individuals whose loyalty to institutional norms was in some doubt.[37] During the rise of Solidarity in 1980 and the ensuing crisis within the PZPR leadership, the party rank and file began to form a 'horizontal movement' which united workers and intellectuals, primarily from large factories and educational institutions.

Condemned by the party central authorities as factionalism, the horizontal movement nevertheless quickly spread to a dozen other provinces, demanding electoral reform within the party and forcing an extraordinary party congress in July 1981. Although the horizontalists managed to have few delegates elected to the congress itself, the political turmoil they had helped foster among other party members led to the delegates' almost total removal of incumbent Central Committee and Politburo members.[38] Fear of the increasing power of the horizontalists in part influenced the decision to impose martial law, as it became increasingly clear that the party membership could no longer be trusted to defend the institutional status quo.[39]

Given the factors and precedents enumerated above it should not be

36. George Kolankiewicz, 'The Politics of "Socialist Renewal"', in Jean Woodall (ed.), *Policy and Politics in Contemporary Poland* (New York: St. Martin's Press, 1982): 56.
37. Joni Lovenduski and Jean Woodall, *Politics and Society in Eastern Europe* (Bloomington, IN: Indiana University Press, 1987): 214.
38. Kolankiewicz, 'The Politics of "Socialist Renewal"': 70. An excellent study of the rise of the horizontal movement in Poland can be found in Werner Hahn, *Democracy in a Communist Party* (New York: Columbia University Press, 1987).
39. Hahn, *Democracy in a Communist Party*: 195–7.

surprising that in Hungary a countryside revolt arose from the ranks of the party intellectuals. The co-optation of local intelligentsia, their isolation from resources or local representation, combined with the corrupt and clan-like nature of county party politics, was a recipe for a rank-and-file backlash. Moreover, the party was not alone in this regard; by late 1988 the Hungarian countryside in general began to experience the widespread mobilization and organization of the populace in general, which rivalled developments in Budapest. Protesters rallied against corruption, environmental pollution and economic conditions, demanding political reform – rural activity with little precedent in Hungarian political history.[40]

This was particularly the case in one county, that of Csongrád, and its county seat, Szeged. A paragon of conservative and clientelistic party power, Csongrád exemplified many of the problems and tensions which dominated rural Hungary. Consequently it was precisely there where the reform circles first took up the battle against the old party order, setting in motion a grassroots revolt that caught the central authorities off-guard and initiated the unraveling of the party itself.

THE SEEDS OF DISCONTENT: CSONGRÁD

Csongrád county is located in the southeastern corner of Hungary, bordering Yugoslavia and Romania. This area, a wide prairie known as the *Alföld* or 'lower lands' in Hungarian, is known primarily for its agricultural output and its largest city, Szeged, a town of some 175,000 inhabitants. Industrial and economic development in the region has traditionally been hindered by the lack of local resources, compounded by the territorial losses Hungary suffered after World War One, when some two-thirds of Hungary and much of its industrial base were granted to Romania, Slovakia and Yugoslavia, lands primarily concentrated to the east and south of Szeged. From its more central position in

40. Annamária Telekes and János Rechnitzer, 'A "vidék" a mozgások évében [The 'countryside' in the year of movements]', *Valóság* **XXXII** (September 1989): 97–108. Among the rural population in general the resurgence of populism has been connected to that population's perception of its abuse and neglect under state socialism: see Lengyel, *Micsoda Év!*: 30–31.

the old Austro-Hungarian Empire, Csongrád county now found itself in the backwater of a truncated and much poorer nation-state.

In part as a result of this, the historical relationship of this area to socialism has been ambiguous at best. Lacking major industry, the region did not serve as a working-class base for communist or social-democratic movements. When a communist 'Republic of Councils' took control of Hungary in 1919, it was in Szeged where an armed counter-revolutionary 'Anti-Bolshevik Committee' was first founded. Its military leader, Miklós Horthy, eventually came to power following the collapse of the communist government and permitted a white terror which claimed the lives of thousands, primarily communists, socialists and Jews.[41] Horthy's oppression of communist leaders during his inter-war reign was not forgotten following the imposition of socialist rule, and many in the county believed that their region was being 'punished' economically in the post-war period for their town's role in the past. Locals complained, for example, of disproportionately low development funds and poor medical facilities despite some of the highest rates of alcoholism and nervous disorders in the nation.[42]

Whatever the source, one impact of the relatively low level of industrial development in the region was that other large organizations, in particular educational institutions, held a greater prominence in the community and party structure than might otherwise have been the case. Szeged boasts the regionally important Attila József Scientific University (AJTE), with the largest social science faculty outside of Budapest, as well as a medical school and several other institutes of research and higher learning.[43] From the inter-war period onwards the city thus took on many of the characteristics of a typical 'intellectual' university town.

Central power in Csongrád, however, reflected few of these traits. Perhaps as a result of lingering mistrust towards the region, party politics in the county became known for the excessive degree to which

41. For historical details see Hoensch, *A History of Modern Hungary*, chap. 3.
42. István Nádor, 'Szentesített szocializmus [Sanctified socialism]', *Élet és irodalom*, 12 May 1989: 16.
43. Árpád Rátkai, 'Az állampárt utolsó évei Csongrádban [The last years of the party-state in Csongrád]' unpublished paper, Szeged, n.d., 6; Károly Bodó, 'Híres város – hírhedt ügyek után [Famous city after notorious affairs]', *Új Fórum*, 4–5 May 1989: 18–23.

power was centralized, conservative and entrenched. From 1960 to 1985 only two party county secretaries held that post: Imre Győri until 1974, and Mihály Komócsin thereafter. Both secretaries were born in the county, and had strong family connections to each other.[44] Mihály Komócsin in particular was well known because of his older brother, one of the Politburo members who in 1972 had led the failed *putsch* against Kádár.

During Komócsin's long reign, party activity in Csongrád was exemplified by its dogmatic and personalistic nature, 'power concentrated in the hands of one individual who could not be contradicted; those who dared could not remain in the county, or if they tried were marginalized, pushed to the periphery of society'.[45] As one of Komócsin's own protégés noted, this was directed particularly against the local intelligentsia, who were consciously shut out of local politics.[46] During this time a large surveillance force under direct control of the local party leadership was even developed to control activity at such institutions as the university.[47] Csongrád soon garnered the nickname 'Pol Pot county' both inside and out of the region.

Matters were made worse by the corrupt nature of many of Komócsin's less-crafty underlings, who gained control over the country apparatus after Komócsin stepped down from his position in 1985. Uninterested in reviving or reforming the ossified party structure, they instead took advantage of this monopolized system inherited from Komócsin to plunder county assets and commandeer well-paying positions – looting the system from within. Among other abuses, during the 1980s members of the local party élite – in particular the new party first secretary and heads of the local government – created the legal means by which they could acquire and then liquidate large amounts of property for a huge profit (as high as thirteen thousand per cent).[48]

44. Nyírő, *Segédkönyv*: 278, 290–91.
45. Ferenc Odorics, 'Miért nem élek Csongrád megyében én sem? [Why don't I live in Csongrád county either?]', *Juss* **II** (March 1989): 19.
46. István Csonka, president of the Szeged Town Council, quoted in 'Híres város – hírhedt ügyek után': 18.
47. Ernő Raffay, AJTE adjunct professor and local MDF leader, quoted in ibid.: 21.
48. The persons credited for eventually breaking the stories of corruption in Csongrád were István Tanács, county reporter for the central party paper *Népszabadság*, and Miklós Halász, who worked for the local *Délmagyarország*, although his exposés initially appeared only in the national paper *Magyar Nemzet*. A collection of Halász's articles can be found in *Suttog a város. Kit segít a varázsgömb?* [The city

Lacking Komócsin's political talents and seeking only personal gain, local party cronies unknowingly undermined their own power structure, further demoralizing the apparatus and spreading cynicism and open hostility throughout the party ranks.

By the mid-1980s the crumbling and stagnant nature of the party system in Csongrád country had brought many of its members to the limits of their tolerance. Signs of increasing discontent, autonomous action and open clashes with the party hierarchy began appearing from within Pol Pot county's lower party ranks. Given the sharp divide between the community and the party, and between the party intelligentsia and its local leadership, the organization of political activity apart from and against the county leadership was perhaps only a matter of time. In particular, by keeping party intellectuals out of any meaningful role in the party, hardliners in essence compelled that segment to band together in order to inform themselves and make their opinions heard.

THE REVOLT OF THE LOCAL MEMBERSHIP

The first conspicuous example of the poor state of relations within the MSZMP in Csongrád was provided by the 1985 parliamentary elections. These elections were noteworthy in that for the first time multiple candidates had been made mandatory in each constituency, a half-hearted attempt at political pluralism.[49] One of the Csongrád candidates for office was Mihály Komócsin, recently retired from his position as county first secretary, who hoped to retire into a parliamentary seat (a fairly common practice). While intentionally paired against an unknown contender, what local party bosses had not anticipated was that a well-known local television reporter, Zoltán Király, would be nominated from the floor and capture nearly half of the votes cast. This was a clear sign of both Király's popularity and rank-and-file hostility towards Komócsin, who subsequently withdrew his candidacy before the runoff

whispers – who is helped by the crystal ball?] (Szeged: Novum, 1989).

49. Information regarding the 1985 electoral reforms and outcomes can be found in István Kukorelli, *Így választottunk …* [This is how we have voted …] (Budapest: Eötvös Loránd Tudományegyetem, 1988), and in Toma, *Socialist Authority*: 48–55.

election. The following years of Király's tenure were marked by his outspokenness in parliament and his radical views on the subject of political pluralism and reform, views which led to his eventual expulsion from the party in 1988 (see Chapter 2).[50]

The most organized political movement within the local party structure was, however, developing within the institutions of higher education. Already in the late 1970s, the party committee of the school of liberal arts at AJTE had been able to wrest some autonomy from the local party oligarchy, although occasional clashes were still common.[51] Under this relative independence unofficial party activity flourished, much of it centred upon the Department of Scientific Socialism. Such departments were typically known for the poor quality and hopeless conservatism of their faculty. AJTE, however, boasted a younger staff who turned the department into a centre for alternative political information. Already in the early 1980s, one of its instructors, József Géczi, had begun an unofficial collection of samizdat and foreign political material for the open use of faculty and students, which grew into the largest single resource of its kind outside Budapest.[52]

50. Zoltán Király interview, *Kizárt a párt*: 183–215; idem, '"Az egész rendszer igényli a megújítást ..." ['The entire system demands renewal']', interview by Tibor Szabó, *Tiszatáj* **XLII** (January 1988): 93–102. One example of Király's outspokenness was witnessed by the author during an address at AJTE in 1987 where Király commented that *Das Kapital* was no longer relevant to modern society and belonged in a museum of the working class.

    A second conflict involved that of the well-respected local journal *Tiszatáj*. *Tiszatáj* was nationally known for its willingness to cover sensitive political issues, notably those which were usually associated with the populist movement – for example, on the plight of ethnic Hungarians in Romania. In 1986 the editorial board of *Tiszatáj* was finally sacked by central authorities, technically for its publication of a poem which the party accused of being counter-revolutionary and questioning the legitimacy of their leadership. Ironically, as in the case of *Mozgó Világ* after the replacement of the editorial board, the journal moved more towards covering the reformist party intelligentsia, whose articles and interviews became the centrepiece of the journal. For details see Sándor Olász, 'Tiszatáj-dráma, 1986 [Tiszatáj Drama, 1986]', *Juss* **II** (March 1989): 2–5; László Vörös and József Annus, former editor and deputy editor, respectively, of *Tiszatáj*, interview by Csaba Könczöl, 'A Tiszatáj-főnix [Tiszatáj Phoenix]', *Kritika* (November 1989): 21–5; László Vörös, interview by László Domokos, 'Egy leváltás története [The story of a dismissal]', *Élet és irodalom*, 17 February 1989: 7.
51. One example is the university student reform movement in 1980–81, which a number of party faculty members assisted.
52. Rátkai, 'Az állampárt': 4–5.

During this same period numerous lecture series were organized by the university and other institutes around the county which invited many of the most prominent reform-orientated intellectuals and politicians in Hungary to speak frankly on a number of sensitive topics: political and economic reform, social policy and local government. In 1987 and 1988, Pozsgay himself gave two prominent lectures on political pluralism, in which he openly criticized the central party leadership, much to the consternation of local party leaders.[53] The mobilizing impact of these forums was undoubtedly great. Reform circle interview subjects in Szeged stressed the impact of these lectures on their own decision to actively organize themselves.

The first formal attempts at horizontal organization were, however, of limited success, blocked by the party apparatus and the limits of their own objectives. Following the MSZMP party conference in May 1988 and its call for the reform and rejuvenation of the party, there was an understanding at the top and bottom ranks of the party that similar conferences would be held at the county and city level, so as to effect a turnover in the regional old guard. But local party secretaries were not so inclined to see themselves forced from power. By the autumn of 1988 14 of 19 county leaders had openly rejected the need for such meetings. Party members throughout Hungary reacted openly and angrily, compelling nearly half the county leaders to backtrack.[54]

In June the Csongrád party county leadership had been the first to formally reject the idea of a conference - which many city committees in Csongrád quickly echoed. In response, 25 party secretaries from larger county institutions - hospitals, factories, cooperatives, AJTE and the school of medicine - drafted and signed a petition to the county party committee in which they decried the 'deep crisis of trust and opposition to the leadership' that had developed among the members. The party secretaries demanded that a county party conference be convened through which a new leadership could be democratically elected. This 'Group of 25', as it came to be known, was the first sign of horizontal organization in the MSZMP, perhaps in its entire history.[55]

53. Ibid.: 5-6; see also Imre Attila Kovács, 'Mállunk vagy reformálunk [We will crumble or reform]', *Juss* **I** (June 1988): 28–47.

54. Telekes and Rechnitzer, 'A "vidék"': 106.

55. A copy of the petition was published in *Juss* **I** (September 1988): 47–8, although the signatories are omitted; they can be found in Árpád Rátkai, 'Végjáték a Tisza mentén [Endgame on the banks of the Tisza]' unpublished paper, Szeged, n.d., 24.

The instigator of the Group of 25 was an individual by the name of Ádám Anderle, party secretary at AJTE and a Latin American historian sympathetic to Eurocommunist ideas. Anderle had been openly calling for a turnover in local leaders even before the national party conference in May.[56] The broader objective was to develop the Group of 25 into an internal interest group on the basis of similar organizational forms found among socialist parties in the West. The local party leadership was not pleased with these actions, branding the Group of 25's activities as factionalism and threatening disciplinary proceedings against it.[57]

The battle over the county conference eventually brought the central leadership into the fray. During August, several members of the party Central Committee declared in the national media that a party conference in Csongrád was clearly necessary. Grósz himself threatened in a Szeged radio interview that should the county party committee continue to reject a party conference, it would be demanded by Budapest. Less than a week later the county committee finally gave in, reluctantly. A county conference would be held in December, and Grósz himself would attend to ensure a desired outcome.[58]

For Csongrád county, the Group of 25 was an organizational catalyst. Shortly thereafter a 'Group of 19' and a 'Group of 35' had appeared, delegates demanding the democratization of forthcoming city and county conferences. Many within the party ranks were mobilized by events, but these groups remained local and issue-orientated, seeking only to transform the county party structure and make it more responsive to the mass membership, rather than making broader demands.

For details on the struggle to force a county party conference see István Tanács, 'A bizalom teherpróbája [The ordeal of trust]', *Népszabadság*, 18 August 1988: 5.

56. Ádám Anderle, personal interview by the author, Szeged, 29 January 1993; Rátkai, 'Az állampárt': 9–14.
57. This included Sándor Székely, first party secretary of Szeged, who had aligned himself against the county leadership since the May conference; Rátkai, 'Az állampárt': 9–14.
58. Ibid.: 13.

THE FOUNDING OF THE FIRST REFORM CIRCLE

But there was one exception - the party reform circle, whose origins lie within the local party apparatus itself. Seeking to remedy the crisis of trust within the local party structure, in the summer of 1988 the county first secretary floated the idea of a consultative body of intelligentsia that would assist the local leadership - an obvious defensive attempt at pacification through co-optation. The body never materialized, but two of those involved in the attempt - József Géczi (the previously mentioned instructor of scientific socialism at AJTE) and József Lovászi (an employee of the county party committee) continued to discuss the idea.

Géczi and Lovászi began to outline the concept of an independent political body within the party, a 'reform cell' which could link local party reformers scattered throughout basic party organizations into one horizontally-based group. By collecting reformers under one organization, it was argued, they could break free from their minority position and increase their effectiveness. Moreover, such an organization could concentrate not simply on the local level, but broaden their objectives and foster similar groupings elsewhere in the country. Taking its cue from the Polish horizontal movement, a grassroots movement or party platform was envisaged as a final outcome which could link up with reformers at the centre of power.[59]

Throughout the autumn a small group of party members had come together to make the idea a reality. The organizers now sought some kind of public declaration that would announce their presence, bringing the group into the public sphere and helping to increase their ranks. With the help of sympathetic editors at two local newspapers, on 29 November 1988 the first declaration of the Csongrád county reform circle appeared in the local press. Entitled 'Reform circles in the party as well!' - a reference to the rise in political 'circles' spreading outside of the party - the declaration opened with a radical call to action:

59. Csongrád county reform circle members, personal interview by the author, Szeged, 9 February 1993, and Budapest, 20 October 1992 and 23 March 1993; József Lovászi, 'Párttagok reformköre Csongrád megyében [The reform circle of party members in Csongrád county]', unpublished document dated 28 March 1989; József Géczi, 'reformkör = pártfrakció? [Reform circle = party faction?]', interview by Ilona Újszász, *Szegedi Egyetem*, 23 February 1989: 6.

> In Eastern Europe, the countries of so-called existing socialism are in deep crisis. This crisis can only be fought against with radical and complex reforms; the historic task is to liquidate the structure of the Stalinist model. The economy, politics, various spheres of society - and our own socialist concept as well - we must irreversibly liberate from the captivity of the bureaucratic mechanism! This will simultaneously require the following: 1. A clear strategy for reintegration into the world economy (above all a functioning market and the revival of rejected bourgeois values); 2. Political and ideological reform which will rediscover and support every legitimate value of the socialist movement; 3. The reform of political institutions, such that they will give space to individual and communal autonomy and regard a multiparty system as a natural state.

The quarter-page statement continued with a discussion of the need for a critical analysis of the past and the role of the party within it; the development of a dialogue with those outside the party; for reformers within the party to unite forces against those seeking to sabotage reform; for party members to join their reform circle and establish others so as to create horizontal connections within the party, a forum which could have the characteristics of a political movement. The article was signed by 26 members from the county party rank and file, the majority of them from educational institutions.[60] Within two days the reform circle received a letter of support from the local branches of FIDESZ, MDF, SZDSZ and TDDSZ (an independent union of scientific workers).[61] The first public meeting of the reform circle on 2 December 1988 attracted some 120 people, and more than 65 signed its founding statement.[62]

In retrospect, those involved in the creation of the Csongrád reform circle noted in interviews that this first initiative was a jump into the dark. Although the dogmatic local leadership was on the defensive, it still held a great deal of power, and events at the party centre did not give one hope that an immediate breakthrough in terms of reform was imminent. Perhaps more disturbing, the open formation of a horizontal movement went against the most fundamental Leninist organizational

60. 'Reformkörök a pártban is! [There are reform circles in the party as well!]', *Délmagyarország*, 29 November 1988: 2, and *Csongrád Megye Hírlap*, 29 November 1988: 2.
61. Letter from regional FIDESZ, MDF, SZDSZ and TDDSZ organizations to Csongrád county reform circle [photocopy], dated 1 December 1988.
62. 'Megalakult a párttagok reformköre [The reform circle of party members has been established]', *Csongrád Megye Hírlap*, 3 December 1988: 3.

tenets of the party structure, 'factionalism', which was traditionally branded as dangerous to party unity and a threat to the realization of party objectives.[63]

NOTORIETY AND SETBACKS

That the reform circle was a risky undertaking was driven home almost immediately. On the same day that the first reform circle declaration was published in Csongrád, in Budapest General Secretary Grósz gave a lengthy public speech to party activists. He eventually turned to the topic of increasing pluralism in Hungary, some of which merits quoting:

> in the cities tensions are increasing, particularly among the youth and within intellectual circles. Furthermore, one can observe that there grow hostile, small in number yet strident, bourgeois restoration-seeking, counter-revolutionary forces as well. ... They overstate the possibilities of a multi-party system, exaggerating its presumed advantages. They disturb our international relations. ... It is apparent that on the basis of a goal-orientated, thought-out concept they want to disturb the socialist institutional order. ... The question is whether we are able to win back our self-confidence, can we win to our side the forces of reason, and if we must, can we act decisively against hostile, counter-revolutionary forces. If so, we can maintain order and stability, pass through our economic difficulties, defend our values and bring about a new, modern and more effective Hungarian socialism. If not, anarchy, chaos, and – let there be no illusions – a white terror will prevail.[64]

The reform circle members were taken aback by the aggressive and hardline nature of Grósz's comments and began to worry about his anticipated presence at the forthcoming county party conference. City party conferences already held in Csongrád had produced mixed results. Party committees experienced large turnovers in incumbent members (more than 50 per cent) in the five largest cities in Csongrád, but many of these new members were themselves ambivalent towards

63. See the definition of factionalism in Dus, *A pártélet kisszotára*: 38.
64. *Kiállni a politikáért, tenni az országért! Grósz Károly beszéde a Budapesti párt-aktíván, 1988. November 29* [Fight for the political, act for the nation! Károly Grósz's speech to Budapest party activists, 29 November 1988] (Budapest: Kossuth, 1988): 6–7.

radical reform, calling into question how much progress had been achieved.[65]

Moreover, central party leadership involvement in the run-up to the county party conference had been on an unprecedented scale, in the form of a campaign to mobilize delegate support for potential secretarial candidate Pál Vastagh, the dean of law at AJTE. Vastagh was known for his close ties to Grósz supporters in the Central Committee as well as for his political opportunism, which had so far garnered him little support from among the local party membership.[66] Delegates worried that the conference would be dominated by Grósz and his allies, who would reform the county leadership to meet Budapest's objectives rather than those of the local rank and file.

The conference opened on 10 December. Despite the intimidating presence of the general secretary, party delegates (including a handful of reform circle members) rose to condemn the current state of affairs in Csongrád and the nation as a whole. Speakers decried the lack of local social investments and the state of infrastructure, censorship and the suppression of the Group of 25's petition.[67] Some went even further. Anderle accused the local leadership of being 'anti-intellectual' and ineffective, calling for their complete removal from power. Reform circle member Imre Keserű stated outright that 'the past forty years cannot be called socialism' and that only revolutionary steps could solve the nation's problems, including the convening of an early national party congress and the transformation of parliament such that it could bring about a democratic constitution.[68] Delegate Zsolt Szoboszlai, noting that the success of significant historical events in Hungary had always hinged on the countryside, welcomed the reform circle declaration as a means to that end.

It was Grósz's turn to speak. Ignoring the concerns raised by the delegates, he immediately took up the topic of his already infamous

65. Rátkai, 'Az állampárt': 21–2.

66. Earlier that September the AJTE party organization elected five delegates to the Szeged city party conference from among eight candidates, including Vastagh. Vastagh came in eighth. Rátkai, 'Az állampárt': 23, n. 70.

67. 'Megtartották a Csongrád megyei pártértekezlet [The Csongrád party conference has taken place]', *Délmagyarország*, 12 December 1988: 1–5.

68. Ibid.: 3.

'white terror' speech, defending his comments and reiterating the threat of right-wing extremism in Hungary. Within this context he then turned to the issue of the Csongrád reform circle and its recent declaration, which, he commented, he had just read. Holding a copy of the offending newspaper in his hand, he condemned the actions of the reform circle as factionalist, reading aloud their calls for a dialogue with those outside the party and the creation of a horizontal movement. In whose name did the reform circle speak, he questioned. By what right did they make these demands? He responded:

> Please, this is not platform freedom. This is a demand for the freedom of factions. ... Where do they think this will lead? Is this a good idea? We should establish two parties. Perhaps there will be three Marxist–Leninist parties, if we continue in this manner. At least let us say that that will be the case. But in one party this is not tolerable. It debilitates the party.

Grósz castigated the editors of the two local papers, questioning why the declaration had even been published. He then concluded:

> I simply want to say one thing. One cannot lead a county in this manner. We must draw a lesson from this. I do not want to reprimand the county first secretary, the secretaries, the city or county committee, I do not wish them to misunderstand. I do not wish to influence you with my speech in how you should vote. I simply want to draw your attention to the fact that should such things continue you will be incapable of continuing your work. And so I ask of you: put your ranks in order![69]

The old guard withered under this upbraiding, clearing the way for the election of a new county committee and Vastagh as the new first secretary. Reform circle delegates and others countered with their own candidate, but with his backing from Grósz, Vastagh won easily.

69. 'Grósz Károly beszéde a megyei pártertekezleten [Károly Grósz's speech at the county party conference]', *Csongrád Megye Hírlap*, 12 December 1988: 3–4. This section of Grósz's speech was omitted in the Szeged party paper *Délmagyarország*, and received national attention only in one article: Zoltán Lökös and Sándor Palkó, 'Tiszta közélet, bizalmat [A clean public life and trust]', *Vasárnapi Hírek*, 11 December 1988: 3–4.

REFORM AT THE CENTRE AND THE THREAT OF A PARTY SPLIT

While the Csongrád reform circle was voicing its grievances and coming under fire, the party stalemate between hardliners and reformers continued to play itself out in Budapest. Although Pozsgay had cancelled the planned meeting of party reformers and opposition figures in November, Grósz's recent hardline statements only reinforced the views of those around him of the need to 'unfurl the flag' of reform, rallying his supporters for a possible split of the MSZMP itself. This was a potentially dangerous step forward, not only with regard to what would happen to party–state relations, but also in that rumours were circulating that Grósz and his party allies had begun to prepare lists of individuals to be arrested within the party should a crackdown against reformers be necessary. For the time being, strengthening the hands of the reformers within the party to bring about the internal transformation of the MSZMP remained the judicious, if somewhat more daunting, strategy.[70]

What reformers were up against was exemplified by a Central Committee meeting on 15 December, where the concept of political pluralism was first taken into explicit consideration by the MSZMP. Members were provided with a set of documents on possible political and economic reform by János Berecz, supplemented by a selection of conflicting quotations on the subject by members of the Politburo as they had appeared in the press. Clearly uneasy with any reforms, a number of Central Committee members rose to denounce the new alternative organizations such as MDF and FIDESZ and their 'manipulation of democracy' in order to garner support, such as their demand for the liquidation of the MSZMP armed unit, the Workers'

70. See Pozsgay, *1989*: 90–91. In his memoirs József Horváth, brigadier-general within the Hungarian Interior Ministry in charge of domestic security, comments that during this period the threat of a conservative *putsch* by forces in the military, Workers' Guard, and/or the party apparatus against party reformers was quite real: see *A Tábornok Vallomása* [The confession of the brigadier-general] (Budapest: Pallas Lap- és Könyvkiadó and PALLWEST, 1990): 188; see also Lengyel, *Micsoda év*: 77, n. 4, and Mihály Bihari, 'A diktatorikus szocializmusból a pluralista demokráciába: a magyar út 1987–90 [From dictatorial socialism to pluralist democracy: the Hungarian road, 1987–90]', in *Demokratikus út a szabadsághoz* [Democratic road to freedom] (Budapest: Gondolat, 1990): 125–6.

Guard. Nyers himself struck a cautious tone, stressing the need to move the party to the centre while warning against a 'Weimarization' of Hungarian politics. Grósz downplayed the notion of a national crisis, arguing that party functionaries were more nervous than was warranted, and ironically mentioning the recent Csongrád party conference as a prime example of the party working together to solve their problems.[71]

Towards the end of the meeting, Berecz made a short speech on the implications of the documents he had submitted. It was proposed that a new constitution would be submitted to parliament in 1990, to precede national elections that autumn. Electoral reform and a law on the right of association could also be drafted during this time. However, Berecz made it clear that the party did not support a 'Western-style' multiparty democracy, speaking of such a system as a 'romantic desire'. He concluded that reforms would not lead to the introduction of a multi-party system, but to the *division* of political power rather than the *sharing* of it.[72] The meeting concluded with the formation of three committees to continue work on the issues of party plurality, alternative organizations and the reform of the electoral system, which were to submit reports for the next Central Committee meeting in late February. The party appeared to be moving forward to reorganize, but not surrender, its monopoly on power.[73]

Pozsgay, however, had plans to undermine this controlled reform. Since the May 1988 national party conference, he had been entrusted to chair several subcommittees to work on a new party programme, in particular dealing with the re-examination of recent Hungarian history. The historical subcommittee's most sensitive question was that of 1956 and its immediate aftermath – now that Kádár was effectively out of the picture, could these events be re-evaluated? Already opposition forces had been pressing to allow the reburial of Imre Nagy and his

71. However, Grósz noted that the biggest weakness of the party at the time was the threat of the press slipping out of the hands of the party – a comment that may have been directly based on the reform circle declaration. Transcripts of the MSZMP Central Committee meeting 15 December 1988, National Archives collection 288f 4/248 ő.e. A summary of the proceeds of this meeting can also be found in Alfred Reisch, 'The HSWP CC Grapples with the Implications of Political Pluralism', *RFER* (12 January 1989): 9–14.
72. Transcripts of the 15 December 1988 Central Committee meeting: 162, 164.
73. For an excellent overview of this period see Béla Faragó, 'Mi történik Magyarországon? [What is happening in Hungary?]', *Századvég* 1–2 (1989): 5–17.

executed associates, to which the party eventually agreed, although this did not indicate any kind of rehabilitation. Yet the need to reassess these events was apparent, should the new leadership truly wish to distance itself from the past.

After much debate, in late January 1989 the party's historical subcommittee drew the general conclusion that 1956 was not in fact a counterrevolution, as the party maintained, but was rather a 'popular uprising'.[74] The findings of the subcommittee were now to be submitted to the Politburo for consideration, which, Pozsgay envisaged, would lead to their watering down or total suppression. Unbeknown even to his closest supporters, Pozsgay decided to make the findings public himself. On 28 January, one day after the final meeting of the subcommittee and while Grósz was out of the country, Pozsgay broke the news in an interview on national radio: the historical subcommittee had reached the conclusion that what had occurred in 1956 was in fact 'a national uprising against an oligarchic form of rule that had debased the nation'.[75] With one stroke Pozsgay gained the upper hand within the party and caused a national sensation. Scrambling to respond, Grósz and other party leaders quickly tried to dismiss Pozsgay's comments as unauthorized and unacceptable, but Pozsgay held fast. Uncertain what to do, the next Central Committee meeting was moved forward to deal with the implications of Pozsgay's action.

Pozsgay's statement had a tremendous impact on reformers within the party, mobilizing their support behind him and giving them something to rally around. In Csongrád in particular it helped shatter the hesitations of the reform circle following the disastrous events of the county conference and their open denunciation by the general secretary. Since that time, the party apparatus in Csongrád had continued with a carrot and stick approach towards local party dissenters. On the one hand, the organization of potentially powerful party officials such as the party secretaries in the Group of 25 were not tolerated; surveillance

74. Alfred Reisch, 'HSWP Study Re-evaluates the 1956 Revolution, Imre Nagy, and 40 Years of Hungarian History', *RFER* (24 February 1989): 3–8. Transcript excerpts from the subcommittee meeting can be found in Emil Kimmel, *Végjáték a fehér házban* [Endgame in the white house] (n.p.: Tibor Drucker, 1990): 8–24. The final report of the subcommittee was published under the title 'Történelmi utunk [Our historical road]' as a special edition of *Társadalmi Szemle*; for the English translation see *JPRS Report: East Europe* (26 July 1989): 1–35.
75. Radio Budapest, 28 January 1989, cited in Reisch, 'HSWP Study': 5.

of that organization continued, and increased to such an extent that its organizer, Anderle, became fearful and temporarily took an academic post in West Germany.[76] In contrast, towards the few dozen unknown figures comprising the reform circle county party, the new First Secretary, Vastagh, struck a more conciliatory tone, stating to the local media that unlike Grósz he did not view them as a party faction.[77] Bolstered by Vastagh's comments and Pozsgay's declaration, Géczi and Lovászi arranged for a second reform circle gathering in early February.

During this next meeting the participants drafted an open letter to the Central Committee, in which they criticized the body as incapable of carrying out reform and expressed their support for Pozsgay's actions. The party was on the verge of a split, they warned, and the danger of a conservative counterreformation had risen. The forthcoming Central Committee meeting should be fully open, take steps towards a multiparty system and schedule a party congress for that year instead of after parliamentary elections in 1990. While the Central Committee did not respond to the reform circle's letter, the media did, broadcasting their demands on national radio and in *Magyar Nemzet*, the newspaper of the Patriotic Peoples' Front (which remained sympathetic to its former boss, Pozsgay). This coverage by a central paper made the reform circle's activity a part of the national political landscape.[78]

Although the Central Committee meeting scheduled for 10–11 February was ostensibly to return to the question of political reform, many expected that its real outcome would be the expulsion of Pozsgay from the party. Despite strong support for his actions from the public and many among the party rank and file, similar backing had not been forthcoming from the Politburo or Central Committee, even from the more reformist Nyers. But Grósz was aware that Pozsgay had staked

76. Anderle personal interview.

77. 'Tájékoztató a megyei pártértekezlet óta eltelt időszak politikai eseményeiről [Information regarding political developments since the county party conference]', *Délmagyarország*, 24 January 1989: 2.

78. *Magyar Nemzet*, 9 February 1989: 3; details of the letter were broadcast on Radio Budapest, 8 and 9 February 1989; both cited in Alfred Reisch, 'HSWP CC Compromises on 1956 and Endorses Multiparty System', *RFER* (22 March 1989): 8, n. 7. For details surrounding the drafting of the letter see 'Romlottak a reform esélyei [The chances for reform have deteriorated]', *Csongrád Megyei Hírlap*, 9 February 1989: 3.

the party's legitimacy to his own fortunes. By expelling him, Pozsgay would be made a martyr, strengthening whatever political base he might subsequently join (or take with him), and the party would lose what little credibility remained. When the Central Committee meeting opened, numerous members condemned Pozsgay for his actions, some calling for his removal from office. Grósz, however, quickly moved to block this action, rallying nearly all members in favour of a statement of confidence in Pozsgay.[79] Pozsgay himself was surprised by the outcome. Grósz was too clever to let the event become a breaking point for the party or nation as a whole.[80]

The question of political pluralization still remained on the agenda, and had been made all the more pertinent by the crisis initiated by Pozsgay's actions. It was now obvious to the Central Committee that some action on this issue was necessary to reassert an image of the party as unified and proactive. Members conceded that some kind of democratization would be 'unavoidable', although many spoke of society not being ready for such a system, and that without the hegemony of the party reforms would lead to anarchy.

Nyers, showing himself to be still thinking of reform in the same terms as he had in the 1960s, perhaps best captured the mood of the Central Committee. Multiparty democracy is unavoidable, he conceded, although he had hoped he would not live to see it. However, steps in this direction must be taken now, he stressed, while the party was still the decisive political force in the country.[81] The example of Spain was cited by several, among them Prime Minister Németh, as a long-term controlled transition from above in which elections consolidated the post-Franco regime.[82] Grósz agreed that a multiparty system should be initiated only in a limited form and over the course of the next decade.[83]

Consequently, when details of the Central Committee meeting appeared in the newspapers the following Monday, they were notable

79. Transcripts of the MSZMP Central Committee meeting 10–11 February 1988, National Archives collection 288f 4/251 ő.e.; see also Pozsgay, *1989*: 108–9.
80. Pozsgay, *1989*: 109; see also Tőkés, *Hungary's Negotiated Revolution*: 298–303.
81. Ibid.: 161.
82. Transcripts of the 10–11 February 1989 Central Committee meeting: 145.
83. Ibid.: 39.

for the dramatic events that had not occurred. The year 1956 was now viewed as an uprising that had degenerated into counterrevolution. A minor chastising of Pozsgay was noted. A series of constitutional changes would form the basis for the introduction of a multiparty system and a powerful presidency; however, the population was not yet ready for the unfettered introduction of such institutions and rapid change could destabilize the nation. Most importantly, any political reform would be predicated on the *constitutional inviolability* of socialism, and a multiparty system would incorporate only those parties which accepted the constitution. Therefore, non-socialist parties would be unconstitutional. As Grósz responded in an interview shortly thereafter, 'if they do not accept the constitution, then they could not function legally. It's that simple'.[84] Moreover, this vague determination of eligibility would be made by the MSZMP-controlled courts.

Even under these limitations, actual open elections were not expected until 1995.[85] Consequently, as László Bruszt commented, uneasy party conservatives were able to reassure themselves that 'after all, even North Korea had a multiparty system'.[86] Opposition parties and organizations had little popular backing to oppose these steps, as compared to, for example, Poland. Public opinion surveys around this time showed that in open elections nearly 40 per cent polled would vote for the MSZMP, while only 11 per cent would vote for the MDF, 6 per cent for SZDSZ, or 2 per cent for FIDESZ.[87] Lacking the unifying force of simple oppression, civil society remained fragmented, disinterested in challenging the system as a whole. The discord unleashed by Pozsgay's declarations had for now been brought under control.

84. *Magyar Nemzet*, 13 February 1989; cited in Faragó, 'Mi történik Magyarországon?': 10, n. 5.
85. *Magyar Nemzet*, 24 February 1989; cited in ibid.: 12, n. 19.
86. Bruszt, '1989: The Negotiated Revolution in Hungary', in Bozóki, Körösényi and Schöpflin, *Post-Communist Transition*: 51. Unlike most other East European states Hungary had not had a pseudo-multiparty system of satellite parties, and therefore the announcement that parties would be tolerated did not necessarily mean a political breakthrough.
87. Bruszt and Simon, 'Politikai orientációk': 65, Table 25. The survey was taken in March 1989.

THE REFORM CIRCLES SPREAD

Although reformers at the centre of the party were making limited headway, at the grass-roots level the Csongrád reform circle was beginning to have an effect. With the exception of *Magyar Nemzet*, the national media continued to ignore the reform circle. However, here and there word of their existence had spread - often by word of mouth - and elsewhere in the country others began to follow their lead. In late February, a reform circle appeared in the southwestern town of Kaposvár, citing the example of Csongrád as their impetus. Elsewhere in the area several others followed shortly thereafter. A reform circle appeared in Budapest around the same time. A party draft proposal on platform freedom in mid-March helped push this groundswell forward, although the party still remained opposed to 'factionalism' and was unclear on what separated the two.[88]

By the middle of March, reform circles or cells had emerged in the counties of Somogy, Hajdú-Bihar, Bács-Kiskun, Zala and Békés. By the end of the month others had appeared in Fejér, Tolna, Szolnok and Györ-Sopron, representing over half of the total counties in Hungary. Reform circles were particularly strong in Csongrád, Zala, Somogy and Bács-Kiskun - all southern counties well known for lower levels of

88. 'A platformszabadságról: A pártion belüli politikai kezdeményezés szabadságának, a kritika, a nézet-, a vélemény- és a vitaszabadság érvényesítésének elvi és gyakorlati kérdéseiről [On platform freedom: theoretical and practical questions on the freedom of political initiative within the party, and the realization of the freedom of criticism, viewpoint, opinion, and debate]', *Népszabadság*, 17 March 1989: 6. On the confusion as to what constituted a platform versus a faction see Central Committee member Jenő Kovács, 'Kié a párt? [Whose party is this?]', interview by István Gábor Benedek, *Népszabadság*, 18 March 1989: 13.

The difference which the MSZMP argued existed between platforms and factions was that while platforms were temporary groupings of congress delegates based on specific issues, factions would be institutionalized, formally arranged subunits (such as one finds in Italy). The party's justification for permitting platforms rather than factions was based on the claim that while platform freedom within communist parties was supported by Lenin, he specifically opposed factions as an organizational threat. In reality, several loose groups did form during the early years of the Soviet communist party, which were encouraged to form *platforms* at the Tenth Party Congress in 1921. These platforms were then promptly attacked by Lenin as 'factionalist' and banned: see Leonard Schapiro, *The Communist Party of the Soviet Union* (New York: Random House, 1960): 198-212.

heavy industry, underdeveloped infrastructures and conservative, often corrupt, local leaders.[89]

Despite the lack of direct connections, the spreading reform circles mirrored one another to an amazing extent, indicating their relationship to a specific party cohort and set of solidarity groups. Although a few prominent individuals tended to direct and inspire each reform circle, none incorporated a formal leadership, explicitly eschewing any semblance of hierarchy or vertical organization. Nor did there tend to be any registered or delimited membership, allowing both party and non-party members to participate - sometimes including local members of the opposition camp. Participants themselves were usually 35–40 years old, university graduates (many with advanced degrees) who held minor positions in party cells or committees at the workplace - rather than full-time employees of the party apparatus - and who felt marginalized by the tactics of local party counter-selection. The reform circle was their new instrument for political influence.[90]

The reform circles thus represented the organizational expression of the post-war generation discussed in the previous chapter. Educated and socialized under the period of reform communism, this intellectual cohort formed a strong bond to the egalitarian and progressive values of the socialist ideology while developing a critical view of state socialism as found in Eastern Europe. For the rural segment of this cohort, in particular, this was later reinforced by the lack of opportunities and resources, combined with their isolation from local power structures. Few options were open to them politically. Either they could withdraw from political activity or take advantage of their position within and utilize an organizational format that was itself an expression of protest,

89. A thorough discussion of these issues as they relate to Bács-Kiskun and Zala counties can be found in Gergely, *A pártallam varázstalanítása*. On Kecskemét (county seat of Bács-Kiskun) see also Veronika Torkos, 'Mezővárosi fejlődés, polgarosodás Kecskeméten [Agricultural-urban development and *embourgeoisement* in Kecskemét]', in Veronika Torkos, Zoltán Kárpáti and András Vágvölgyi, *Középvárosok a mérlegen* [Intermediate cities in the balance] (Budapest, MTA Politikai Tudományok Intézete, 1992): 3–17. Incidentally, one source of the lower levels of industrialization in the south of Hungary stemmed from the lack of natural resources in the area such as iron or coal; see Bernat Tivadar, *An Economic Geography of Hungary* (Budapest: Akadémiai Kiadó, 1989).

90. György Kerényi, 'Reform kor-kör-kór-kép [a portrait of the reform time/circle/malady]', *Jelző* 1 (1989): 22–6.

consciously rejecting the rigid, vertical nature of the party with a loosely organized, leaderless and horizontal form.

Reflecting this common socialization, early reform circle declarations shared a set of similar themes. The nation is in crisis, for which the party is responsible. Stalinism, rather than socialism, has ruled Hungary in the post-war era, and despite the aspirations of 1956 a Stalinist organizational structure still dominates the nation. This system has brought the country to an economic and political dead end. Among the mass membership, those who seek reform are leaving the party in droves – particularly in the countryside, where reform has been delayed by local leaders – only increasing the power of conservatives and raising the threat of counterreform. The party must recapture the ideals of the *original* MSZMP, the communist successor party formed just prior to the Soviet intervention in 1956. Socialism can only be predicated on true democracy and not vice-versa. To that end, the institutional framework for a true multiparty democracy must be created, both within the nation and the party. This would include the formation of a horizontally-based MSZMP reform platform to press for the transformation of the party into one which could compete and function in a system of party pluralism. The reform circles, as public forums open to all, could serve as an instrument to this end.

Beyond these general points, various detailed proposals emerged. State and party leadership should be uncoupled as soon as possible, and direct negotiations begun with opposition forces to forge a national consensus on political and economic reform. Party cells in the workplace, seen as a Stalinist method of control, should be reorganized on a territorial basis, and greater power devolved to the local government level. The large party bureaucracy of full-time employees should be radically cut back and replaced with those whose livelihood is not dependent on the MSZMP. Party members must be given the power to freely elect and recall party officials on a yearly basis, with any member eligible for any position. All of this would need to be introduced through an extraordinary party congress in the autumn, rather than through Grósz's current suggestion for an expanded Central Committee meeting to enact reforms.[91]

91. This summary of issues is based on unpublished reform circle documents and published statements and interviews taken from national and county newspapers from February to mid-May 1989, approximately 75 in all. For good examples of

No matter how radical these objectives, the reform circles' impact was attenuated by their size and strength. Although their numbers were increasing, with new groups appearing in different cities almost weekly, they still represented a minority. Their connections to one another remained fragmentary. Press coverage was slowly on the increase, at both the local and national level (including the party daily *Népszabadság*), but their influence on politics remained minimal. Party first secretaries in the counties welcomed their appearance in the spirit of reform, tolerated some coverage in the local paper, and then promptly ignored them. These frustrations took place within the context of continuing fears among many that party hardliners, enraged by recent events, might resort to a *putsch*. In Csongrád county, members of the Workers' Guard suggested that the reform circle notable Keserű should be hanged; reform circle leaders in Zala county, fearful of a crackdown, kept their car fuel tanks full should they need to flee across the border.[92] Despite such obstacles, the reform circles were becoming more than a scattered set of dissenters. They were slowly becoming a political movement.[93]

these various documents in English, see the excerpts from the April declaration of the Budapest reform circle, *Népszabadság*, 17 May 1989: 7; translated in *JPRS Report: East Europe* (23 June 1989): 5–8; also excerpts from *Új fórum*, 4–5 May 1989, translated in *JPRS Report: East Europe* (26 June 1989): 14–18.

92. On events in Csongrád see Imre Takacs, 'Nem jogi, hanem politikai kérdés [Not a legal, but rather a political question]', *Népszabadság*, 29 March 1989: 5; Zala reform circle members, personal interview by the author, Nagykanizsa, 4 April 1993.

93. The development of the reform circles into a movement would at first glance seem to necessitate a discussion of their activity within the framework of analysis provided by those who study similar phenomena. Many of the ideas found in social movement theory are in fact incorporated into this study. However, I have resisted incorporating too much of this literature for two reasons. First, the question under scrutiny is not one of social movements (how or why they function) but why such a movement took place within the MSZMP, something I believe is better answered by institutional theory. Second, given that the reform circle movement occurred within and was a part of an existing organization, it raises questions as to the applicability of social movement theory in this case, since the reform circles existed as a manifestation of an existing party-state structure and not as an independent formation. Despite these reservations I have nevertheless attempted to follow the research agenda put forth by Mayer N. Zald and John D. McCarthy for analysing social movements: 'Epilogue: An Agenda for Research', in Mayer N. Zald and John D. McCarthy (eds), *The Dynamics of Social Movements* (Cambridge, MA: Winthrop, 1979): 238–46.

Given these developments, the question remains as to why the party chose to tolerate horizontal organization within the MSZMP itself. Grósz correctly realized from the beginning that such action threatened vertical party control and only played into the hands of the opposition, yet neither the Csongrád leaders nor other reform circle figures elsewhere were expelled from the party in an early effort to blunt the movement. In part this can be explained by the fact that the central leadership was not overly concerned with political turmoil in the countryside, concentrating instead on struggles both within and against the party at its organizational centre.

Another important reason lies within the institutional construct of the party itself, paralleling the party's inconsistent response to civil organization. Because the institutionalization of the party was based so heavily on a broad policy of co-optation as a means of legitimation, the option of actually purging party members representative of a particular social segment ran contrary to the most basic institutional tenets of the MSZMP. Kádárism as a means of institutionalization represented control through absorption, incorporating dissent in an effort to neutralize its effects. Consequently, although this policy eventually led to the formation of organized opposition within the party itself, the party continued to respond in the only way it knew how – by appropriating aspects of that dissent, and tolerating its existence in the hopes of denying it a clear target to rally against.

ABOVE AND BELOW: PARTY REFORMERS SEEK A COMMON PLATFORM

The reform circles' frenetic activity soon caught the attention of reformers higher up in the party. Since the February Central Committee meeting, those around Pozsgay remained frustrated as a result of his outflanking by Grósz. Instead of a political breakthrough, the party had followed its tried and true policy of tolerating and swallowing up dissent so as to control it better. Party officials and intellectuals around Pozsgay met again in secret to discuss coordinated actions which could help them regain the initiative. Their long-delayed 'reform conference' should be rescheduled for as soon as possible, although the idea of including participants from the opposition was shelved. Instead, the conference was now envisaged as a way to unite important party reformers, serving as the source of a new party platform or even the foundation of a separate socialist party – although Pozsgay still wavered on this idea, while other participants, notably Nyers, warned against such an action.[94] With its goals still uncertain, the *reform-műhely*, or reform workshop, was scheduled to take place in the southern town of Kecskemét on 15 April.[95]

Added to the list of invited participants were delegates from the reform circles.[96] Some around Pozsgay hoped that the reform circles would provide the basis for a regional network that could undergird support in the party for activists at the top. Such an alliance of reformers at the party centre and periphery could create a formidable challenge to hardliners in the MSZMP, and perhaps even form the initial structure for a new party, should Pozsgay choose to make that step. In fact, speculation was now rampant that the reform workshop would in fact serve as the event where Pozsgay would finally 'unfurl the flag' and declare the formation of a new democratic socialist party.[97]

Reform circle members had mixed feelings about such an idea. It was recognized that in order to save the party some kind of divorce

94. Rezső Nyers, personal interview by the author, Budapest, 27 May 1993. On 15 March 1989 this group published a special newspaper in which the participants provided articles on the aspects of radical political change (and thus serves as a useful list of those connected to the reform initiative at the party centre). A somewhat oblique reference to the meetings of this party reform group can be found on the back page of the paper: László Nagy Császár, 'Politikai tájkép [Political landscape]', *Március Tizenötödike*, 15 March 1989: 12.

    The anniversary of the revolution against Habsburg rule, 15 March, traditionally carried anti-Russian overtones, and was not an official holiday until 1989. A number of opposition groups attempted to use the event to mobilize mass support against the regime, with limited success. For an analysis of the 15 March holiday in 1989 see Tamás Hofer, 'Harc a rendszerváltásért szimbolikus mezőben; 1989 március 15-e Budapesten [Battle for the transition in the field of symbolism; Budapest, 15 March 1989]', *Politikatudományi Szemle*, no. 1 (1992): 29–51.

95. Pozsgay's early positions in the party during the 1960s were in the city of Kecskemét, and his connections were still strong in the local apparatus – hence the decision to hold the reform workshop there.

96. Tőkés mistakenly describes this event as primarily a reform circle meeting, when in fact the reform circles played a relatively minor role: *Hungary's Negotiated Revolution*: 322.

97. Zoltán Lökös, 'Ha pártszakadás … [If there is a party split …]', *Vasárnapi Hírek*, 16 April 1989: 3; Gombár Csaba, interview by Péter Kurucz, *Mai Nap*, 17 April 1989: 3.

between reformers and conservatives would be necessary. However, many feared that a unilateral split from the MSZMP could lead to unforeseen consequences for the reform process as a whole. This reluctance was reinforced by what some saw as a lack of open support by central party reformers for the reform circles. Yet now they were invited to the conference in Kecskemét, perhaps to be manipulated in the continuing power struggle at the top.[98] Uncertainty over the objectives of the forthcoming reform workshop was reinforced by several developments behind the scenes. In mid-March, Pozsgay took advantage of an official visit to the Italian Communist Party congress to consult with Soviet delegates in attendance, notably Alexander Yakovlev, about the state of party affairs. He came away discouraged, as the Soviets expressed their unreserved support for Grósz and his policies. Further consultations with Polish Prime Minister Mieczysław Rakowski drove home the view that a party split without the direct approval of the Soviets would be dangerous.[99] Meanwhile Grósz, fully cognizant of the possible outcome of reform workshop, responded with increasing calls for party unity, warning of the dangers that any split or independent organization might involve, and stepped up his attacks on the reform circles as well. The general secretary criticized their attempts to organize horizontally as anarchic, factionalist and dangerous to the party as a whole.[100]

98. József Géczi, László Kovács and József Lovászi, 'A Csongrád megyei párttagok reformkörének vitájáról [On the debate of the Csongrád county reform circle]', *Csongrád Megyei Hírlap*, 29 March 1989: 3; 'A Somogy megyei reformkör platformjából [From the platform of the Somogy county reform circle]', *Magyar Nemzet*, 11 April 1989: 4; Ida Bárdi and Tivadar Molnár (reform circle members from Hajdú-Bihar county) 'A válság katasztrófába torkollhat [The crisis can lead to catastrophe]', interview by József K. Horváth, *Népszava*, 15 April 1989: 4.

99. Pozsgay, *1989*: 116–22, 127; Pozsgay personal interview. In a later interview Nyers also argued that the uncertainty of international conditions at that time convinced him that a split at Kecskemét would be unwise; Rezső Nyers, 'A piaccsináló antikapitalista [The market-building anticapitalist]', interview by Katalin Bossányi, *Mozgó Világ* (September 1992): 12.

100. Károly Grósz, personal interview. Statements by Grósz to this effect can be found in 'Várható-e változás a párt vezet testületeiben? [Can we expect changes in the leading bodies of the party?]', *Népszabadság*, 7 April 1989: 7; László Szabó, 'Kisebb, de cselekvőképesebb csapat – Grósz Károly nyilatkozata a *Népszabadság*nak [A smaller team but more capable of action – Károly Grósz's statement to *Népszabadság*]', *Népszabadság*, 13 April 1989: 5, and his opening speech to a conference of county and city party first secretaries, reprinted in 'A párt egyértelműen

Grósz moved once again to outflank Pozsgay and his supporters. At a Central Committee meeting just three days before the reform workshop, Grósz and others confronted Pozsgay on his intent. Was the meeting a party function, a gathering of those interested in reform, or the basis for a party split? Backing away from his earlier intentions, Pozsgay responded that the meeting would not lead to a party split, or even a party platform. The reform workshop would be no more than its name suggested. The general secretary then concluded that if the meeting were in fact a party conference, it should be open to all – thereby suggesting to conservatives in the Central Committee and the Politburo that they attend and confuse the participants. Finally, Grósz took the dramatic step of initiating the resignation and re-election of the entire Politburo, including himself.

Dropped from the Politburo were four members, among them the unpopular Berecz, replaced by two new figures allied with Grósz, Budapest party First Secretary Mihály Jassó, as well as Csongrád First Secretary Vastagh (who prior to this had not even been a member of the Central Committee). Grósz was re-elected general secretary by an almost unanimous vote, thus reconfirming his power at the top. Contrary to analyses in the Western media, the Politburo 'shake-up' was no victory for reformers, but rather was intended to give the impression of increasing change towards reform in the party while consolidating the general secretary's own political base and serving as a show of strength.[101]

It was with high expectations and anxieties that the five hundred delegates gathered on 15 April for the reform workshop. Some came expecting the foundation of a new party. Others hoped for the creation of a formal platform that could unite reformists inside the party. Again using Hirschman's terms, the conflict came down to the locus of action: could reform be better achieved by 'exiting' the party? If so, would this be a betrayal of the MSZMP, and what would be the penalties of such a

reformelkötelezett [The party is unambiguously resolved towards reform]', *Népszabadság*, 15 April 1989: 5. See also 'A platform szabadság nem jelent frakciószabadságot [Platform freedom does not equal the freedom of factions]', *Népszabadság*, 14 April 1989: 1, 5.

101. Károly Grósz personal interview; see also Pozsgay, *1989*: 125; Kimmel, 97–100; 'Újjáalakult a Politikai Bizottság [The Politburo has been reorganized]', *Népszabadság*, 13 April 1989: 1, 5; Endre Bilecz, 'Kecskemét után – reformok előtt [After Kecskemét and before reforms]', *Kapu* (May 1989): 30–31.

step? Would the organization of some kind of internal reform voice be perhaps a wiser strategy instead? Whatever the outcome – and despite the attendance of Central Committee and Politburo conservatives – the meeting seemed certain to be a milestone in the party's history, perhaps for the nation as a whole.[102]

Yet like the actions taken before it, the reform workshop would be no watershed event. There would be no exit, and little voice. Unnerved by recent developments and still fearing retribution by Grósz, Pozsgay in his opening address was extremely restrained and cautious, stressing the need to hold the party together for the sake of reform – a call also echoed by Nyers.[103] Many delegates were taken aback. This was to be the event where the party reformers finally 'unfurled the flag', yet now they appeared to be sounding the retreat. There had been of late signs that Pozsgay was backing away from his earlier radicalism, but not to this extent. The meeting saw no split, no platform, no organization or manifesto – a workshop that did no work. The meeting had been constructed solely as a dramatic backdrop and lacked the dramatic event. Many delegates were angry and confused, accusing Pozsgay of betraying all they had worked for and placing political reform itself in danger.[104]

However, at another level the reform workshop was in fact a turning-point – notably for the reform circles, eighty of their delegates representing some thirty reform circles in all. Shunted to an auxiliary hall and connected to the conference by closed-circuit television, reform circle delegates enjoyed their first opportunity to meet one another, share ideas and take stock of their growing movement. Ignoring the insinuation of their subordinate status to central party reformers, they gave some of the most forceful and radical speeches of the day.[105] József Géczi implored the participants to organize into a

102. See the coverage in *Magyar Hírlap*, 17 April 1989; *Magyar Nemzet*, 17–18 April 1989; *Népszabadság*, 17 April 1989; and *Vasárnapi Hírek*, 16 April 1989.

103. A complete transcript of the speeches given were published in László Vass (ed.), *Reform-műhely* (Budapest: Kossuth, 1989).

104. These points are based on interviews with participants as well as the following articles: 'Reform-műhely: szakíts, ha bírsz [Reform workshop: Break, if you can bear it]', *Heti Világgazdaság*, 22 April 1989: 6; Bilecz, 'Kecskemét után': 30–31; Gábor László, 'Ket korszak határán [On the border of two eras]', *Hevesi Szemle* **XVII** (July 1989): 35–9; Lengyel, *Micsoda év!*: 21.

105. 'Reform-műhely: szakíts, ha bírsz': 6.

platform which would include the demands of the countryside. Imre Keserű spoke of the need for a national consensus, a pact which would form the basis for a political coalition. Budapest reform circle member Zoltán Szabó asserted that a parliamentary democracy and market economy were both inescapable. The reform circle delegates overall stressed that reformers below needed leaders above and vice-versa, although this call went unheeded.

Towards the end of the day it was clear to the reform circle participants that they could not expect reformers at the party centre to lead or incorporate them into a larger movement. The reformists at the party centre had become overly dependent on Pozsgay, and for reasons still unclear to his supporters he had backed away from his own challenge. Pozsgay himself met with the reform circle delegates, but commented that he would not presume to be their leader, although this was apparently not motivated by modesty. Pozsgay, who had already met with several individual reform circle members, worried that their movement might be more political opportunism than anything else.[106]

But the reform circles were not deterred. When the workshop came to a close it was only their group who had drafted a common declaration, the first joint document of the reform circle movement. The Central Committee and Politburo were not capable of carrying out reform, it stated; they had undermined trust in the party and its capacity to serve the people. This crisis requires changes in the leadership itself. The need for a party congress in the autumn was reiterated. The declaration also called upon others to found their own reform circles, to develop horizontal links and utilize the resources of the party to facilitate their objectives. To further this impetus and continue the battle for political change, the reform circles would organize their own conference for the following month in Szeged.[107]

The meeting in Kecskemét was to all intents and purposes the last chance for central MSZMP reformers to translate popular expectations into dramatic organizational action, either by splitting off from the party or by forming their own platform within it. But their lack of a clearly defined objective and a dependence on one hesitant leader instead brought them to disarray. Yet for the reform circles the

106. 'Reformműhely Kecskeméten [Reform workshop in Kecskemét]', *Petőfi Népe*, 17 April 1989: 3.

107. The declaration was printed in its entirety in *Magyar Nemzet*, 17 April 1989: 3.

outcome was the opposite. Now effectively connected to one another, they could engage in a dialogue on reform. Shorn of any illusions that those at the centre would lead their movement, they began to coordinate their own actions, to take up the battle on their own. The initiative within the party had now shifted to them.

4. The Organization of the Reform Circle Movement and the Party in Disorder

LOCAL AND NATIONAL STRUGGLES SPREAD WITHIN THE PARTY

Despite the ambiguous outcome of the reform workshop in Kecskemét, the call for radical change had now been clearly brought out in the open, drawing battle lines within the party over the future of reform. A resolution of this conflict seemed increasingly unavoidable as the contours of a reform wing within the party took shape. In particular, the strong showing of the reform circles raised their prominence from a collection of rural troublemakers to that of a national movement. Of course, this only troubled conservatives at the centre all the more. In response to their declaration at Kecskemét, Grósz again attacked the reform circles' horizontalist character, arguing that it did not correspond to platform freedom and was more dangerous to the MSZMP than a party split itself.[1] At least on the last point, Grósz would prove to be correct.

These developments within the party were slowly threatening the MSZMP's centralized political power - particularly that of the general

1. Károly Grósz interview, 'Törekvéseink külföldi fogadtatásáról, a pártról - válasz a reformkörök bírálata [On the foreign reception of our endeavours and the party - response to the criticism of the reform circles]', interview by István Zalai, *Népszabadság*, 18 April 1989: 3; Éva Terényi, 'Az MSZMP a reformok pártja - a párt főtitkárának előadása a veszprémi aktívaülésen [The MSZMP is the party of reorm - the address by the general secretary at the session of party activists in Veszprém]', *Népszabadság*, 27 April 1989: 4; see also the comments by Central Committee member István Petrovszki, 'A munkahely ne legyen politikai csatározás színtere [The workplace should not become a battlefield]', *Népszabadság*, 20 April 1989: 5.

secretary, despite his recent successes in blunting the offensives of reformers. This was further undermined by developments in Poland, where in mid-April the communist party agreed to legalize Solidarity and permit limited elections, with the blessing of the Soviet Union. But rather than yield to the momentum, Grósz took the opposite tack, attempting to further centralize his own personal power. Already Pozsgay and others believed that Grósz was developing his own links to the army and police should he need them in case of a power struggle.[2]

Such fears were reinforced during the next Politburo meeting on 19 April, when the general secretary introduced the motion that a 'state of economic emergency' be declared to deal with the current national crisis. Members of the Politburo, suspecting that this was in fact an attempt by Grósz to accrue greater political power (and perhaps even pave the way for a coup within the party) rejected the proposal. Undeterred, three days later Grósz, in an address to the party's communist youth league, publicly raised the issue, arguing that a state of emergency would be unavoidable and that although the Politburo did not back him in this regard he enjoyed the support of the prime minister. That evening, Prime Minister Németh himself contacted the national media and flatly denied that he supported Grósz's initiative. That Németh, heretofore seen by many as a puppet of the general secretary, would go against the latter's wishes was a great surprise to many (including, no doubt, Grósz). The technocratic-staffed state apparatus, caught up in the power struggle within the party and anticipating an increasing role for an autonomous state structure in a future liberalized Hungary, was taking steps to assert its own organizational power independent of the MSZMP.[3] Outnumbered, Grósz backed down, claiming

2. Imre Pozsgay, 'Itt semmi, valóban semmi nem változik [Here nothing, truly nothing ever changes]', interview by Katalin Kékesi, *Kritika* (November 1991): 20; see also Tőkés, *Hungary's Negotiated Revolution*: 296–8.
3. For details on this event see Attila Mélykuti, 'Még ma sem tudjuk, kinek van igaza ... [We still don't know who is telling the truth ...]', *Magyar Nemzet*, 25 April 1989: 1; Pozsgay, *1989*: 127–8; also idem, 'Itt semmi, valóban semmi nem változik': 20. For more on the prime minister's growing independence, see Károly Németh, 'Nem tekintem átmenetinek, sem a kormányt, sem magamat [I do not regard either myself or the government as transitional]', interview by Ákos Mester, *168 óra*, 16 May 1989: 4–5; also Lengyel, *Micsoda év!*: 78, n. 6.

instead that he had been misquoted and never actually intended any such action.[4] The general secretary was losing the upper hand.

As for the reform circles, with the call for a national conference in May the movement swelled, attracting more and more members to its ranks and propelling the 'internal pluralization' of the party forward.[5] Press coverage in national newspapers (particularly the party paper *Népszabadság*) jumped dramatically, furthering the reform circles' recognition and fostering their development.[6] By early May one list of major reform circles contained more than 75 such groups, not including a number of circles in smaller towns and institutions. Reform circles could now be found not only at the city and county level, but also within a number of universities and large factories, most districts of Budapest, and inside the state itself, including the Central Statistical Office, the Foreign Ministry, the Ministry of Culture, as well as the Patriotic Peoples' Front.[7]

The reform circles' effectiveness was to a large extent facilitated by their unique position as an internal revolt within a larger institution. Unlike other external civic movements, the reform circles were able to draw their resources from within the system, for example utilizing party buildings, presses, photocopy machines, typists, fax and phone lines. Any opposition to their actions by local party figures was typically countered with the argument that the reform circles had the right to access party resources as the 'real' representatives of the party as a whole, and that their activity, as party activity, gave them the right to use the resources of the MSZMP. Given the increasing momentum of the movement, many cadres chose to accede to these demands, rather than openly confront the shibboleth of 'reform'.

At the rank-and-file level of the party, support for the reform circles

4. Károly Grósz, 'Egy korszak visszafordíthatatlanul véget ért [An era has irreversibly come to an end]', interview by Andrea Balogh, *Észak-Magyarország*, 27 May 1989: 3.
5. András Bozóki, 'Hungary's Road to Systemic Change: The Opposition Roundtable', *East European Politics and Society* 7 (Spring 1993): 287.
6. See, for example, the roundtable interview with reform circle members in 'Reformkor - reformkör [Reform era - reform circle]', *Népszabadság*, 22 April 1989: 4; and 'MSZMP-reformkörök tanácskozásai [The meetings of MSZMP reform circles]', *Népszabadság*, 24 April 1989: 5.
7. 'Az MSZMP reformköreinek "gyorslista" [The MSZMP reform circles' short list]', *Ötlet*, 11 May 1989: 8.

also continued to grow, aided by the reform circles' emphasis on the public and open forum nature of their movement. The largest reform circle in Budapest even publicly invited Grósz to their meetings, although the general secretary politely declined.[8] In addition, many reform circles developed expanding ties with local opposition figures. As we have noted, these actions were above all a conscious anti-organizational policy, in direct contradiction to the traditionally secretive, hierarchical and undemocratic nature of the party.[9]

REFORM CIRCLES ON THE OFFENSIVE

From late April onwards work began on organizing the first reform circle conference in Szeged. Already by early May more than 400 delegates were expected to attend, including Nyers and Pozsgay as key speakers. Information and invitations were in fact sent to all members of the Politburo, although most did not respond. The prime minister - whose political ambitions now appeared more directed towards strengthening the state apparatus rather than saving the party - also declined to attend, claiming other obligations, although he expressed his support for the movement and its goals.[10]

Plans were for delegates to be divided into five working groups, which would deal with the issues of the party's role in the past, the future of the party, reform of the economy and property relations,

8. 'Táviratváltás az MSZMP budapesti reformköre és Grósz Károly főtitkár között [Exchange of telegraphs between the Budapest reform circle and General Secretary Károly Grósz]', *Magyar Hírlap*, 21 April 1989: 6.
9. Not all participants could be so open, however; one example was Lieutenant László Rekvényi, a Budapest police officer who was responsible for founding the first independent police union in Hungary in 1989, of which he was elected first secretary. Rekvényi had fought an uphill battle in this regard, with his attempts first blocked in September 1988 and his interview on the matter for the Ministry of Interior journal *Belügyi Szemle* suppressed. Given the traditionally hardline nature of the police, Rekvényi's own participation in the activities of the reform circles was secretive. For details on developments within the police and Ministry of the Interior during the transition, see Károly Lencsés, 'A belügy belügyei [The internal affairs of internal affairs]', in Kurtán, Sándor and Vass, *Magyarország Politikai Évkönyve 1990*: 237–45.
10. Letter from Prime Minister Miklós Németh to József Lovászi, Csongrád reform circle delegate [photocopy] dated 18 May 1989.

social reform and the transition to a democratic state of law. From the work of these sections it was hoped that a formal party platform could be hammered out by a smaller committee, despite the still-uncertain status of such structures in the party.[11] Already documents were flooding in from various reform circles as contributions to a single platform manifesto for radical change.[12]

While this growing prominence helped garner rank-and-file support for the reform circles, it also contributed to the reform circles' unpopularity among many conservatives within the central party apparatus. One illustration was provided during a forum organized in Budapest for May Day celebrations, which counted among the invited guests the general secretary as well as Budapest reform circle representatives. The reform circle representatives caused an uproar when they argued that they should be allowed to take a seat on the stage alongside Grósz, as equals. Grósz and Budapest party First Secretary Mihály Jassó both blasted the reform circles as impetuous and factionalist, to loud applause, but the circle delegates held their ground and defended their activities.[13] Other circles were drawing upon their increasing prominence to better influence local party structure, personnel and activities. In Tolna, prior to the county party conference, local reform circles demanded a turnover in the party leadership and the apportionment of delegates on the basis of platforms; one of the circle's founders, known for his open attacks on Grósz and the one-party system as a whole, was elected by the conference to a secretarial post in the county party

11. Letter from László Brúszel, Gyula Gráner and György Kerényi, Kecskemét reform circle, to Csongrád reform circle [photocopy] dated 27 April 1989; letter from Mihály Révész, József Lovászi, József Géczi and Béla Szabó, Csongrád reform circle, to Politburo [photocopy] dated 21 April 1989; József Lovászi, 'Feljegyzés a reformkörök országos tanácskozásának előkészítéséről [Notes on the preparations for the reform circles' national conference]', unpublished document, dated 5 May 1989.
12. These were published under the auspices of the Csongrád newspaper, *Délmagyarország*, as a special periodical entitled *Platform*, 20 May 1989.
13. The event is covered, although lacking most details, in 'Új szellemben ünnepelte május elsejét az ország [The nation celebrates 1 May in a new spirit]', *Népszabadság*, 2 May 1989: 4, and 'Grósz Károly és Jassó Mihály válaszai [Károly Grósz and Mihály Jassó's answers]', *Népszabadság*, 6 May 1989: 7, and 8 May 1989: 7; much better coverage can be found in 'Pártvezetők kérdésekre válaszoltak [Party leaders respond to questions]', *Szolnok Megyei Hírlap*, 2 May 1989: 2.

committee.[14] Similarly, at the county conference in Somogy the local reform circle called for the party cells to be withdrawn from the workplace and for the local party leadership to resign. Their proposals were rejected, although a compromise figure was elected as the new county first secretary.[15] Reform circles in Györ, Szolnok, Komárom and Békés counties, as well as cities such as Sopron and Nagykanizsa also tried to push through changes in party structure and leadership, with mixed results. However, a number of conferences did vote in favour of the reform circles' demand for an early national party congress.[16] Despite these skirmishes, the core objectives of the circles remained national in scope. Successes at the city or county level could only achieve so much; a real political transformation would have to be enacted at the top, or rather foisted upon it. This, the reform circles knew, could be achieved only by undermining the old structure, neutralizing opposition and mobilizing the party ranks to their cause.

CENTRAL COMMITTEE ATTEMPTS AT PACIFICATION

Some successes at the national level seemed to be forthcoming. At the Central Committee meeting on 8 May, the party confronted the increasing pressure, spearheaded by the reform circles, for the convocation of an early party congress, as well as the topic of the reform circles themselves. This took place within the context of discussion over the contentious issue of platform freedom within the party. As background information, István Petrovszki, the director of the Central Committee

14. 'A paksi reformkör javaslatai a megyei pártértekezlet anyagához [The Paks reform circle proposals to the text of the county party conference]', *Tolna Megyei Népújság*, 29 April 1989: 3; 'Reformpárti jelöltek: radikális és higgadtabb végrehajtással [Reform party candidates, with radical and more moderate enactments]', *Tolna Megyei Népújság*, 27 April 1989: 4–5; 'A reformgondolatok áttörése jellemezte az MSZMP megyei értekezletet [The breakthrough of reform ideas characterizes the MSZMP county conference]', *Tolna Megyei Népújság*, 2 May 1989: 1–4.
15. 'A reformerek bukása Somogyban? [The failure of reformers in Somogy?]', *168 óra*, 25 Ápril 1989: 7.
16. 'Kongresszus összehívást sürgették [The convening of a congress has been urged]', *Népszabadság*, 2 May 1989: 1.

Office on Party and Mass Organizations, submitted a report to the Central Committee on the reform circles, which had previously been forwarded to the Politburo.

Petrovszki's summary outlined the reform circles' origins within the young party intelligentsia and their perspective on political change, overall painting a favourable picture of the movement, although Petrovszki looked on their increasingly national demands (such as the Kecskemét declaration), as well as the 'extremist' and 'intolerant' views of some of its members, with apprehension.[17] Most interesting was the lack of response from the Central Committee with regard to the document, which generated no debate and few comments – indicating that as of yet they were unable to comprehend fully or respond meaningfully to this movement among their own ranks.[18]

The Central Committee next turned to the matter of the party congress. Grósz had up to now adamantly opposed any significant party assembly, fearing that a delegate revolt similar to that which swept the general secretary into power in 1988 would now be used against him. Grósz conceded that before the parliamentary elections in 1990 a national meeting of the party would be necessary (rather than merely an expanded Central Committee meeting as proposed earlier) in order to reconcile the increasingly factional tendencies that were destabilizing the MSZMP. However, he proposed that a party conference (rather than an early congress) should be convened in the autumn. Although seemingly an issue of semantics, the reform circles had been specifically pushing for an early congress, which would necessitate new regional party conferences for the election of delegates and also provide another opportunity to oust conservative local leaders and shake up county party structures. Moreover, any outcome of a party national meeting would carry the greatest authority if enacted by a congress, which was technically the highest body of the party.

17. István Petrovszki, 'Tájékoztató a Politikai Bizottságnak a reformkörök működésének kezdett tapasztalatairól [Information to the Politburo on the initial experiences of the functioning of the reform circles]', document from the MSZMP Politburo meeting 2 May 1989, National Archives collection 288f. 5/1063 ő.é.: 153–61. The document was released (in one copy, marked 'Secret') to the Central Committee on 8 May: see transcripts from the MSZMP Central Committee meeting, 8 May 1989, National Archive collection 288f. 4/261 ő.é.: 44–56.
18. Transcripts of the MSZMP Central Committee meeting, 8 May 1989.

By contrast, only two party conferences had ever been held by the MSZMP, and this ad hoc assembly lacked a clear set of electoral rules or jurisdiction (which were left to the discretion of the Central Committee). Grósz and other conservatives thus wisely continued to oppose the idea of an extraordinary congress, precisely for fear that the reformist wing of the party would use the event to transform radically the MSZMP itself.[19]

In the end the Central Committee approved the proposal for a party conference, with the method of delegate selection to be determined at a later date.[20] In a subsequent press conference spokesmen for the Central Committee admitted that their decision to hold a conference was a necessary response to party pressure from below. However, with regard to the issue of platform freedom, the Central Committee backed away from their earlier inclinations, reiterating the Grósz view that the formal organization of platforms would destroy party unity and pointing to the reform circles as an example of this.[21]

Other decisions made by the Central Committee indicated the party's desire to reassert its image of reform: the infamous Workers'

19. Grósz personal interview; see also transcripts of the Central Committee meeting 8 May 1989.
20. Some of the proposals included the bypassing of the normal method of delegate selection via city and county conferences, which had produced many 'permanent' delegates, as well as the direct election of the general secretary by the entire party membership: see Jenő Kovács, 'Javaslat a Központi Bizottságnak az országos pártértekezlet előkészítésével és megrendezésével összefüggő főbb feladatokra [Proposal to the Central Committee on the interdependent main tasks for the preparation and organization of the national party conference]', document from the MSZMP Politburo meeting, 16 May 1989, National Archive collection 288f. 5/1065 ő.é.: 28–33; also 'Javaslat a Központi Bizottságnak az MSZMP elnöke, főtitkára választásának, valamint az MSZMP köztársasági elnök-jelöltje állításának pártszavazás útján történő lebonyolítására [Proposal to the Central Committee on the election of the MSZMP president and general secretary, as well as the standing of a MSZMP candidate for president of the republic through party elections]', ibid.: 38–43.
21. 'Közlemény a Magyar Szocialista Munkáspárt Központi Bizottságának 1989 május 8-ai üléséről [Report on the 8 May 1989 session of the Central Committee]', *Népszabadság*, 10 May 1989: 3; see also 'Ősszel országos pártertekezletet tart az MSZMP [The MSZMP will hold a national conference in the autumn]', *Népszabadság*, 9 May 1989: 1, 5; and Alfred Reisch, 'HSWP To Hold Another National Conference To Set Election Program and Strategy', *RFER* (30 May 1989): 9–14.

Guard was to be placed under state authority, the scope of the *nomenklatura* lists was to be reduced, and the guidelines for a new law on political parties were to be approved. Finally, the party, which had in April unsuccessfully attempted to hold talks with the opposition (the most prominent of which had by now coalesced into the Opposition Roundtable *(Ellenzéki Kerekasztal*, or EKA), called for a new round of discussions, although shortly thereafter these reached a stalemate over the organization, scope and authority of the talks.[22] Grósz himself continued to insist that open elections would only occur in 1994 or 1995, and that the party did not foresee giving up its monopoly on power until that time, and then only to another socialist party.[23]

The 8 May Central Committee meeting was a clear sign that although the party still retained considerable power, the growing organization and pluralization of civil society combined with the internal pressure of the reform circles was undermining party authority. The party possessed the resources to resist and envelop external pressure; it had the means to silence internal critics; but it was hard pressed to do both. Furthermore, having staked the institution on the ideology of reform, the usurping of this key party instrument by an opposition from within was devastating. This two-front battle was steadily closing off the MSZMP's policy options, forcing them into defensive positions which conceded important political ground.

OBSTACLES TO ORGANIZATIONAL POWER

Yet as the reform circles prepared for the Szeged conference, their own growing strength was beginning to underscore the limits of their movement. Until now, the reform circles had drawn upon their unique

22. An excellent history and analysis of the EKA and its negotiations with the government can be found in András Bozóki, 'Hungary's Road to Systemic Change'; see also Anna Richter, *Ellenzéki Kerekasztal* (Budapest: Ötlet, 1990), and Tőkés, *Hungary's Negotiated Revolution*, Chap. 7. Not surprisingly, although the hardline party organization known as the Ferenc Münnich Society was brought into these negotiations by the MSZMP as part of a 'third side' supposedly between party and opposition, the reform circles were not invited to participate.
23. Henry Kamm, 'In Hungary, the Political Changes are Tempered by Economic Fears', *New York Times*, 15 May 1989: A1, A6; excerpts of the article were reprinted in *Magyar Hírlap*, 16 May 1989; also Grósz personal interview.

location inside the institution both to manipulate and to attack the internal structure of the party, manifesting a loose unorganized structure which made it hard to take action against them. Reform circle members in fact liked to refer to themselves as a 'reform virus', attacking the host from within. However, when the movement grew large enough that it sought to take coordinated action as an autonomous organization, this amorphous structure proved to have serious disadvantages, good at attacking the host but unable to create its own internal structure.

The difficulties sprang from a number of levels, but their most fundamental they divided into questions of authority and ideology, central pillars for any organizational development. One early source of contention among and within the reform circles was the question of how far reform could or should go, and what the movement's objectives should be in response. While the reform circles shared a number of common views on political and economic reform, the limits to change remained uncertain, with views differing from person to person. This was the dilemma of *modellváltás* versus *rendszerváltás* – the change of the model versus the change of the system, reform versus transformation.

How far should the reform circles push, and how to change the current order while still preserving the socialist movement? As an internal opposition movement, the reform circles drew their legitimacy from a critique of the existing order rather than as an independent civil organization with a policy alternative. Consequently, one clear weakness of the reform circles was that most knew better what they wished to get rid of than what they wanted to replace it with. Animosity was already beginning to develop over the activities of the largest Budapest reform circle, which had been responsible for some of the most strident attacks on the party so far and some of the most radical proposals for political change.[24] Some in the movement began to believe that the leaders of 'Budapest Reform Circle Number One', as it had dubbed itself (much to the irritation of others, who saw this as a hierarchical ranking), were in fact more interested in destroying socialism than saving it, expressing

24. The Budapest reform circle was, for example, involved in the row with Grósz at the party forum on 1 May. They also sharply criticized the General Secretary's statements in his interview with the *New York Times*; their criticisms were in turn disparaged by the party as 'malevolent' and 'tasteless': see the exchange of vituperation in *Magyar Hírlap*, 19 May 1989: 11.

reckless and impudent views closer to the radical opposition than to the rest of the movement.[25]

This contributed to a second problem within the movement, one centred upon the anti-hierarchical and anti-organizational aspects of the movement. With the development of the conflict over the activities of the Budapest reform circle, the traditional cleavage of rural versus urban began to assert itself among the reform circles as well. Having grown prominent within the movement during the spring, the Budapest reform circle leaders were characterized by other circle members as uncreditworthy and haughty, and accused of trying to form a de facto movement leadership out of their own circle. Moreover, in keeping with the traditional rural–urban split, this criticism carried anti-Semitic undertones. Several within the Budapest Reform Circle Number One were Jewish, and this fact was not lost on other reform circle members.

Similarly, attempts to unify reform circle activity with the work of the central party intelligentsia also bore little fruit. A number of reform circle activists bore a lingering antagonism towards these figures – notably those in Pozsgay's camp, reinforced by the reform circles' snubbing at Kecskemét. While many still hoped that Pozsgay would declare a formal party faction or separate party which they could join, others were less reverent of the reformist leader and suspicious of his personal motives. Such misgivings created a hesitancy to cooperate with these potential allies, fearing that they would somehow usurp or manipulate their rural movement.

On 9 May, a group of reform circle delegates met a number of reform intellectuals close to Pozsgay, as well as his deputy minister, László Vass, to discuss the forthcoming Szeged conference and the possibility for the creation of a formal reformist platform.[26] There still remained hopes that Pozsgay, perhaps with the help of the ever-growing reform circles, could form an organized political movement within the MSZMP. The meeting ended inconclusively. The reform circle representatives were pressed by those supportive of Pozsgay to invite opposition representatives from the EKA to the Szeged conference, but they resisted this idea, preferring that the meeting

25. See Győző Lugosi, 'Taktika és etika? [Tactics and ethics?]', *Új fórum*, 30 June 1989: 13.
26. For details, see Attila Szűcs, 'A közös platform felé [Towards a common platform]', *Ötlet*, 18 May 1989: 6.

remain by and for party reformists. Reform intellectuals at the meeting clearly sensed a latent hostility towards them from some of the reform circle delegates present, which convinced many of them to put an end to further cooperation.

A final source of continuing contention remained the reform circles' relationship to the party and the possibility of transforming the movement into an independent organization. Some members argued that the movement should seize the opportunity of the Szeged meeting to leave the party. But where to go? Although the reform circles could now count a 'membership' in the thousands, how many would go along with such an action? What kind of national support could a party of former communist intellectuals attract?

One possibility would have been to merge with the Hungarian Social Democratic Party (*Magyarországi Szociáldemokrata Párt*, or MSZDP), historically a powerful force in Hungarian politics that had re-emerged by early 1989, to initially strong popular support. Early on the MSZDP had the highest levels of potential voters after the MSZMP itself.[27] But by spring the MSZDP began to disintegrate as fault lines appeared between pre-war social democrats and reformist ex-communists, older original members and new younger supporters. Internal battles, turnovers in leadership and expulsions rocked the party and decimated both its ranks and its popular support, effectively eliminating the MSZDP as a political player and a potential ally of the reform circles.[28] Members of other opposition parties also urged the reform circles to stay within the MSZMP, to help advance the cause of political transformation from within by neutralizing party conservatives. Shortly before the Szeged reform circle conference the EKA publicly hailed the meeting, urging them to help push the party leadership towards real negotiations with the opposition.[29]

27. Bruszt and Simon, 'Politikai orientációk Magyarországon': 65, Table 25.
28. For details, see László Lengyel, 'The Character of Political Parties in Hungary', in Bozóki, Körösényi and Schöpflin, *Post-Communist Transition*: 41–4; Jeremy King, 'Social-Democratic Party Hurt by Internal Squabbles', *RFER* (14 July 1989): 37–9.
29. 'Nyílt levél az MSZMP reformkörei országos tanácskozásának [Open letter to the MSZMP reform circle national conference]', *Magyar Hírlap*, 20 May 1989: 3; see also Bruszt, '1989: The Negotiated Revolution in Hungary': 54.

THE FIRST NATIONAL REFORM CIRCLE CONFERENCE

On 20 May 1989 the first reform circle conference convened in Szeged, with some 440 participants from 110 reform circles, as well as Politburo members Nyers, Pozsgay, Vastagh and several reformers from within the Central Committee.[30] Unlike Kecskemét, however, few of the Budapest party intelligentsia allied with Pozsgay were in attendance. Discouraged by Pozsgay's inconsistent behaviour and their cold reception by reform circle delegates, this group was now backing away from the political arena. However, a new stratum of party *apparatchiki* appeared in their place, testimony to the growing prominence of the movement and the weakening of central authority. These cadres increasingly saw the reform circles as potential winners in the continuing internal MSZMP conflicts, and wanted to ensure that they would end up on the winning side.[31]

The conference opened with short opening speeches by the organizers, who stressed that the burden was now upon them to move the party clearly towards reform, down the 'road to Damascus' that would produce the kind of radical conversion as experienced by the apostle Paul. Reformist officials within the party could act as their allies but should not be seen as their leaders. The reform circles would have to fight the battle for themselves, and force an early party congress upon the party. József Géczi, pointing to the lessons of Hungarian history (that is, 1956) stressed that the reform circles should fight for a national

30. For details on the conference, see István Tanács and Éva Terényi, 'Békés átmenettel a demokratikus szocializmusba [Towards democratic socialism with a peaceful transition]', *Népszabadság*, 22 May 1989: 1, 4–5; Attila Mélykuti, 'Reformkörök országos tanácskozása Szegeden [Reform circles' national conference in Szeged]', *Magyar Nemzet*, 22 May 1989: 3; András György Lengyel, 'Pártkongresszus összehívását sürgették az MSZMP reformkörök szegedi tanácskozásán [A party congress has been urged at the Szeged reform circle conference]', *Magyar Hírlap*, 22 May 1989: 1, 3; László Gábor, 'Mi is az a reformköri mozgalom? [What is the reform circle movement?]', *Hevesi Szemle* **XVII**, no. 4 (August 1989): 51–7; Judith Pataki, 'First National Conference of HSWP Reform Circles', *RFER* (30 May 1989): 25–9.

31. It is also possible, as many interview subjects suspected, that some of these individuals in fact came to the reform conference with the sole intention of sabotaging the outcome.

elszámolás (a reckoning of past events), instead of a *leszámolás* (a settling of scores or revenge).[32] György Kerényi called upon delegates to remain committed to their original objectives, not to leave the party, but rather to occupy it:

> Why have the reform circles come into existence? One of the roots, causes and consequences of the social change of model [*modellváltás*] is the Stalinist party structure. We are seeking liberation from its captivity. Not a more comfortable jail cell, not better guards, but rather a free and genuine movement organized according to one's own norms and ethics. The reform circles have consequently come forth above all as an unambiguous criticism of the party's performance up to the present. The party is collapsing. Who is falling away, who is disappointed? The most valuable [members], in ever greater proportions, from every level. ... Party reform has been arrested and in this present structure we cannot go any further. The paralysis of the structure has most strongly and spectacularly felt in the countryside, where post-Stalinist and feudalistic relations are intertwined. ...
>
> What do the reform circles want and not want? They wish to transform the MSZMP into a democratic reform party that serves the people. To clarify the nature of the reform programme and its contents, as well as to recognize dissent within the party. ... We seek the fundamental and radical transformation of the party, through calm measures, taking into account domestic and international reality.[33]

Armed with proposed platform contributions from various reform circles, delegates broke into their five sections. Debate, sometimes stormy, went on for most of the day. Participants in the section dealing with 'our past in the present' struggled with the legacies of Marxism (how relevant was this work to the present?), Leninism (described by one as a temporary condition of wartime Russia that was never rescinded), and Kádárism. The party, a number of individuals argued, was in dire need of 'de-Bolshevization' - in effect a call for the de-institutionalization of the Soviet-type party order. Seeking alternatives, others raised the examples of the immediate post-war period in

32. Transcripts of the reform circle national conference [unpublished, incomplete], Szeged, 20 May 1989, opening plenary section: 1–22; see also Tanács and Terényi, 'Békés átmenettel': 4; Mélykuti, 'Reformkörök országos tanácskozása': 3; Lengyel, 'Pártkongresszus összehívását sürgették': 1, 3.
33. Speech by György Kerényi, transcripts of the reform circle national conference opening plenary section: 4–10; see also excerpts from Kerényi's speech in 'Mit és kinek? [What and for whom?]', *Magyar ifjúság*, 26 May 1989: 11; many of these points were recapitulated in Géczi and Kerényi, 'A tétlenség anarchiája': 18–19.

Hungary, when a coalition government and free elections were permitted by the Soviets. Others pointed to the development of workers' councils and spontaneous self-government during the uprising of 1956 – an event which some delegates now argued should be openly declared a true revolution.

In the section concerning the future outlines of the party, discussion centred on the need for the party to surrender its information monopoly and property assets, for the right of recall and minority opinions, and for congresses that would be held on a yearly basis. Recognizing their almost exclusive intelligentsia base, delegates acknowledged the need to broaden the reform circles' support to include the working class. Section three addressed economic and property reform, reaching consensus that radical transformation of this sector was imperative, which would include privatization, joint-stock companies and capital markets, as well as a social safety net to compensate for the unemployment that would follow.

Delegates in the section on society and reform considered the idea of a social compact to facilitate political transition; in the last section, dealing with the transition to a democratic state of law, participants rejected Grósz's unwillingness to accept fully open elections. Some envisaged an electoral pact that would prevent any one party from suffering a serious defeat, so as to keep all political forces on board and pave the way for a broad coalition government (although others contended that the MSZMP should not be guaranteed a role in the next government). During these sessions the idea of a party split was again raised by some, but this remained a minority view. Most supported the idea instead that an extraordinary party congress could serve this function, facilitating a peaceful and mutually-agreed divorce of conservatives and reformers into two parties. For now, such a unilateral act would be political suicide.[34]

That evening the delegates met to debate the work accomplished during the afternoon. Section leaders gave an account of their group's work and proposed contributions to the platform, and Vastagh and Pozsgay followed with short speeches of support. Delegates, however,

34. This summary is based upon the transcripts of the reform circle national conference; for short summaries of each section debate, see in particular Tanacs and Terényi, 'Békés átmenettel': 4, and Gábor, 'Mi is az a reformköri mozgalom?': 54–6.

did not know that Pozsgay intended to use the occasion to declare the formation of a new independent political organization, the Movement for a Democratic Hungary. Yet, as in Kecskemét, Pozsgay remained wary of the reform circles, and unsure whether his future lay with a reformed MSZMP, some fraction of it, or in a completely new mass movement. The declaration remained in his pocket, unread.[35]

The evening plenary session did not go smoothly for the reform circle delegates, reflecting the overly democratic and unorganized aspect of the movement. For four hours participants argued over the various proposed platform contributions. A number of participants began to question the very idea that the conference formally accept a platform at that time, arguing instead that the reform circles wait for September (when a second conference was already scheduled) to compose such a document. Delegates, hostile to expressions of vertical authority through their long experience within the party, were hesitant to assume the power to accept a manifesto on behalf of others. Irritated with this indecision, Zoltán Szabó, a delegate from Budapest Reform Circle Number One, accused some of the delegates of intentionally sabotaging the chances for a platform and the formal organization of an MSZMP reform wing. This provoked an angry response that drowned out his speech and intensified the rural–urban split within the movement.[36]

The Szeged meeting showed the constraints of the reform circle movement. The reform circles' effectiveness was in part based upon their lack of structure, making them dangerous to a party structure whose rigid vertical institutionalization made it ill-prepared for such a threat – particularly one among its ranks. But such an amalgamation could not easily coordinate its activities or take unified action, or easily contemplate the idea of formally organizing itself. In fact, the main solution to this problem, to create a reform circle leadership, had been early on rejected by the Szeged conference organizers as contrary to the spirit of the movement.[37]

35. László Vass (former deputy state minister under Pozsgay), personal interview by the author, Budapest, 19 November 1992.
36. Lugosi, 'Etika és taktika': 13; Mélykuti, 'Reformkörök országos tanácskozás Szegeden': 3.
37. József Lovászi, 'Feljegyzés a reformkörök országos tanácskozásával összefüggő néhány kérdésről [Notes on a few questions relating to the reform circles' national conference]', unpublished document, dated 25 May 1989.

A compromise was eventually reached. The delegates would not adopt a platform, but would instead edit and release a draft document for all reform circle members to return to in September. The following day some three thousand persons came to the closing session of the conference, which was open to the public. Nyers and Pozsgay addressed the audience, calling for fundamental political reform and praising the reform circles' contribution to this effort, while reform circle delegates József Lovászi and Imre Keserű gave details of the previous day's work and outlined the reform circles' demands.

Although still only a draft document, the reform circle platform programme was the first comprehensive document of the movement, a radical challenge to the party status quo. The document opened with a scathing description of the current order as an 'Asiatic, despotic, post-Stalinist system' which despite numerous modifications was no longer able to function. The document continued: dogmatism and self-serving pragmatism had to be replaced by ideological concepts found in European and Hungarian progressive movements, drawing from socialist, bourgeois radical, liberal and populist values. The party must bear responsibility for the current crisis within Hungary. Any reform which is not comprehensive, transforming all sectors of society, is doomed to failure. The party must withdraw from the state; reject its anti-intellectual dogmas; bind itself to fundamental human values – individual liberty, democracy, openness, security; community autonomy must be supported through the reorganization of civil society and through the strengthening of local government. The economy must be transformed as well. Real democracy cannot be predicated on state ownership of the means of production. The party must surrender its anti-market attitudes. Property forms must be pluralized, which would create real owners and block the reconcentration of economic power in the hands of party managers. Foreign capital should be welcomed. Relations with COMECON should be restructured.

The document also stressed the need for multiparty democracy within the framework of pluralistic political institutions and a *rechtsstaat*. To achieve this an extraordinary party congress would be necessary in the autumn, which could create new party statutes and a new leadership, turning the MSZMP from a class- and cadre-based monolith into a modern, progressive and fully democratic socialist party. The party should also seek a compromise with forces external to it (namely, the EKA) to ensure a peaceful transition and division of power, which would form part of a broader 'national compact' upon which a new constitution could be based. The draft platform concluded with two open letters, one calling on the party to rehabilitate Imre Nagy and to delegate party representatives to his forthcoming reburial, and the other asking party members to begin collecting signatures to force an extraordinary party congress in the autumn.[38] The conference also sent a letter directly to the EKA, offering to engage in direct negotiation with them at the national and local level. However, the reform circles, no matter how prominent, possessed no direct authority or organizational power that would make them a legitimate negotiating partner. The EKA declined the offer.[39]

THE BALANCE OF POWER SHIFTS

Despite the shortcomings of the Szeged conference, the size and strength of the reform circles was now plain to see. Party conservatives and opportunists, who just weeks before had stridently attacked the movement as factionalist and destructive, had good reason to wonder if the tide was turning against them. Many began to fall into increasingly conciliatory positions towards the reform circles, a last-ditch effort to curry favour and hopefully co-opt their views. Politburo member Mihály Jassó, who three weeks before had disparaged the reform circles as impetuous, now praised the movement as 'giving an intellectual impetus to the party that would help the formation of party unity' and stated that a party congress should be held if the ranks demanded it.[40] Central Committee Secretary György Fejti, a staunch ally of Grósz, held talks with reform circle delegates regarding negotiations with the

38. 'Az MSZMP reformköri mozgalom platformja [The MSZMP reform circle movement platform]', *Népszabadság*, 23 May 1989: 4.
39. Letter from József Lovászi on behalf of the first reform circle conference delegates to the EKA [photocopy], dated 22 May 1989; for the EKA's response see 'Kimozdulni a holtpontról [To move out of the deadlock]', *Népszabadság*, 23 May 1989: 4; Bozóki, 'Hungary's Road to Systemic Change': 287.
40. Mihály Jassó, 'Ha igény van kongresszusra, akkor legyen [If there is a demand for a congress, then there should be one]', *Magyar Nemzet*, 23 May 1989: 4.

EKA, supporting their idea of a national roundtable that would widen the circle of participants.[41]

The influence of the reform circles was, however, most clearly shown at the Central Committee session on 29 May, where representatives confronted a number of significant topics raised at the reform circle conference, such as the party's re-evaluation of Imre Nagy, talks with the EKA, and the forthcoming MSZMP national conference.[42] The assembly heard an anonymously-written, confidential report on the 20 May Szeged conference and the unfolding of the movement to date. Although even the department from which the document had originated was omitted, the report's detailed contents clearly showed that the reform circles were under observation.

The document spoke in largely positive terms about the conference, describing the debates and speeches as 'responsible', and 'free from extremism', although the excesses of some delegates was mentioned (notably in connection with the move to have 1956 declared a revolution, as well as the speeches of Budapest Reform Circle Number One delegates). It added that the reform circles were attracting increasing amounts of interest and support within the party, as indicated by the large numbers which attended the conference and the thousands which came to its closing session.[43]

In contrast to the past the Central Committee was now clearly aware of this, as a number spoke of the increasing pressure from below for a party congress to be convened in place of the party conference. Members' growing apprehension over the rank and file overrode their traditional obedience, seeking to acquiesce despite the fact that Grósz continued to oppose a congress.[44] Only three weeks after it had agreed

41. Kornélia Dolecskó, 'Kezdődjön meg a párbeszéd [The dialogue should begin]', *Népszabadság*, 29 May 1989: 4.
42. For details see *Népszabadság*, 30 May 1989: 1–3; Judith Pataki, 'HSWP Faces Sensitive Issues', *RFER* (16 June 1989): 7–10.
43. 'Tájékoztató az MSZMP Központi Bizottságának az MSZMP reformkörök 1989 május 20-án Szegeden rendezett munkatanácskozásáról [Information for the MSZMP Central Committee regarding the MSZMP reform circles' 20 May 1989 work conference in Szeged]', dated 26 May 1989, document from the MSZMP Central Committee meeting, 29 May 1989, National Archives collection 288f. 4/263 ő.é.: 125–9.
44. Transcripts of the MSZMP Central Committee meeting 29 May 1989, National Archives collection 288f. 4/262 ő.é.; see also Károly Grósz, 'Eleget tettünk a

to a party conference, the Central Committee retreated once more and approved an extraordinary party congress for the autumn. Grósz complained in a subsequent interview that the party was unprepared for a congress, but had to yield to demands from the party ranks, such as those heard at the reform circle conference.[45] In another, more indirect victory for the reform circles, the party effectively (although not officially) rehabilitated Imre Nagy.

Helped along by the first reform circle conference and the subsequent concession of the Central Committee on many of their demands, from May onwards the political situation in Hungary changed dramatically from that witnessed at the beginning of the year. By early summer the party underwent a serious enervation of its organizational power, as the reform circles and reformist leadership undermined its monolithic position and pushed it further down the path of reform by challenging the status quo. This weakening of party power in turn helped increase the political 'space' for opposition forces to coalesce and manoeuvre, forcing the party to take increasingly radical steps forward to maintain the initiative, shore up popular support and appear in control of events. These included the dismantling of the barbed-wire fence between Hungary and Austria, a suspension of the controversial joint Hungarian–Czechoslovak dam project across the Danube, and the eventual commencement of negotiations with the EKA.

Imperceptibly a turning-point had been reached, of which the population, the party and the opposition were now quite aware: although the MSZMP was still the dominant force in the country, it could no longer simply dictate events. Granted, polls still indicated that the party would do well in elections, capturing close to a third of the vote, and Pozsgay and Németh in particular continued to enjoy widespread popularity in comparison to those within the opposition camp. In addition, many in the opposition leadership still questioned whether they possessed the popular legitimacy or skills to actually take over the reins of power were they to win an open election. For example, the president of the most popular opposition party, the MDF, argued that they were not yet

párttagság kívánságának [We have done enough of the membership's wishes]', interview by László Szabó, *Népszabadság*, 30 May 1989: 4.

45. See the text of a television interview with Károly Grósz, 'Tagadom, hogy a négy évtized zsákutca volt [I reject that the last four decades were a dead-end]', *Magyar Hírlap*, 31 May 1989: 4–5.

ready to govern alone, necessitating a parliamentary coalition with the communists.[46]

However, the overwhelming victory of Solidarity in the Polish elections in June showed the possibilities of political change, bolstering opposition forces even as it struck fear into the MSZMP. While strong, support for the MSZMP as a whole and the general secretary in particular was on the decline (by June it had dropped to 45 per cent of those surveyed), and nearly half of *party members* surveyed in June believed it would be better for the MSZMP to split apart.[47] By July the party had lost nearly 60,000 members since the beginning of the year.[48]

Pozsgay further exacerbated the division within the party leadership with his eventual founding of the Movement for a Democratic Hungary (*Mozgalom a Demokratikus Magyarországért*) on 7 June. Described as a non-party mass movement in support of democratic transition, it was headed by a committee made up of notable intellectuals, independents and MSZMP members, including several from the reform circle movement. According to one of its organizers, within the first week it had attracted several thousand members.[49]

Although Pozsgay denied it at the time, his intention was to develop the Movement for a Democratic Hungary as a potential political party, an alternative and a threat to the MSZMP should its transformation be unsuccessful. The organization also reflected the fact that Pozsgay had his eye on the state presidency, which under current constitutional

46. See Zoltán Bíró (president of the MDF), 'Hungary's Rulers Undergo Crisis of Confidence', interview by Jyrki Palo, *Helsingin Sansomat* (Helsinki), 22 June 1989: 32, translated in *JPRS Report: East Europe* (9 August 1989): 18.
47. See the opinion survey results of the Hungarian Public Opinion Research Institute, in Kurtán, Sándor and Vass, *Magyarország Politikai Évkönyve 1990*: 443–51. The party leadership at this time still expected that they would get some 40–50 per cent of the vote: see Rezső Nyers, 'Közelkép [Close-up]', interview by Tamás Vitray, *Kritika* (June 1989): 3.
48. The data can be found in *Kongresszus '89*, no. 8 (27 September 1989): 2. This party publication, produced by the Central Committee Department of Party Politics (*Pártpolitikai Osztálya*), appeared from mid-August as an information source for congress delegates.
49. Ferenc Gazsó, personal interview by the author, Budapest, 11 March 1993. For details on the organization's founding meeting see Attila Vödrös, 'A csöndes többséget várják a reformerek [The reformers anticipate the silent majority]', *Magyar Hírlap*, 8 June 1989: 1, 3; Alfred Reisch, 'New Political Movement Formed to Support Radical Reform', *RFER* (23 June 1989): 21–5.

proposals would be directly elected and wield considerable power.[50] The Movement could serve to build for Pozsgay a base of personal support which would bridge both the party and society – a more promising strategy than to throw in his lot with the reform circle movement alone, which he continued to hold at arm's length and view with some suspicion.[51] In fact, the Movement very much resembled an early form of the populist opposition party, the MDF, as an agglomeration of populist–socialist views and members from both camps.

In general, the reform circles welcomed the fact that Pozsgay had finally created the political platform they had been expecting for months. However, because of Pozsgay's earlier ambivalence towards the reform circles, and with their own fortunes on the rise, many no longer looked to him as their natural leader. The Movement and the reform circles overlapped in membership and objectives, but their actual merger was never considered. Grósz, meanwhile, responded to Pozsgay's action by branding the Movement 'a step tantamount to a party split'.[52]

Yet it was too early for anyone to declare victory. The reform circles had achieved what they had desired – an early party congress, to be held before national elections. Now they faced the task of being the decisive force at that congress. Original proposals by the Central Committee were that the congress would be held some time in the autumn, and delegate selection completed by mid-July.[53] In addition, it was proposed that the offices of general secretary and party president should be filled through direct election by all party members, rather than through election by party delegates at the autumn congress. Central Committee members, it was further proposed, would also have

50. Pozsgay personal interview. For details on the struggle over the presidency in Hungary see Patrick H. O'Neil, 'Hungary: Political Transition and Executive Conflict: The Balance or Fragmentation of Power?', in Ray Taras (ed.), *Post-Communist Presidents* (Cambridge: Cambridge University Press, 1997): 195–224.

51. Pozsgay personal interview; see also Imre Pozsgay, interview by Zoltán Bíró, *Egy év után, választás előtt* [After a year, before elections] (Budapest: Püski, 1990): 18–20, where Pozsgay clearly discusses his reservations with regard to the reform circles.

52. 'Pártszakadással egyenértékű lépés? [A step tantamount to a party split?]', *Magyar Hírlap*, 10 June 1989: 4.

53. 'A tagság nyomására lesz pártkongresszus [Due to membership pressure there will be a party congress]', *Magyar Hírlap*, 31 May 1989: 5.

automatic voting rights at the congress.[54] Reform circles protested that the last two proposals were a subterfuge, intended to hinder reformers by diluting their power.

The reform circles suggested instead that delegate selection be based on candidates nominated by party platforms, which would compete in territorial-based electoral districts. Proportional shares of votes would determine the number of delegates sent from each platform list. Other proposals suggested that the congress be held in November, and that delegate selection be extended to mid-September, so as to give opposing platforms time to organize their campaigns. Above all, reform circles wanted the selection of delegates to be as direct as possible, rather than the traditional method of congress delegates being handpicked by local party bosses at the intermediate city and county party conferences by so-called 'nominating committees', instruments of democratic centralism created for just such a task.[55] Budapest reform circles themselves clashed with the city party committee over their attempt to limit the deadline for Budapest delegate selection even further, a transparent attempt to prevent reformers from organizing their ranks.[56]

THE DOWNSIDE OF SUCCESS

Beyond these manoeuvres, the reform circles were also finding it increasingly difficult to deal with the effects of their own success. As first glimpsed at the Szeged conference, the growing momentum

54. For details, see 'A Központi Bizottság két vitaanyag-javaslata [Two Central Committee proposals for debate]', *Népszabadság*, 3 June 1989: 4; Alfred Reisch, 'New Caretaker Leadership Under Nyers Averts Party Split', *RFER* (14 July 1989): 4–5.
55. Examples of these proposals include 'Ajánlás a kongresszusi küldöttválasztás alapelveire [Proposal for the basic principles of congress delegate election]', unpublished document, Csongrád county reform circle, dated 13 June 1989; 'Reformkongresszust! Felhívás az MSZMP tagsághoz [Reform congress! Call to the MSZMP membership]', unpublished joint document of six reform circles, dated 14 June 1989; 'Felhívás a reformkörökhöz! [Call to the reform circles!]', unpublished document, Kecskemét reform circle, n.d.; 'A Budapesti Reformkörének állásfoglalása a pártkongresszusról [The Budapest reform circle statement regarding the party congress]', *Népszabadság*, 12 June 1989: 7.
56. 'A fővárosi reformkörök a párt feladatairól [The capital reform circles on the tasks of the party]', *Népszabadság*, 7 June 1989: 4.

towards political change within Hungary and the bloc as a whole served to attract individuals to the reform circle movement whose cohort origins and political motivations were not necessarily identical to those of the movement founders. Radical political change was becoming less a subversive idea and more a common part of political discourse. Whereas initially participation in a reform circle was seen as an act which could conceivably jeopardize one's personal position, now, barring a hardliner *putsch*, a lack of credible 'reformist' credentials was the potentially more risky course to take, condemning one to fall behind the course of events.

Consequently, by summer the reform circles attracted growing numbers of more moderate reformers, who now saw change as inevitable and were willing to play a role in a movement which drew open support from a number of powerful party leaders. In addition, there were undoubtedly large numbers of sheer opportunists, party careerists who saw the reform circles as part of the likely winning team in the party struggles and who wanted to keep their power and status within a future socialist order. Because of its very nature, the reform circles, as an open, weakly-organized and informal movement, had no way to check this unintended effect. This development was first felt at the Szeged conference, and undoubtedly contributed to Pozsgay's decision to delay his founding of the Movement for a Democratic Hungary. The movement now had to struggle with this growing 'centrist' camp within their ranks which was frustrating more radical members, who had anticipated a radical step forward at the Szeged conference and were bitterly disappointed by what they saw as its derailment.[57] Ironically, some now accused the reform circles of having turned into little more than a new class of party intellectuals striving for nothing more than to gain power for themselves.[58]

Meanwhile, while reform circles were still struggling with the idea of formal organization, conservative and left-wing forces within the party were founding their own platforms. In late May hardliner Robert

57. See for examples the interview with former member of the Central Control Committee and reform circle participant, Flórián Kováts, 'Elszakadás [Splitting off]', interview by István Hegedüs, *Világ*, 6 July 1989: 22.

58. Zsolt Szoboszlai, 'Egy az utunk? Én (is) kiléptem az MSZMP-ből [Do we have a single path? I (too) have left the MSZMP]', *Juss* **II** (September 1989): 62–3. This article provides an excellent overview and analysis of developments within Csongrad during 1988 and early 1989.

Ribánski founded the Marxist Unity Platform (*Marxista Egység Platform*), comprising older Kádárist functionaries who supported the status quo – and hinted at the use of force, if necessary, to retain it. June and early July saw the formation of another platform, Solidarity for the Renewal of the MSZMP (*Összefogás az MSZMP Megújításért*). Headed by former Politburo member Berecz, this platform collected somewhat younger cadres around a policy of party unity and moderate reform – the standard Grósz line. The Solidarity platform attacked 'reform arrogance' and 'reform anarchy', stressing the need to preserve party unity for sake of national stability.[59] A third group formed around this period was the Peoples' Democratic Platform (*Népi Demokratikus Platform*), based largely on anti-liberal, neo-Marxist ideology – also critical of the status quo, but from a quasi-Trotskyite perspective.[60] With this growing factionalization within the MSZMP, many were calling for the party to finally acknowledge this growing tendency and formally sanction party platforms.[61]

Finally, the success of the reform circles was changing their relationship to the opposition as well. One point made earlier about Kádárism is that one of its major achievements was its ability to effectively pacify and atomize Hungarian society, eliminating the communist party as a symbol against which opposition could organize and build support. As a result, when the move towards political change was initiated in 1988, it was a largely independent act of the party, a response to the deepening economic and political crisis rather than a reaction to any specific pressure from dissident organizations (as in Poland). Opposition groups, while on the rise, remained small and fragmented, attracting limited attention from most in society. But by the early summer of 1989

59. See, for example, the text of Berecz's speech to the second national congress of the Solidarity platform in *Kongresszus '89: 'Összefogás az MSZMP Megújitásáért'* [Congress 1989: 'Solidarity for the Renewal of the MSZMP'] (Budapest: Szikra, 1989): 3–8.
60. For details see Alfred Reisch, 'HSWP Leadership Caught Between Reform Circles and Party Factions', *RFER* (14 July 1989): 16; Zoltan D. Barany, 'Factions Form in the HSWP Before the Party Congress', *RFER* (10 November 1989): 9–13; For a collection of documents chronicling the development and of the People's Democratic Platform, see Péter Szigeti (ed.), *Balra, ki a zűrzavarból!* [Leftward, out of the chaos!] (Budapest: n.p. 1990).
61. Antal Gyenes, 'Féljünk-e a frakcióktól? [Should we be afraid of factions?]', *Magyar Nemzet*, 22 June 1989: 7.

this had changed dramatically as the MSZMP began to disintegrate in the face of reform circle pressure below and power struggles at the top.

These developments changed the political field entirely. The ability of the MSZMP to dominate forthcoming parliamentary elections, either through legal trickery or through passive social support, was becoming less certain by the day. This in turn raised the very real possibility that the final battle for parliament might not be between the MSZMP and the opposition but between the opposition parties themselves. This was particularly important for the liberal–urban SZDSZ and the youth-based FIDESZ, which still lagged far behind both the MSZMP and the populist MDF in terms of popularity. Both parties thus began to step up their attacks on the MSZMP in order to gain attention as the most strident critics of the old order.

The SZDSZ also complemented this tactic with an attack on the MDF. The MDF had a base of rural support much larger than the Budapest-centred SZDSZ, whose leaders earlier doubted that they would even enter parliament. It was widely assumed that the MDF would gain the second-largest share of votes after the MSZMP, forming a coalition with the communists as a junior partner.[62] But as the centralized authority of the MSZMP began to decay, the SZDSZ capitalized on this close association between the MDF and the MSZMP (Pozsgay in particular) to tar the MDF as little more than a vehicle for crypto-communists to retain power. This was a powerful tool. The president of the MDF, Zoltán Bíró, was in fact one of the four intellectuals expelled from the MSZMP in 1988, and one will recall that Pozsgay had played an important role in the creation of the MDF through their first meeting in Lakitelek in 1987. In response to these accusations the MDF returned fire, pointing out the communist pedigrees of major SZDSZ figures who had been close to the radical new left movement of the 1960s. The traditional rural–urban split, never far below the surface, returned to the fore.

An important outcome of these battles was that they forced the opposition as a whole to distance themselves from any earlier political tenets which could be identified as socialist. The SZDSZ and FIDESZ moved from a social–liberal position further towards a more classic

62. János Kenedi (founding member of the SZDSZ), 'Emberekről, eszmékről, politikáról [On people, ideas, and politics]', interview by Ervin Csizmadia, *Valóság* (April 1990): 48–9.

liberal perspective, while the MDF began to cultivate a conservative, Christian–nationalist line.[63] Anti-communism now grew as a central piece of political rhetoric for all opposition forces as they attempted to outflank and stigmatize each other *vis-à-vis* their association with or position towards the MSZMP. These tactics hit the reform circles particularly hard. Previously they had regarded the opposition as their natural allies, partners in the move towards democracy. But as one of the founders of the SZDSZ noted, by summer 1989 association with the reform circles had become a liability to the opposition.[64]

The first clear sign of this new turn in political strategy appeared during the reburial of Imre Nagy and his compatriots on 16 June. The reform circles had demanded at the Szeged meeting that the party officially send representatives to Nagy's reburial, something the MSZMP eventually chose not to do (Pozsgay and Németh both attended the ceremonies, but as representatives of the government and not of the party). As a result, several reform circles decided to send their own representatives. However, much to their surprise and dismay the reform circle representatives were shut out of the formal ceremonies by the opposition organizers of the event.[65] More injurious was the forceful speech at the ceremony by Viktor Orban, one of the leaders of FIDESZ:

> We do not understand that the very same party and government leaders who told us to learn about the revolution from textbooks falsifying history can today vie with each other in seeking to touch these coffins as if they were lucky charms. We do not think that there is any reason for us to be grateful

63. Ibid. These developments are also covered extremely well in Ervin Csizmadia, 'Utak a pártosodáshoz: az MDF és az SZDSZ megszerveződése [The roads to party organization: The formation of the MDF and the SZDSZ]', in Mihály Bihari (ed.), *A többpártrendszer kialakulása Magyarországon 1985–1991* [The formation of multiparty system in Hungary, 1985-91] (Budapest: Kossuth, 1992): 7–39; and Tamás Kolosi, Iván Szelényi, Szonja Szelényi and Bruce Western, 'The Making of Political Fields in Post-Communist Transition (Dynamics of Class and Party in Hungarian Politics, 1989-90)', in Bozóki, Körösényi and Schöpflin, *Post-Communist Transition*, esp. 152–5.
64. Kenedi, 'Emberekről': 49–50.
65. 'A Budapesti Reformkör a Törtenelmi Igazságtétel Bizottságához [From the Budapest Reform Circle to the Committee for Historical Justice]', *Népszabadság*, 21 June 1989: 7.

> for being allowed to bury our dead. We do not owe thanks to anyone for the fact that our political organizations can be alive and working today.[66]

The opposition had in effect appropriated 1956 entirely as their own, portraying the MSZMP and all those within it as culpable for its suppression. A number of interview subjects stressed that this dealt a serious moral blow to the reform circle movement, which until that time had seen itself as an opposition force just like those outside the party. Now it was clear that party membership, and not one's political views, was the central litmus test.

THE BATTLE FOR POWER INTENSIFIES AT THE TOP

During the summer, conflicts within the party leadership re-emerged with a vengeance. The political power which Grósz once wielded had rapidly atrophied, and Prime Minister Németh's 'rebirth' as a reformer as well as the growing paralysis of the Central Committee cost the general secretary key allies. By mid-June Grósz was admitting publicly that serious conflicts had emerged within the party leadership, which he blamed on the 'personal ambitions' among some Politburo members. Also, his attacks on the reform circles continued unabated, charging them with fomenting a possible party split.[67] In turn a number of reform circles grew bolder in their criticism of Grósz, demanding his immediate removal as the only way to restore internal confidence in the party and isolate the conservative wing.[68]

66. Quoted in Judith Pataki, 'Speech by Federation of Young Democrats' Delegate at Nagy's Reburial Ceremony', *RFER* (14 July 1989): 27–8.
67. See the comments by Grósz in 'Marxista szellemű, politizáló pártot akarunk [We want a Marxist-spirited, politicizing party]', *Népszabadság*, 12 June 1989: 1, 4.
68. For the comments of the Csongrád reform circle see 'Válságmenedzselő főtitkárra voksolnak [Elect a crisis-managing general secretary]', *Magyar Hírlap* (23 June 1989): 6; see also the statements by the Nagykanizsa and Pécs-Baranya reform circles in *Magyar Nemzet*, 23 June 1989: 7. Similar comments by Central Committee Foreign Affairs Department deputy head Csaba Tabajdi to the Italian daily *L'Unità* led to his suspension pending a disciplinary investigation, an action apparently directed personally by Grósz. A number of reform circles protested against the action, and he was eventually cleared of any wrongdoing: see Alfred Reisch,

By the time of the Central Committee meeting of 23 June, the party was in open crisis, which much of the party leadership feared would soon split the party in two. Yet despite pressure from within the party Grósz refused to resign, and as before Pozsgay remained apprehensive as to the consequences for reform should he respond by taking steps towards a party split.[69]

The result was another compromise. After an apparently stormy debate in which no one was able to decisively gain the upper hand, Grósz, having lost much of his support in the Central Committee, was forced to submit to the creation of a collective party presidium with Pozsgay, Németh and Nyers. Grósz retained his position as general secretary, and Nyers was elected to the post of party president (which had remained vacant since Kádár's dismissal in early May).[70] Unlike the other party leaders, Nyers, who was considerably older and had a long history within the party, enjoyed widespread support among different factions within the MSZMP – for example, he was more favoured among party conservatives than was Grósz himself.[71] While Nyers had been known for his relatively radical views on economic reform in the 1960s, by mid-1989 the rapidly changing political situation had made many of these ideas anachronistic, placing Nyers more towards the centre of the party. This made him more palatable to various factions in the MSZMP. Nyers also had kept his distance from reformers within the party even as he courted them, for example criticizing the reform circles' radical demands and harsh analysis of Hungarian socialism as extremist and 'ultrareformist'.[72] Nyers thus became a key mediator between the party leadership and the MSZMP

'New Caretaker Government Under Nyers Avoids Split', *RFER* (14 July 1989): 6.

69. Pozsgay, *Egy év után*: 17–18.
70. For details on this event see *Népszabadság*, 26–27 July 1989; Alfred Reisch, 'New Caretaker Government'; and Tőkés, *Hungary's Negotiated Revolution*: 330–31. See also the personal accounts in Pozsgay, *1989*: 149–54; Kimmel, *Végjáték a fehér házban*: 135–56. For the reaction of reform circle members see Sára Pogány, 'Reformkörök képviselői a KB-ülésről [Reform circle representatives on the Central Committee session]', *Magyar Hírlap*, 4 July 1989: 3, and 5 July 1989: 3.
71. See 'A közvélemény 1989-ban' in Kurtán, Sándor and Vass, *Magyarország Politikai Évkönyve 1990*: 454.
72. See, for example, Rezső Nyers, 'Szélsőségek akadályozzák a pártban az intergráló centrum létrejöttét [Extremes obstruct the creation of an integrative centre within the party]', *Népszabadság*, 22 June 1989: 1, 3; see also Reisch, 'New Caretaker Government': 8.

as a whole, bridging the widening rifts and essentially holding the fractious party together.

The Politburo itself was also expanded to become the Political Executive Committee (*Politikai Intéző Bizottság*, or PIB) of some 21 members, effectively appropriating much of the power of the Central Committee. Elected into the expanded body were a number of new figures, among them Foreign Minister Gyula Horn, who had in recent months become quite radical in his public pronouncements on foreign policy. However, two other Pozsgay backers, Minister of Interior István Horváth and President of Parliament Mátyás Szűrös, did not receive enough votes from the Central Committee. Overall the new PIB composition could be described as ideologically centrist – an essentially stop-gap measure to hold the party together until the forthcoming congress.[73] Another party split had been avoided, but any pretence of unity within the MSZMP leadership was clearly gone. Outside the area of leadership battles, the Central Committee officially set the party congress to take place on 6 October, with the closing date for the election of delegates set for the end of August (both of these dates were still earlier than many reform circles had demanded, although the deadline for delegate election was eventually extended to late September). Earlier proposals for the direct election of general secretary and party president by the membership were also dropped shortly thereafter, but the automatic participation rights of the Central Committee remained. Most importantly, the contentious issue of how delegates would be elected was left to local party organs to decide. The only stipulation was that each county send one delegate per 600 party members under their jurisdiction.

While the reform circles had sought to overturn the hidebound process of delegate selection via local party conferences, the central authorities' failure to make a clear decision was no great comfort. With no clear rules from Budapest, power remained in the hands of local committees to choose the eventual method of selection. Whether the reform circles would be able to overcome the entrenched local party machinery to force clear changes in the electoral process was an open question.

73. Even Horn was barely elected into the PIB, gaining the second-lowest number of votes; Kimmel, *Végjáték a fehér házban*: 154–5.

LOCAL ELECTIONS, NATIONAL COORDINATION, AND THE REFORM CIRCLES

In response to the results of the Central Committee meeting, the reform circles began a new effort to coordinate their actions prior to the party congress. Already in a number of places reform circles were holding county-wide or regional meetings in order to better facilitate local action. In late June and early July, reform circles from western Hungary proposed the idea of a national coordinating committee, as a necessary tool for the movement to gain representation to the congress and to prepare tactics. The need was underscored, they noted, by the short deadline for delegate selection and fears that the vague stipulations for delegate selection would be manipulated by the party machinery.[74]

In fact, already by early July Budapest reform circles had created their own coordinating council and convened their own city conference, which some 600 attended, including Nyers, who contrary to his recent criticisms praised the movement as a necessary and useful element of the party's renewal.[75] Shortly thereafter the Budapest coordinating council invited rural reform circle representatives to meet on 28 June in preparation for the second reform circle conference scheduled for September. Discussion turned on the forthcoming reform circle conference, problems of delegate selection and widening the movement's support, and how to prepare the MSZMP for parliamentary elections. The session was also marred by angry comments from several rural reform circle members that the Budapest coordinating committee had through its establishment unilaterally assumed the leadership mantle for itself. In response, a standing 'preparatory committee' comprised of both Budapest and rural reform circle members was formally established. Despite the obvious friction at this first meeting, the autonomous reform circles were at last attempting to unify their movement, effectively creating a leadership to integrate their activity towards a common goal.[76]

74. 'MSZMP Reformkörök Kaposváron [MSZMP reform circles in Kaposvár]', *Somogyi Néplap*, 26 June 1989: 1, 3; 'Felhívás és állásfoglalás [Invitation and statement]', *Somogyi Néplap*, 3 July 1989: 3.
75. Zsusza Láng, 'Vissza kell szerezni a szocialista mozgalom becsületét [We must win back the honour of the socialist movement]', *Népszabadság*, 6 July 1989: 1, 5.
76. Minutes of the 28 June 1989 reform circle preparatory committee session,

While it was apparent that the movement was still uneasy with the idea of national coordination and leadership, the need for the reform circles to better consolidate their actions had been driven home in recent days. During the spring, a number of seats in parliament had come available through resignations by senior deputies, several of which were prompted by recall petitions led by opposition forces. In four cases circumstances forced the calling of by-elections for 22 July: Szeged, Kecskemét, Gödöllő and Kiskunfélegyháza. These were to be the first open elections in Hungary for more than forty years, and an early test of the political waters.[77]

For the MSZMP, the results were not promising. In Szeged the local MSZMP apparatus was by this time so discredited that before the first round of elections the two candidates put forward by the party did not receive the necessary one-third support from the mandatory public nominating conventions. and MDF candidate Ernő Raffay swept the elections on a strident anti-communist platform.[78] In Kiskunfélegyháza, the local reform circle attempt to field their own candidate similarly failed at the nominating level.[79] In Kecskemét, the reform circles took the unusual step of running their own candidate, Gyula Gráner, against the official candidate of the MSZMP itself, István Kiss.[80] However, in the first round of elections Gráner won less than 9 per cent of the vote,

unpublished document, dated 30 June 1989.

77. For details see Judith Pataki, 'Parliamentary By-Elections as First Step Toward Multiparty National Election', *RFER* (27 July 1989): 3–7; János Simon, 'A nem-választók szabadsága [The freedom of not voting]', in Kurtán, Sándor and Vass, *Magyarország Politikai Évkönyve 1990*: 199–208; on elections in Kecskemét in particular, see László Bruszt and János Simon, 'Két választás Magyarországon a demokrácia serdülőkorában [Two elections in Hungary during democracy's adolescence]', in Bruszt and Simon, *A lecsendesített többség*: 89–104.
78. During the second round of elections the MSZMP had been able to field a candidate backed by a strong campaign propaganda, yet Raffay still won 61.5 per cent of the vote (in the first round he had won 59 per cent). His MSZMP opponent received only 21.9 per cent, and the rest of the vote went to a third independent: Simon, 'A nem-választók szabadsága': 200–201.
79. 'Bizalmat kapott: Dr. Garai László, Dr. Vas László, Fekete Pál [Dr László Garai, Dr László Vas and Pál Fekete win the vote of confidence]', *Petőfi Népe*, 3 July 1989: 1.
80. For details, see István Tanács, 'Kiélezett választási küzdelem Bács-Kiskun megyében [Sharp election battle in Bács-Kiskun county]', *Népszabadság*, 20 July 1989: 7; and 'A kecskeméti reformkör a választásokról [The Kecskemét reform circle on the elections]', *Népszabadság*, 10 August 1989: 4.

against 22 per cent for Kiss (Kiss himself lost to the MDF candidate, who received 70 per cent of the vote in the second round). As an aside, in both Szeged and Kecskemét voter turnout had been less than 50 per cent - hardly the turnout expected from a populace being given its first chance for democratic participation in forty years.

The lessons drawn from these elections were not comforting to the MSZMP or to the reform circle movement. First, it was clear that at least in single-member districts much of the populace would not support MSZMP candidates, even those from the reformist wing, as evidenced by the overwhelming victories of the opposition in three of the four by-elections (the MSZMP candidate winning only in Kiskunfélegyháza). Second, support for the reform circles within the party ranks was also open to serious question, given the poor showing of their candidates in both Kiskunfélegyháza and Kecskemét.

This raised a troubling question for the reform circles. What sort of reception could they expect from the rank and file during delegate elections to the forthcoming MSZMP congress? The by-elections were a strong incentive to organize a central reform circle leadership, having given substance to fears that the party was losing its last chance to redeem itself in the eyes of the populace, not to mention that the reform circles perhaps did not enjoy the kind of rank-and-file party support they had imagined.

Shortly thereafter the reform circles were buoyed by a spectacular local victory. In Zala county, where several reform circles were particularly active, one group in the town of Nagykanizsa proposed the fundamental reorganization of the county party structure to prepare for and better reflect the needs of a multiparty system. The proposal involved replacing the party committee with a much larger executive board and coordinating bureau, headed by a county party president.[81] During a marathon county party conference on 29 July, the incumbent leadership tried to dissuade the delegates from accepting the reform circle proposal with a more moderate alternative, while PIB member Fejti, a strong ally of Grósz and a guest of the conference, spoke against

81. For the original proposal, see 'Javaslat az MSZMP zalai válaszmányának és koordinaciós irodájának létrehozására [Proposal for the creation of an MSZMP board and coordinating bureau in Zala]', *Új forum*, 18 August 1989: 16; the proposal's original date is given as 10 July.

exclusory and impatient tactics, 'internal party cannibalism' that would result in the party's loss of power.[82]

Despite this pressure, the reform circle proposal was voted in by the conference delegates, and an entirely new leadership of reformists elected into the highest offices, the majority with no previous political experience (including the new party president). The following day, the county party paper *Zalai Hírlap* stripped the usual slogan 'Proletariat of the world, unite!' from its masthead.[83] A number of other county papers soon followed their lead, contending that the MSZMP should no longer have control over the content of the press.[84] The victory in Zala was widely regarded as a major breakthrough for the MSZMP reform circles, and terrified a number of more conservative party leaders. PIB member Vastagh, for example, commented shortly afterwards that if the events in Zala were to develop into a tendency within the party it would threaten party organization, which required 'professional' politicians.[85]

Bolstered by this success, throughout August reform circles worked feverishly to seize the momentum and turn the disparate movement into the core of a new socialist party. The idea of the 'Zala model', as it was being called, was taken up by the movement as a possible blueprint for local party conferences, as well as a structure that could be duplicated at the national level. Reform circles also continued to demand that the Central Committee be stripped of its automatic voting rights at the

82. 'Új pártmodell született, amely biztató kisérlet lehet [A new party model has been born, from which an encouraging experiment is possible]', *Zalai Hírlap*, 31 July 1989: 5.
83. A summary of the proceedings and results of the Zala conference were published as *Ébresztő, elvtársak! avagy a zalai modell* [Awake, comrades! or, the Zala model] (Budapest: Kossuth, 1989); see also László Ráb, 'Kedves elvtársak, jó reggelt! [Dear comrades, good morning!]', *Népszabadság*, 31 July 1989: 1, 5; and the interview with the new Zala party president László Vári, 'A zalai fordulat üzenete [The message of the Zala turnabout]', interview by István Bőle, *Délmagyarország*, 6 September 1989.
84. This was the case in, for example, Veszprém, Somogy, Fejér and Vas counties. For a discussion of the rationale behind these actions see 'A reformok szellemében: a Napló szerkesztőbizottságának állásfoglalása a lap fejlécének megvaltoztatásáról [In the spirit of reform: the Daily's editorial committee position on the change of the masthead]', *Veszprém Megyei Napló*, 18 August 1989: 1.
85. Lajos Pogonyi, 'Ettől még nem kell pánikba esni ... [We must not break into a panic over this ...]', *Népszabadság*, 1 August 1989: 1.

forthcoming congress, arguing that they should be required to win their mandates just like all other delegates. The party Mandate Committee in charge of overseeing these matters eventually compromised, ruling that the issue be decided at the congress by the delegates themselves.[86] Other reform circle declarations during this time ranged from denunciations of the party's recent attempt to transfer MSZMP assets and state property into a front corporation to a call for the party to condemn its role in the intervention in Czechoslovakia in 1968, with which the PIB concurred some days later.[87]

The number of reform circles themselves continued to spread, notably within state and para-statal structures. One example was the national trade union, where reform circles sought to separate the union from the MSZMP, making it fully autonomous. Another, more striking example was the appearance of reform circles within the hardline party paramilitary force, the Workers' Guard. Reform circles developed within the army as well. Originating within the military academies, their numbers grew large enough to convene their own conference in early September, at which representatives called for the end to party cells in the military and the restoration of parliamentary control over the armed forces.[88]

During this time the reform circle preparatory committee struggled to disseminate the views of the movement among the party and society,

86. 'Ülésezett a Mandátumvizsgáló Bizottság [The session of the Mandate Committee]', *Kongresszus '89*, no. 2 (25 August 1989): 4.
87. For details on the issue of party assets see Zoltan D. Barany, 'Playing Unfair: the HSWP's Financial Manipulations', *RFER* (4 October 1989): 17–20; for the reform circle response, see Zsusza Láng, 'A baloldal, a párt hitele a tét [The left wing, the party's credit is at stake]', *Népszabadság*, 29 August 1989: 1, 5. On the Hungarian intervention in Czechoslovakia in 1968 see 'A Budapesti Reformkör a csehszlovákiai bevonulásról [The Budapest Reform Circle on the Czechoslovak intervention]', *Népszabadság*, 11 August 1989: 5; see also the statement of the Debrecen reform circle in *Népszabadság*, 12 August 1989: 5. The PIB statement to the same effect was issued on 16 August.
88. 'Az MSZMP Honvédségi Reformkörei szeptember 10-én, 10.00 órakor a Magyar Néphadsereg Művelődési Házaban megtartandó tanácskozásának állásfoglalás-tervezete [The draft statement of the MSZMP Army Reform Circles' conference, held on 10 September at 10:00 a.m., in the Hungarian People's Army House of Culture]', unpublished document; a short statement from the conference was published in *Népszabadság*, 15 September 1989: 4. For details on the conference, see Béla Valkó, 'Komisszárok végnapjai [The last days of the commissars]', *Ötlet*, 14 September 1989: 7–8.

and force changes in the format of the forthcoming congress so as to better suit their planned tactics. Work was still under way on finalizing a platform document that could attract widespread delegate support at the congress. Fears were that the reform circles, because of their relatively small size within the party, would inevitably be in the minority at the congress. There was thus a strong sense that the movement must appeal to a presumably reform-inclined, but still irresolute majority among the rank and file.

Proposals to modify the structure and sequence of the congress were also elaborated. This included the proposal that the tentative schedule of the congress be reversed, so that the election of a party leadership, on the basis of closed, platform-based lists, would precede any discussion of party organizational change. Here the reform circles hoped that this would force an early split among the delegates, leading to a defeat of conservatives who would then leave or be excluded from the rest of the congress.[89] The actions of the preparatory committee were not lost on the Central Committee, which invited its representatives to join in discussions over proposed changes to party statutes.[90]

In the area of expanding party support, the preparatory committee set up a smaller group charged with developing contacts with sympathetic individuals within the press. These contacts paid off. During the month of August the party paper *Népszabadság* published longer articles regarding the activities of the reform circles almost every other day, including a number of interviews and circle proposals on changes in party policy. A new weekly party publication, *Új forum*, devoted an entire special issue to the reform circles, reprinting many of their declarations on various topics.[91] An international news conference was also held by representatives of the committee, who in response to questions stated frankly that even a radically transformed MSZMP would now be

89. Minutes of reform circle preparatory committee meetings unpublished documents, 12 August and 26 August 1989; 'Az MSZMP Reformkörök és Reformalapszervezetek Országos Koordinációs Tanácsnak tárgyalási álláspontja a kongresszusi napirend és ügyrend tervezetéhez [The MSZMP Reform Circle and Reform Cell National Coordinating Council points of discussion for the planned programme and statutes of the congress]', unpublished document, n.d.

90. For details see Lajos Pogonyi, 'Óvakodjunk a túlszabályozástól! [We must be careful not to overregulate!]', *Népszabadság*, 30 August 1989: 6.

91. *Új fórum*, 19 August 1989.

likely to suffer defeat in open elections.[92] This frenetic activity of the reform circles eventually attracted the attention of the Soviet Embassy, which invited representatives from the preparatory committee to discuss the current political situation in Hungary.[93]

THE SECOND NATIONAL REFORM CIRCLE CONFERENCE

The culmination of much of this work was the second national reform circle conference. Held in Budapest on the weekend of 2–3 September 1989, it was attended by some 357 delegates from 158 reform circles, along with a number of observers and representatives from the Central Committee and PIB (although several noted party reformers such as Horn and Szűrös kept their distance and did not attend).[94] The conference began on a note of optimism, with Csongrád reform circle delegate József Lovászi opening his speech with the cry 'Good morning, comrades!' – the first words of the new Zala party president following the reform circles' victory there in June. A new day for the party is dawning, Lovászi declared, thanks to their efforts.

Yet despite the major steps forward by the movement in recent weeks, it was obvious from the opening speeches by Lovászi and others that the reform circles were in many aspects still frustrated by their lack of progress both inside and outside the party. Lovászi noted that the reform circles faced a climate of mistrust, both from the opposition – such as was seen at the Nagy reburial – and from reformist party leaders themselves. As for the latter, Lovászi noted that 'it is as if

92. Zsuzsa Láng, 'Szocialista eszméket hordozó radikális baloldal [A radical left wing bearing socialist ideas]', *Népszabadság*, 30 August 1989: 5.
93. This is based on interviews with reform circle members and the minutes of preparatory committee sessions, August–September 1989.
94. The proceedings of the conference were published in György Kerekes and Zsuzsa Varsádi (eds), *Reformkörök és reform-alapszervezetek budapesti tanácskozása* [Reform circles and reform cells Budapest conference] (Budapest: Kossuth, n.d. [1989]). See also Alfred Reisch, 'HSWP Reform Circles Call for a New, Radically Reformed Party To Be Set Up', *RFER* (4 October 1989): 3–8; and the coverage in *Magyar Nemzet*, 4 September 1989; less detailed coverage can also be found in *Magyar Hírlap* and *Népszabadság*, 4 September 1989.

they were conducting themselves with an aristocratic distance towards the 'lesser nobility' (*köznemesség*) reform circles'.[95] Reform, he concluded, will succeed only if reformers at the top and reform circles below can combine their efforts, linking the movement to the leadership.

Budapest reform circle delegate Miklós Szántó argued that given the fact that the current political model was unreformable, the reform circles must openly embrace the concept of the change of system rather than a change of model, accepting the fundamental transformation that this implies. A multiparty democracy is fast becoming a reality, he warned, but the party leadership still refused to believe it.[96] Conference chairman Attila Ágh noted the rising wave of panic among many party conservatives, and he cautioned against seeking party unity at all costs which would result in a compromise of principles.[97]

Following opening addresses, the delegates broke into ten plenary sessions to work on sections of the movement's platform. But as with the Szeged conference, the reform circles struggled to find common ground over several fundamental issues. Szántó's proposal that the conference unambiguously place itself behind the concept of the *rendszerváltás* - the change of system - was one breaking-point. While many at the conference backed the concept, they feared that the use of the term could provide ammunition to both party hardliners and opposition forces. Consequently they chose to utilize the more moderate reference of a change of model instead.

A second conflict broke out over how a transformation of the party structure would affect the idea of party continuity. That is, whether a new party under the reform circles' terms would be defined as a 'reformed' MSZMP (and therefore its legal successor) or an entirely new political organization. Some delegates even argued that the reform circle conference should above all be involved in building a new and separate organizational structure, which could be installed at the party congress were the reform circles to be victorious. If they were defeated, this same structure could serve as the foundation for their own separate

95. Kerekes and Varsádi, *Reformkörök és reformalapszervezetek budapesti tanácskozása*: 6.
96. Ibid.: 8-11.
97. 'Országos MSZMP-tanácskozás [National MSZMP conference]', *Magyar Hírlap*, 4 September 1989: 4.

party. In other words, with the de-institutionalization of the party as the central goal of the movement, some believed that the reform circles should prepare the organizational groundwork to either absorb the membership and physical remnants of the party, or leave it. This idea did not win over the majority of delegates. Indeed, even less controversial plans, such as a proposal for conference delegates to submit Central Committee members to a reform circle 'vote of confidence', met with resistance and had to be withdrawn.

The conflict generated by these issues was again symptomatic of the problems generated from the growing size and diversity of the reform circle movement. Some delegates specifically blamed much of the friction on opportunistic *apparatchik* delegates, whose increasing presence within the movement was viewed as hindering the formation of a common programme.[98] Other observers and conference participants, however, maintained that the real problem stemmed not from the intransigent views of a few opportunists, but rather from the fact that many reform circle members in general were still trapped by their inability to break away from their reliance on criticism of the existing order, and were therefore unable to use the conference to replace this harangue with a clear concept for a new socialist party.[99] Many within the movement, like those within the party in general, were still unable or unwilling to completely disassociate their socialist views from the institutions which claimed to embody them. Thus, while they supported the creation of a 'new' socialist party and its realization through radical action, destroying the MSZMP as they knew it or creating an organizational alternative to it remained hard to accept. The means versus ends of socialism were still easier to separate in theory than in practice.

These conflicts underscore the fact that, consistent with the structure of a movement, the reform circles possessed a radical core of individuals, numbering no more than fifty persons, who were instrumental in mobilizing other participants and formulating the fundamental arguments of the movement as a whole. These key individuals were

98. Ibid.

99. István Cseri, 'Reform-hétvége [Reform weekend]', *Ötlet*, 7 September 1989: 14–15; 'Miért lépett ki az MSZMP-ből a reformkör két tagja? [Why have two reform circle members left the MSZMP?]', *Hajdú-Bihari Napló*, 12 September 1989: 1; Mihály Nagy (Gazdagréti reform circle), 'Mit is talaltunk? [And what have we found?]', *Új fórum*, 22 September 1989: 7–8.

responsible for the creation of the first reform circles, and tended to think alike on most of the major issues that concerned them. However, outside this core among the movement ranks, for many individuals participation was more indirect, temporary, or, later on, opportunistic in nature, creating a weaker sense of commitment and contributing to fault lines within the membership when attempts were made to create a common political accord. The reform circles were united by their opposition to the status quo, but once confronted with the task of having to produce a concrete political alternative these differences within the movement became readily apparent.

Both days of the conference were capped off by speeches from Pozsgay and Nyers. Pozsgay took up the question of compromise between the party factions at the forthcoming congress, drawing a comparison with the historical debate between those who believed that the earth was flat and at the centre of the universe, rather than those who had experienced a 'Copernican turnabout' in their way of thinking. Both views had the right to exist, he concluded, but there was no way that the two could be reconciled within one body.[100] Nyers took a more cautious line, stressing the continuity of socialism in Hungary and the *reform* of the system, and the need to transform the MSZMP into a 'party of the people'. As the limits to political change kept expanding, moving from political reform to political transition, Nyers found himself caught between these two poles, a reformer of the old guard whose once radical views were being outstripped by the demands of younger party radicals.

One other important address was made by a new figure among the reform circles – Prime Minister Németh, who had heretofore not participated in the activities of the reform circles to any extent. Németh's appearance at the conference signalled a clear departure from his earlier position as the state instrument of Grósz. Indeed, in his address Németh himself admitted that until that time his true political orientation had been a mystery to many within the party. Németh's identification with the state institutions over which he presided had in recent months overshadowed his loyalty to Grósz or even to the party as whole. Now the prime minister attempted to place himself clearly within the reformist camp through the radical tenor of his speech, in which he lauded the

100. Kerekes and Varsádi, *Reformkörök és reformalapszervezetek budapesti tanácskozása*: 31–3.

reform circles for their important contribution to the changes taking place within the party and their creation of a programme for radical reform. The prime minister also stressed that the congress must bring about fundamental changes in the structure and leadership of the party, noting that many who had taken up the label of reform sought compromise more than change. Németh warned that should the party fail to overcome these obstacles and transform itself, it would result in unforeseeable consequences not only for Hungary but for the region as a whole. However, despite Németh's sudden support for the reform circles, he remained detached from the movement. This was made clear by his limited participation in the conference, as Németh came only to make his evening speech, something many delegates viewed as a purely opportunistic gesture.

On Sunday the conference concluded with the reports of the various sections (both majority and minority views), whose material was synthesized into what was called a 'statement of platform reconciliation' as opposed to a formal platform, so as to avoid a repeat of the conflict in Szeged. The statement was in large part a reflection of the earlier draft platform, opening with a critical analysis of Hungarian socialism, which was described as a 'dead-ended attempt at modernization'. The document included a broad outline of proposed reforms in every conceivable area, from property reform to import liberalization and foreign investment, cultural, health and environmental policy, as well as human rights and free elections.[101]

Furthermore, despite the various disagreements the conference managed to reach accord on a number of more specific demands. One such document was a resolution calling for the nationalization of MSZMP assets in response to recent revelations of the party's financial manipulations. A second statement called for the withdrawal of party cells from the workplace. This was undoubtedly prompted by a Central Committee decision one day before the reform circle conference, which had rejected a proposal by Pozsgay that the party withdraw from the workplace as part of a compromise with the opposition roundtable. Pozsgay's proposal was not only attacked by Grósz, but also by Nyers, who also supported the idea of retaining party cells in the workplace.

101. *Magyar Nemzet*, 13 September 1989: 5. The platform was also reprinted in Kerekes and Varsádi, *Reformkörök és reformalapszervezetek budapesti tanácskozása*: 61–77.

Both leaders criticized Pozsgay's unilateral offer on this matter to the opposition, arguing that he had no authorization to do so, and the Central Committee soon afterwards followed their lead.[102]

The conference delegates also approved a set of proposed party statutes, which, drawing from widespread calls for greater party democracy, included such mechanisms as the right of the membership to initiate congresses and recall party officials and the right of any party member to be directly elected into any post. These measures, which earlier in the year would have been seen as radical, in fact did not differ much from the proposed statutes which the central party apparatus had itself recently drafted with the help of reform circle representatives.[103] Reform circle delegates from the army submitted their own call for the disbandment of party cells in the military, while delegates from the Workers' Guard proposed that their forces be dissolved, replaced by a National Guard.

One last important outcome of the conference was the formal election of a permanent organizing committee to oversee the objectives and strategy of the reform circles up to the congress. The *ad hoc* preparatory committee, created earlier to organize the Budapest conference, was now recast as the National Coordinating Council (*Országos Koordinációs Tanács*, or OKT), with representatives delegated from the capital and every county, and also from the armed forces. Much of the OKT leadership was carried over from the preparatory committee, comprising some of the most active and best-known reform circle figures in the country.[104] The group was charged with the daunting task of building a central strategy to dominate the party congress – in less

102. For details, see Edith Oltay, 'Conservatives Show Residual Strength at CC Plenum', *RFER* (4 October 1989): 9–16; for Pozsgay's perspective, see *1989*: 158–61.
103. For the reform circle proposed statutes see 'A párt szervezeti felépítésének és működésének alapelvei [Basic statutes on the structure and function of the party]', *Kongresszus '89*, no. 4 (7 September 1989): 1–4. Compare this document with that produced by the Party Politics Committee of the Central Committee in late August: 'Javaslat a Magyar Szocialista Munkáspárt alapszabályára [Proposal for the Hungarian Socialist Workers' Party basic statutes]', *Kongresszus '89*, no. 3 (5 September 1989): 1–8.
104. The list of members can be found in Kerekes and Varsádi, *Reformkörök és reformalapszervezetek budapesti tanácskozása*: 86.

than one month. The immediate goal was to win as many congress mandates or win over as many delegates as possible, to build a reformist bloc that could carry out the transformation of the party for which they had so long agitated. This would prove to entail unexpected hazards of its own.

5. The Final Party Congress and the Reform Alliance: Victory or Defeat?

SETTING THE STAGE

September 1989 represented the peak of activity for opposition forces, the MSZMP and its reform circles. By mid-September, negotiations with the EKA finally concluded with an agreement over general constitutional amendments which would form the basis of a multiparty system. Unable to dictate the course of these negotiations and increasingly fragmented, the MSZMP had by now conceded on a number of issues, although such legislation was still incomplete and a source of conflict. Most notable was the provision to hold early direct elections for the office of president. Fearing that this would give the popular Pozsgay an easy opportunity to jump from the party into the state apparatus before open parliamentary elections, both FIDESZ and the SZDSZ refused to sign the final accord.[1]

Within the MSZMP itself, in preparation for the forthcoming congress and 1990 parliamentary elections, the MSZMP was busy drafting a new set of documents which would realign the party more with common sentiment and the demands for reform. The party's programme manifesto spoke, among other things, of an independent Hungary, enjoying open and direct elections within a multiparty system, the clear division of power, and a mixed market economy established by a new MSZMP based on both Marxist and modern socialist ideology.[2]

1. For details see Edith Oltay, 'HSWP and Six Opposition Groups Agree on First Steps Toward Multiparty Elections', *RFER* (4 October 1989): 37–40, and O'Neil, 'Hungary: Political Transition and Executive Conflict'. The text of the roundtable agreement can be found in Tőkés, *Hungary's Negotiated Revolution*, Appendix 7.1.
2. The first draft of the MSZMP programme declaration was published as a

Clearly the party had come a long way in the last twelve months, a slow, almost imperceptible erosion of party power and resolve, resulting in what were hoped to be open elections by the following spring. However, these claims of rejuvenation and reform on the part of the MSZMP remained nothing more than a set of documents, with no actual changes in party politics having yet taken place. It was evident that conservatives in the party, such as Grósz, remained adamantly opposed to any political change that would jeopardize the party's political monopoly. Others favoured a policy of pseudo-reform which would endow the political system with the façade of pluralist institutions while the MSZMP continued to dominate elections by means of the various state and para-statal institutions it controlled.

As for the reform circle movement, sights were now set on gearing up for the expected battle at the forthcoming party congress. This involved producing manifestos and proposals for party reform, gaining support from the uncommitted party ranks and isolating conservatives, and coordinating reform circle efforts with party reformists in positions of leadership.[3] The congress was seen as the culmination of all of their previous efforts and the years of quiet dissent within the party. Thus, for most of these participants the congress was cast in stark, zero-sum terms: either the reform circles would score a dramatic victory, expelling conservatives from the party and radically transforming its structure, or the opponents of change within the MSZMP would succeed in blocking their demands, leading to the expulsion of the reform movement and perhaps even triggering off a counter-reform that would bring political change to a halt.

supplement to *Népszabadság*, 19 August 1989; the revised version can be found in *Kongresszus '89*, no. 11 (30 September 1989): 1–8.

3. For the activities and statements of the OKT in particular during this period see 'Baloldali szocialista pártot, demokratikus Magyarországot – az MSZMP reformköreinek sajtótájékoztatója [For a left wing socialist party and a democratic Hungary – the press conference of the MSZMP reform circles]', *Népszabadság*, 8 September 1989; 'A platformok a nyilvánosság előtt méressenek meg [The platforms should be considered before the public]', *Népszabadság*, 11 September 1989: 4; and 'Név szerint szavazzanak a küldöttek! [Delegates should vote by name!]', *Népszabadság*, 18 September 1989: 4. See also the shortened platform statement of the OKT, 'A párt radikális megújulása: reformplatform az MSZMP októberi kongresszusára [The radical renewal of the party: reform platform for the MSZMP October congress]', *Magyar Nemzet*, 13 September 1989: 5.

While in retrospect these fears may seem exaggerated, we must place Hungarian developments at that time in context.[4] June had witnessed the violent crackdown against political opposition in China. Dramatic political change had so far taken place only in Poland, while in Czechoslovakia, East Germany and Romania conservative retrenchment was at its height, with much of the hostility directed at Hungary for its 'anti-socialist' reform course. This was underscored by the flood of refugees from other socialist states who fled to Hungary to escape repression at home. This peaked with the dismantling of the barbed-wire fence between Austria and Hungary; by the autumn, more than 100,000 'tourists' from East Germany had poured into the country, seeking to use their open border as an escape route to the West.

Faced with the choice of forcibly repatriating the East Germans (as demanded by their government) or breaking their treaty obligations with East Germany and letting their citizens pass through the border to the West, the Hungarian government – in particular Foreign Minister Horn – chose the latter option.[5] This only increased hostility between Hungary and the 'little entente', as Hungarians referred to their conservative socialist neighbours, and raised fears in Hungary of an eventual conflict or the possible external participation in a *putsch* by hardliners.[6] According to one report, during this time General Secretary Grósz even contacted the Soviet leadership, asking for possible military support should events in Hungary get out of hand. The Soviets refused.[7] Another scenario saw the complete disintegration of the MSZMP, due to its internal conflicts, leading to a dangerous power vacuum that could destabilize the nation.[8]

4. This point is made most clearly by László Vass, 'A Magyar Szocialista Párt', in Bihari, *A többpártrendszer kialakulása Magyarországon*: 147–8.
5. For a personal account of these events see Gyula Horn, *Cölöpök* [Pillars] (Budapest: Zenit, 1991): 236–55.
6. Frigyes Varjú, 'A had állapota [The state of the army]', *Ötlet* (28 September 1989): 12–13.
7. Pravda, 'Soviet Policy Towards Eastern Europe in Transition': 26.
8. See, for example, the discussion of this point as raised by Lengyel in September 1989: *Micsoda Év!*: 28.

THE ELECTION OF CONGRESS DELEGATES

Despite the fears of such repercussions, fanned to a large extent by party conservatives, the reform circles continued to struggle to gain control over the forthcoming party congress. Most pressing in this regard was the continuing delegate selection process. Local and national reform circle activity had been focused on this process for some time, and while the reform circles' demands to codify delegate election procedure (such as election by platform) had been unsuccessful, they countered with various forms of propaganda as well as an attempt to field as many candidates as possible in the various electoral forums. Given the lack of central directives on how they were to be chosen, delegate selection for the congress varied widely from county to county, from district to district, and even from party committee to party committee in some of the larger institutions.[9]

This unprecedented diversity in electoral mechanisms stemmed from the decision by many local party leaders to jettison the standard form of delegate selection, by means of a county party conference. The reform circles had strongly opposed the use of these easily manipulated forums, and no doubt their strident criticism contributed to local party bosses agreeing to democratize the delegate selection process. However, the decision not to hold conferences may have also been prompted by fears among the party leaders themselves that such convocations, as technically the most powerful regional political body, would provide local reform circles with a chance to oust the party leadership as well – as had been the case in Zala.

This is supported by the fact that those party conferences which were actually held tended to be in regions where conservative party committees remained powerful and well entrenched. This was the case, for example, in Nográd county, where General Secretary Grósz himself, alongside county party First Secretary László Szalai and his predecessor Miklós Devcsics were unilaterally made congress delegates by

9. For details, see Judith Pataki, 'Elections of Delegates for the HSWP Congress Not Easy', *RFER* (10 November 1989): 3–7. The author found that more than a dozen different methods of selecting delegates were employed in Budapest alone, ranging from district and regional party conferences (the most common method), to delegates chosen by closed or widened sessions of party committees, open party elections, platform competition, even elections by mail.

the county party leadership.[10] The local reform circle attacked this back-door decision, demanding that these delegates be confirmed at the local party conference where the remainder of delegates were to be chosen. Although they succeeded in this demand, at the conference Grósz, lauded by the delegates, was easily confirmed by the overwhelming majority of candidates, as was the first secretary (although Devcsics was not). In contrast, the reform circle's own candidate was barred from the conference.[11] Similarly, at the Borsod county conference a reform circle proposal for the reorganization of the party structure on the basis of the Zala system received only 37 votes out of 410 cast, and a more conservative variant was accepted in its stead.[12]

In most counties the process of delegate selection by county conference was replaced by a dispersal of allotted delegate seats on the basis of electoral districts, thus creating smaller forums or conferences in which the candidates were chosen. In some districts delegates were even selected by means of open balloting, in which all district members could vote.[13] These alternative methods gave reform circle candidates a greater opportunity to mobilize support among smaller groups of party members, helping to avoid their being outflanked by the party apparatus. Consequently, in many of these smaller districts reform circle candidates did well, able to draw on their local reputation for support. In some larger electoral forums there were also victories. In Szeged, reform circle-backed delegates won 15 out of 25 seats allotted to the city.[14]

10. As indicated by the case of Grósz, although party delegate shares were divided proportionally by county, candidates could run in any region.
11. For details surrounding the Nógrád delegate selection process, see 'A reform közösség tiltakozik [The reform community protests]', *Nógrád*, 2 September 1989: 2; 'Új küldöttség lesz Nógrádban [New delegation in Nógrád]', *Népszabadság*, 16 September 1989: 5; 'Tanácskozott a megyei pártértekezlet [The county party conference has convened]', *Nógrád*, 25 September 1989: 1–5.
12. For the reform circle proposal, see 'Levél a pártértekezlet küldötthöz [letter to the party conference delegates]', *Észak-Magyarország*, 18 September 1989: 5; 'Ügyvezetők a megyei pártbizottság élén [Directors to head party committee]', *Déli Hírlap*, 25 September 1989: 1.
13. As was the case in the city of Pécs. For details, see '61 jelölt küzd 19 mandátumért [Sixty-one candidates struggle for 19 seats]', *Népszabadság*, 14 August 1989: 4.
14. For the reform circle delegate list, see 'Levél a szegedi MSZMP-tagokhoz [Letter to the Szeged MSZMP members]', unpublished document, dated 18 July 1989.

However, elsewhere reform circles complained that they still had to struggle against delegate manipulation by local party leaders, who maintained 'delegate nominating committees' to filter out unwanted candidates and even select some delegates themselves.[15] For example, whereas in Nográd the back-door election of Grósz by party leaders was wholeheartedly affirmed by the party conference, the nomination of Pozsgay for a delegate seat in Debrecen by the local reform circle outraged conservative party members, who prevented his election. When the reform circle charged that the voting process had been manipulated by the party committee in charge of elections, the local leadership countered that Pozsgay's defeat resulted from opposition to having a candidate from outside the area thrust upon the membership (Pozsgay was eventually elected as a delegate from Kecskemét instead).[16]

In Budapest, where delegate selection had been widely dispersed among various districts and institutions, reform circles similarly protested that party leaders were in many cases preventing the democratic selection of delegates through such tactics as the use of prepared lists of nominees in order to ensure that their own candidates would win.[17] This tension culminated in a bitter conflict between reform circle members and representatives of the party apparatus at the Budapest party conference in late September. Although reform circle proposals were largely defeated and many of their nominees for congress routed, some argued that the almost comic tactics of apparatus conservatives against them only supported the argument that radical change in the party structure was critical. Others were not so confident, worrying that what had occurred was in effect a dress-rehearsal for the forthcoming congress.[18]

15. Attila Ágh, 'Kongresszusi aggodalmak [Congress anxieties]', *Népszabadság*, 18 September 1989: 9.
16. For details, see 'Harmincnégy név a kongresszusi küldöttjelöltek listáján [Thirty-four names on the congress delegate list]', *Hajdú-Bihari Napló*, 28 August 1989: 1, 3; Péter Sajó, 'Jön a bal? [Is the left coming?]', *Világ* (14 September 1989): 22–3; Ágnes Szépesi, 'Debreceni fiaskó [Debrecen fiasco]', *Ötlet* (28 September 1989): 2–3.
17. 'Reformkörök levele az MSZMP Elnökségéhez [Reform circle letter to the MSZMP Presidium], *Népszabadság*, 22 July 1989: 5; 'Milyenek a fővárosi küldöttválasztás tapasztalatai? [What are the experiences of delegate election in the capital?]', *Népszabadság*, 27 July 1989: 5.
18. For details on the conference, see Katalin Kékesi, Károly Rimoczi and Éva

But the biggest obstacle to the reform circles in these delegate battles was their minority status within the party. Despite the fact that the membership of the movement could be counted in the thousands, with more than a hundred reform circles functioning nationwide, such a figure was minor within a party of more than 700,000 members. The movement simply could not field enough candidates to dominate delegate election proceedings. Moreover, the bulk of the party ranks, the MSZMP white-collar 'middle class', remained uncertain over events unfolding within the MSZMP. This cut both ways. Just as the reform circles were unable to dominate delegate elections, nor was the party apparatus capable of exacting the kind of membership compliance it had once enjoyed. The party had for decades relied on a hierarchical system of political control, filtering out undesired members through the numerous levels of the apparatus. Now, with electoral decision-making devolved to the margins of the party, congress power was to a great extent in the hands of an unpredictable membership. Despite their best efforts, neither the apparatus nor party radicals could decisively command the election of the bulk of elected candidates.

WINNING OVER THE UNCOMMITTED

When the delegate selection process for the party congress finally came to an end in late September, prospects were no more certain than before. In one area, that of the delegates' demographics, there was reason for hope. More than 80 per cent of delegates were under fifty, possessed some form of higher education, and were classified as either white-collar or intelligentsia. Nearly 90 per cent had never taken part in a party congress before.[19] In this aspect, at least, they clearly resembled the reform circle cohort.

But how many would commit themselves to the reform circles' general platform was less clear. By one estimate, more than 40 per cent of the same delegates came from the ranks of the *nomenklatura* and party

Terényi, 'Meg kell nyerni a társadalom többségének bizalmát [We must win the confidence of the majority of society]', *Népszabadság*, 25 September 1989: 4; for the perspective of one reform circle participant, see Attila Ágh, 'A pártosodás éve: válságok és szervezetek [The year of party formation: crises and organizations]', in Kurtán, Sándor and Vass, *Magyarország Politikai Évkönyve 1990*: 16.

19. See *Kongresszus '89*, no. 23 (6 October 1989): 1.

apparatus, particularly those delegated from Budapest.[20] The OKT's own estimation concluded that the number of those sympathetic to the reform circle platform made up less than a quarter of the more than 1200 delegates, and within that group only about 100 were actually reform circle participants.[21] Organizers hoped that this base of delegate support could be widened before the congress, although the OKT and outside observers acknowledged that in many cases they had damaged their own cause, in that their militancy both hurt their own candidates and widened the gulf between delegates sympathetic to reform and the reform circles themselves.[22]

As the reform circles were looking to broaden their base of support, conservatives within the party were also attempting to sway delegates in their direction. To put it more accurately, conservatives sought to paralyse the delegates, thus reducing the chances for radical reform. Most influential in this effort was PIB member and Grósz supporter György Fejti, who attended a large number of regional delegate meetings with the obvious intention of frightening the participants. Fejti continuously spoke of the threat of 'destabilization' should the MSZMP split apart and lose its commanding position in society, and warned that the 'extremist' reform circles, as 'political prima donnas' were not far removed from those who demanded *leszámolás*, getting even or revenge.[23] These tactics were to a large extent effective in sowing confusion as to the appropriate objectives of the party congress.[24]

20. László Bihari, 'A múltat végleg eltörölni [To finally break with the past]', *Kapu* (October 1989): 4–5.
21. This information was provided in the invitations for the first meeting of the Reform Bloc, unpublished document, dated 25 September 1989, supplement 2.
22. Minutes of the 23 September 1989 reform circle national coordinating council (OKT) meeting, unpublished document, dated 27 September 1989: 2; see also Andor Kloss, 'A jövő a tét, nem a múlt [The future is the stake, not the past]', *Kisalföld*, 12 September 1989: 3.
23. See, for example, excerpts of addresses by Fejti in 'Az ország érdeke a megegyezés [Compromise is in the interests of the nation]', *Déli Hírlap*, 7 September 1989: 1; 'Az MSZMP-nek képessé kell válnia a válság kezelésére [The MSZMP must become capable of handling the crisis]', *Népszabadság*, 25 September 1989: 5; 'A pártszakadást nem szabad kiprovokálni [We are not free to provoke a party split]', *Népszabadság*, 28 September 1989: 1, 5; 'Küldött-találkozó Tatabányán [Delegate meeting in Tatabánya]', *Népszabadság*, 3 October 1989: 5; also his comments in Székesfehérvár, *Népszabadság*, 13 September 1989: 5.
24. This was also to some extent aided by local members of the opposition, who warned delegates against too radical a step at the party congress so as not to

Yet it remained evident to congress delegates that the party required some form of major renovation to stem its continuing political decline. The status quo could not be maintained – power was slipping out of the hands of the party. The June by-elections had been clear evidence of that, and, if more proof were needed, in late September another set of parliamentary by-elections took place as a result of an MDF-initiated recall. Unlike most of the earlier by-elections, however, where weak or divided local party organizations put up a half-hearted struggle against the opposition, this time the by-election was held in Zalaegerszeg, where the reform circles had overthrown the previous party leadership and instituted the radical organizational reforms known as the Zala model.

Local party organization and reform circles united in support of MSZMP parliamentary candidate István Győrffy, the well-known young editor of the county daily, whose own campaign resembled that of the opposition in its attacks on the existing political order. A final contrast to the previous by-elections was that popular central reformers, such as Pozsgay and Horn, publicly campaigned on Győrffy's behalf. Despite all of this support, and the fact that the MSZMP spent more than six times the amount of money as the opposition on the campaign, Győrffy still lost to the MDF candidate, who received 59 per cent of the vote. This defeat shed serious doubt on the ability of party reformers to recast the MSZMP as a politically viable party. However, reformers tried to use this electoral rout to their advantage, portraying it as an ominous sign of the party's fortunes should they not carry out a radical transformation of the MSZMP at the forthcoming congress.[25]

EXPANDING THE BASE OF SUPPORT: THE REFORM ALLIANCE

With the completion of delegate selection, the reform circles had less than two weeks to build majority support among the bulk of vacillating and uncommitted congress delegates. At the local level, reform circle

provoke a conservative backlash that would endanger their continuing negotiations.

25. For details, see the coverage in *Zalai Hírlap*, 18–29 September 1989; Simon, 'A nem-választók szabadsága', 202–3, and Judith Pataki, 'HSWP Loses Fourth Parliamentary Seat to the Opposition', *RFER* (4 October 1989): 27–30.

members continued to agitate for delegate support. At the national level, in late September the OKT finally created a formal platform to collect congress delegates – a 'reform bloc' which stressed its aim to unify both reform circle and reform-committed delegates.[26] This platform was established on 1 October as the *Reformszövetség*, or Reform Alliance.[27] The Reform Alliance's head, Ferenc Kósa, was not a reform circle member, but rather a prominent film maker with close ties to Pozsgay. The choice to place Kósa at the head of the Reform Alliance indicates the extent to which the reform circles wished to broaden their base – both to leaders above and delegates below – by downplaying their own role within this new platform (although the OKT acted as its organizational centre).

Simultaneously the OKT began to conduct meetings with the reformist party leadership, discussing their congress objectives and attempting to elicit support from Pozsgay, Horn, Németh, Nyers and Szűrös, the five party leaders considered most desirable for the new party leadership. The current MSZMP proposal for the congress was to retain the existing structure of party president and a collective executive, with its leadership unchanged (Nyers, Grósz, Németh and Pozsgay) and a smaller executive committee below it, much like the PIB.

A main reform circle objective was to make certain that conservatives, including Grósz, were excluded from these leadership bodies. This they hoped to achieve early at the congress by proposing that Central Committee members not directly elected as delegates be stripped of their voting rights. The second step would then be to initiate the election of the party leadership as early as possible in the congress, instead of the current programme, under which it would not occur until the third or fourth day.[28]

26. Open invitation to congress delegates by the Reform Bloc, unpublished document, dated 26 September 1989.
27. 'Reformszövetség alakult [The Reform Alliance has been established]', *Népszabadság*, 2 October 1989.
28. For the drafts concerning the new party leadership structure and proposed membership, as well as the timetable of the congress see *Kongresszus '89*, no. 20 (5 October 1989): 5–8; the OKT's reaction is detailed in 'Az MSZMP Reformkörök és Reformalapszervezetek Országos Koordinációs Tanácsának tárgyalási álláspontja a kongresszusi napirend és ügyrend tervezetéhez [The reform circle and reform cell national coordinating committee protocol statement on the draft timetable and order of the congress]', unpublished document, n.d.

In addition, the OKT wanted the new leadership elected by means of closed electoral lists. Under this proposal, each platform would submit a specific ranked list of candidates. Representation in the new executive leadership would be based on the total percentage of votes given to that list, or in a more radical variant the list with the most votes would win outright.[29] A closed list would allow for the creation of a unified group of reform leaders and Reform Alliance candidates, preventing the compromise behind the scenes. Ideally, the Reform Alliance hoped that if they could force the early election of the leadership or approval of new party statutes, that would lead to a clear victory for their side, dealing such a blow to party conservatives that they would walk out or be ejected from the congress, leaving reformers in control.[30]

The ability of the Reform Alliance platform to mobilize the majority of delegates in favour of this reform leadership would be contingent on the support of Nyers. Relations between Nyers and the reform circles had always been somewhat ambiguous, made more so by his opposition (alongside Grósz) to removing party cells in the workplace. However, precisely because of his centrism Nyers commanded broad party support, the greatest of any single figure in the party. As the minutes of the 28 September OKT meeting noted, 'Resző Nyers is the voice of moderation; a good deal depends on him, whether there will be a party split, or whether the majority will stand behind a credible reform leadership'.[31] His integration into the Reform Alliance platform could spell the difference between victory and defeat.

This led to a second issue, one which the movement had not yet dared to address. What if in fact the congress precipitated a rout of the reformers, or claimed a 'pseudo-victory' based on compromise and a veneer of change as had occurred so far? What should the reform circle movement do in response? This question had, in one form or another, been plaguing the movement since its inception. At Kecskemét the reform circles expected Pozsgay to 'unfurl the flag', creating a new political movement or splitting the party itself. No such thing occurred.

29. For details, see 'Testület választása zárt listás módszerei [Election to bodies by means of closed lists]', *Kongresszus '89* (20 September 1989): 2–4.
30. 'Tájékoztató az MSZMP KB személyi kérdéseket előkészítő bizottsága 1989. szeptember 14-ei üléseiről [Information on the MSZMP Central Committee personnel preparatory committee 14 September 1989 session]', OKT publication, n.d.; see also the minutes of the 23 September 1989 OKT session: 2.
31. Minutes of the 23 September 1989 OKT session: 2.

The same issue resurfaced at the Szeged and Budapest reform circle conferences, and was never resolved. Now the movement was seeking to achieve its demands not through manifestos and piecemeal action, but by forcing the sudden transformation of the party itself. And if this should fail?

Several prominent reform circle figures argued that this question should no longer be pushed aside. The strong presence of the party apparatus within the congress delegates raised fears that they would be able to block the transformation of the MSZMP; some reform circle leaders were publicly warning that such an outcome could lead to the total withdrawal of reformers from the MSZMP and their foundation of an alternative party.[32]

The OKT had in fact taken up the question as part of its discussion with party reform leaders, hoping to reach consensus on 'breaking-points' at which they should no longer commit to remaining within the party.[33] Pozsgay's Movement for a Democratic Hungary presented one option to regroup in case of a defeat, but since the creation of the collective presidency within the MSZMP, Pozsgay had let the Movement atrophy, and there were worries about seeking refuge in an organization created for the personal ambitions of one man. Others argued that to prepare for the eventuality of defeat, the OKT should prepare a set of contingency plans: a party platform, leadership, name, organizational framework and other necessary aspects, so that in case of defeat the reform circles could found a new party immediately following the congress.[34]

While there appears to have been a general consensus on the need for such contingency measures, they were not followed through. The reform circles, built upon the MSZMP and defined by their institutional relationship to it, were still unable to conceive of themselves as an autonomous political organization. Moreover, they feared the repercussions of such a step, leaving the party-state in the hands of conservatives before a multiparty system had been institutionalized, or

32. Attila Ágh, 'Forgatókönyvek [Scripts]', *Ötlet*, 28 September 1989: 9.
33. Minutes of the September 16, 1989 OKT session: 1.
34. Balázs Mészáros, 'Hogyan győzhetünk vereség esetén [How can we win in case of defeat]', unpublished document, dated 13 September 1989; see also idem, 'A látszatgyőzelem veszélye [The danger of a pseudo-victory]', interview by Ferenc Biró, *Somogyi Néplap*, 9 September 1989: 6.

perhaps worse, touching off the complete disintegration of the MSZMP.[35]

THE PARTY CONGRESS BEGINS; THE REFORM ALLIANCE ADVANCES

The party congress opened on Friday, 6 October.[36] Notable was the way in which the event itself had been designated, not as the fourteenth congress of the MSZMP, but simply 'Congress '89'. Also missing were guests from fraternal socialist countries whose presence was customary. All this contributed to the overwhelming sense that the congress would be a landmark event for the party, from which there would be no turning back. As delegates flooded into the capital, the various congress platforms were already beginning to build their ranks and plan strategy.

35. On this point, see László Rekvényi, 'Érvek a szakadás mellett és ellen [Arguments for and against a party split]', interview by Katalin Kékesi, *Népszabadság*, 5 October 1989: 4, and Jenő S. Horváth, 'A pártszakadás és a pártegység [Party unity and party split]', *Új fórum*, 22 September 1989: 13–15.

36. The following discussion of the MSZMP party congress is based on both written documents and a number of interviews with congress participants. The best documentation of the congress is found in the dailies *Népszabadság*, *Magyar Hírlap* and *Magyar Nemzet*, 6–10 October 1989, and in Emil Kimmel (ed.), *Kongresszus '89: rövidett, szerkesztett jegyzőkönyv az 1989 október 6–9 között tartott kongresszus anyagából* [Congress '89: abbreviated, edited transcripts of the material of the 6–9 October 1989 congress] (Budapest: Kossuth, 1990); the best coverage in English can be found in *RFER* (10 November 1989): 3–43.

Personal analyses of the process and outcome of the congress include Judit Benkő, György Kerekes and János Patkós, *A születés szépséges kínjai, avagy a rendhagyó híradás az MSZMP kongresszusról 1989 Október 6–9* [The beautiful agony of birth, or irregular information concerning the 6–9 October 1989 MSZMP congress] (Budapest: Kossuth, n.d.); László Kéri and Mária Zita Petschnig, 'Ez a név lesz a végső [This name will be your last]' parts I–II, *Első kézből* (9, 16 December 1989): 3–7, 7–10; Attila Ágh, 'Öt fontos nap: közérdekű magánvélemény az MSZP alakuló kongresszusáról [Five crucial days: personal recollections for the public interest on the formation of the MSZP]', unpublished paper, n.d. [October 1989]; 'Az állampárt végórái [The final hours of the party-state]', in Bihari, *Demokratikus út a szabadsághoz*: 98–117; Lajos Gubcsi, *4 nap, amely megrengette az országot* [Four days that shook the nation] (Eger: Agria, 1989), and Tőkés, *Hungary's Negotiated Revolution*, 351–6.

The real reckoning was in the first counting of delegates by platform, prior to the opening of the congress on 5 October (see Table 5.1).

Table 5.1 Congress delegates according to platform registration

Platform name	5 October 10:00 p.m.	6 October 10:00 p.m.	7 October 10:00 a.m.	7 October 10:00 p.m.	8 October 3:00 p.m.	8 October 11:30 p.m.
Reform Alliance	464	479	491	469	521	496
Peoples' Democratic	68	105	111	214	289	255
Solidarity	30	36	24	20	*dissolved*	
Platform for MSZMP	35	33	33	27	24	31
Equality of Countryside	43	46	45	56	62	60
Youth Platform	26	26	30	29	32	31
Agricultural Platform	28	27	38	51	101	63
Workers' Delegate	–	39	39	39	52	58
Platform for a Healthy Hungary	–	43	43	33	38	32

Source: Judit Benkő, György Kerekes and János Patkós, *A születés szépséges kínjai, avagy a rendhagyó híradás az MSZMP kongresszusról 1989 Október 6–9* [The beautiful agony of birth, or irregular information concerning the 6–9 October 1989 MSZMP congress] (Budapest: Kossuth, n.d.): 20.

As suspected, extreme hardline party factions had not been successful in sending enough delegates to the party congress to form party platforms. However, Berecz's Solidarity for the Renewal of the MSZMP did appear, with some thirty delegates, as well as the Peoples' Democratic Platform.[37] Unanticipated platforms included the conservative Platform for the MSZMP (*Platform az MSZMP-ért*), and interest-group

37. For the comparative positions of the Peoples' Democratic Platform, Solidarity for the Renewal of the MSZMP, Platform of the MSZMP and the Reform Alliance with regard to the tasks of the congress, see the statements of the platform leaders in *Népszabadság*, 6 October 1989: 16.

platforms such as the Platform for the Equality of the Countryside (*Platform a Vidék Esélyegyenlőségéért*), the Youth Platform (*Ifjúságért Platform*) and the Agricultural and Food Producer Platform (*Agrár- és Élelmiszergazdasági Platform*). On the second day, two other platforms, the Workers' Delegate Group (*Munkás Küldöttcsoport*) and the Platform for a Healthy Hungary (*Egészséges Magyarországért Platform*) sprang up as well.

Yet to everyone's surprise, none of these platforms compared in size with that of the Reform Alliance. Not only had that platform been able to gather the reform leadership within its ranks (Pozsgay, Németh, Horn and Szűrös, although Nyers remained unaffiliated), but hundreds more had also flocked to their ranks, making the Alliance dwarf the others. The Reform Alliance still did not command an absolute majority, but they held the largest voting bloc by far at the congress. But despite this encouraging news, it remained unclear how many of these delegates were actually committed to radically transforming the party, rather than merely joining what they presumed to be the winning side.

With this kind of electoral weight, the Reform Alliance sought to score some crucial early victories. The first topics of debate, the order and statutes of the congress, were crucial to how the rest of the congress would unfold (several versions of statutes and programme order had been produced by the party in advance, but the final decision had been left to the delegates). As both conservatives and reformers alike were well aware, the sequencing and structure of the congress could easily be arranged in such a way as to advantage one side or another – as had always been the case with party congresses, and all too evident at the Budapest party conference just two weeks before.[38] The first battle lines formed around this issue on the Friday morning, and went on for half a day. Delegates fought over who would have voting rights at the congress, how decisions would be debated and enacted, and how the new party leadership would be nominated and elected into office.

Initially the Reform Alliance was successful in having its proposals

38. Gubcsi, *4 nap, amely megrengette az országot*: 69; Benkő, Kerekes and Patkós, *A születés szépséges kínjai*: 12–13.

accepted. Members of the Central Committee who had not been elected as congress delegates (some two-thirds in all) were from the outset denied voting rights, stripping them of their traditional privilege in this regard. As to how points of debate would be scheduled, the Reform Alliance's proposal that the party's new name and programme be decided early on was also approved, over charges by conservative delegates that this amounted to an intentional provocation to create a party split.[39] The Reform Alliance would soon come to regret this move as well. In one major setback for the Reform Alliance, the proposal for the early election of the party leader and collective presidency (which had been counted on to secure control of the congress) was not accepted.

The biggest achievement of the Reform Alliance, however, was how the party leadership would be elected. Over the strong objections of conservatives and some non-platform affiliated delegates, delegates approved the election of the presidium by means of winner-take-all, closed lists of nominees - although the election of the party president himself would be based on individual nominations.[40] This represented a significant accomplishment for the Reform Alliance, which held the greatest number of delegates and was thus in the best position to win. A victory would give them control over the entire presidium, and exclude conservatives in the process. Many candidates argued against the proposal as undemocratic, preventing independent delegates from having a say in the formation of nomination lists and effectively blocking any compromise. Yet this is precisely what the Reform Alliance and many others wanted, in the hope that this formula would deliver a total victory to one side within the party, facilitating the expulsion of the losing faction and the reintegration of the currently-divided party leadership.[41]

39. Kimmel, *Végjáték a fehér házban*: 161.

40. The lists could be submitted by any formally registered delegate group, the president, or the congress's nominating committee, and the list with more than 50 per cent of votes would win. In the case that no one list would win that number of votes, a run-off between the two lists with the highest number of votes would follow: *Kongresszus '89*, no. 23 (morning, 6 October 1989): 6–7.

41. Benkő, Kerekes and Patkós, *A születés szépséges kínjai*: 38–41. Approximately 250 delegates voted against election by means of closed lists: Gubcsi, *4 nap, amely megrengette az országot*: 115.

SHOULD THE PARTY BE SAVED?

With these procedural issues behind them the delegates then faced the question of the new party programme – whether the congress should reform, transform or dissolve the MSZMP. This question was wrapped up as much in self-perception as in legal technicality, involving questions of party continuity and ideological perspective. Nyers opened the session with a strong call for the party to break free of its Stalinist structural aspects, although he hedged on how far this break should go: 'The Hungarian Socialist Workers' Party's historical role has come to an end. Now the Hungarian socialist movement requires a new type of political party which is a successor, but not simply a continuation of the MSZMP'.[42]

Pozsgay took a similar stand, speaking of the MSZMP's past as that of a party-state, something which could be left behind only if the party recast its organization and ideology, following West European left-wing parties. With this act should come a new name: the Hungarian Socialist Party.[43] These views were seconded by the Reform Alliance and the Youth Platform.

On the opposite side Grósz maintained his earlier views, supporting a renewed MSZMP while warning against any changes that would exclude conservatives from the party. Grósz's views were strongly supported by the Solidarity platform, which raised the fear that the membership would turn away from a new party. The Platform for the MSZMP similarly argued that the congress had no right to split up or dissolve the party.[44] Between the conservatives and party reformers, the Peoples' Democratic Platform took a more ambiguous stance. Its spokesman, the historian Tamás Krausz, attacked the MSZMP as 'the élite party of the cadres and careerists' but at the same time noted that a split within the party was being incited by both 'liberal extremists' – that is, reform circle members – and conservatives in the party. Krausz opposed the victory of either group, calling for the formation of a true party of the peoples that would lay the foundation for a political and economic 'third road' based on the experiences neither of the East nor

42. Kimmel, *Kongresszus '89*: 13.
43. Ibid.: 28–33.
44. For Grósz's comments, see ibid.: 15–23, and for the statements of the various platforms: 42–55.

of the West.[45] This debate continued on into the night, as a long succession of delegates rose to defend or condemn the party status quo. All seemed convinced of the need for a change in the party, but in what manner – and at whose expense – depended on the delegate.

When the congress broke for the evening, Reform Alliance delegates met to discuss the day's events. Despite their early victories a number of delegates were convinced that the difference between platforms could not be reconciled. A real transformation of the party would not be possible, and therefore some began to argue that the Reform Alliance should use their newfound support to pull out of the congress entirely and found their own party. Those who supported this move remained in the minority, and they lacked the crucial backing of Pozsgay, who indicated that he would not participate.

One thing this stormy meeting did achieve was to alarm a number of other delegates – such as representatives from the Peoples' Democratic Platform, who had been invited to the Reform Alliance meeting to discuss an agreement on the contours of a new party. By the following day, rumours abounded that the Alliance was preparing to appropriate the congress as their own and exclude the other delegates. Tension rose palpably at the congress.[46]

THE FORGING OF A COMPROMISE

On the Saturday the delegates returned to the question of the party programme, and the heated debate over the fate of the MSZMP continued. The congress continued to be dominated by a general sense of tension, made worse by rumours of a possible coup attempt by conservatives with the military or the Workers' Guard.[47] Under such circumstances many delegates conceded that compromise would be necessary to prevent chaos. Already the real decision-making had shifted elsewhere, out of the congress hall and into closed-door negotiations.

45. Ibid.: 46–8.
46. Ágh, 'Öt fontos nap': 9–10; see also the short interviews with platform spokesmen in 'Kongresszusi napló [Congress diary]', *Első kézből*, 14 October 1989: 4–5; and Kimmel, *Végjáték a fehér házban*: 162.
47. See, for example, the interview with Imre Pozsgay conducted during the second day of the congress. 'Új párt az MSZMP romjain [A new party on the ruins of the MSZMP]', interview by Ákos Mester, *168 Óra* (10 October 1989): 6.

During the course of the day, negotiators from the Peoples' Democratic Platform, the Youth Platform and the Reform Alliance met privately to work out a so-called 'minimum programme', a basic set of principles for the new party which their platform members had agreed to support – albeit reluctantly for many delegates. Animosity and the wide difference of views between members of the Peoples' Democratic Platform and the Reform Alliance in particular made for fragile negotiations.[48] This was complicated by a parallel development, the sudden surge in the size and power of the Peoples' Democratic Platform. With the growing role of closed-door negotiations by platform representatives, non-affiliated delegates found themselves effectively excluded. A platform was a means for collective action, and those without such affiliation lacked power. In addition, centrist and conservative delegates – members of the Budapest party apparatus in particular – grew increasingly frightened by the overwhelming size of the Reform Alliance and the rumours that they would 'hijack' the congress or force a complete dissolution of the party.

Consequently, many of these delegates (as well as some already affiliated with the two smaller conservative platforms or even the Reform Alliance) rushed to join the Peoples' Democratic Platform, whose left-wing, third road ideology seemed an acceptable counterweight to the radical demands of reformist delegates.[49] This slowly transformed the Peoples' Democratic Platform into a large, heterogeneous faction united primarily by its opposition to the Reform Alliance.[50] During the course of 7 October the Peoples' Democratic Platform nearly doubled in size, with more than 40 per cent of the new affiliates from Budapest.[51]

That afternoon, representatives shuttled back and forth between negotiations and meetings of their own platforms, advising them of developments. Debate over the proposed minimum programme was at times stormy, with opposition on both sides fearing that too much was

48. For details on these negotiations see *Népszabadság*, 8 October 1989: 2; 'Kongresszusi napló': 5–6; Ágh',Öt fontos nap': 12.
49. Rudolf L. Tőkés, 'Beyond the Party Congress: Hungary's Hazy Future', *The New Leader*, 30 October 1989: 6.
50. M. Bihari, 'Az állampárt végórái': 100–101; see also 'Kongresszusi napló': 5.
51. Calculated by the author. Nearly half of the Peoples' Democratic Platform was composed of delegates from Budapest, compared with less than a quarter for the Reform Alliance: Vass, 'A Magyar Szocialista Párt': 149.

being given away in the pursuit of compromise. Some continued to argue for the splitting up of party reformers and conservatives into separate parties instead.[52] This opposition was drowned out. By evening a short manifesto was ready for submission to the congress as a whole. The document, no more than twenty-five sentences, formed the ideological foundation for a new Hungarian socialist party.[53]

It opened with the declaration that the MSZMP, as a product of Stalinist-based socialism, had reached a historical end, requiring the formation of a new party that supports socialist values, human rights and liberty, a multiparty democracy as well as a mixed-property form of social economy. One clear compromise in the text was the statement that while the new party decisively set itself apart from its predecessor's past, it considered itself the legal successor of the MSZMP. A related compromise was over the new party's membership. The document did not stipulate that membership would be automatic, carried over from the MSZMP, as conservative delegates had wanted. However, the opposite proposal – favoured by many in the Reform Alliance – for a formal process of membership screening to block conservatives was rejected, strongly opposed by the Peoples' Democratic Platform.[54] The result was the agreement that all MSZMP members would have to re-join the new party, although this would require nothing more than signing a document adhering to the new party's principles and statutes.

On its dissemination a number of delegates criticized the content of the new party manifesto, or rather the lack of it. Questions were raised over the still-unresolved issue of party cells in the workplace, and the lack of clarity over who exactly would comprise the membership of this new party. Some objected to the characterizations of the MSZMP as Stalinist, while others questioned the use of the term 'social market'.[55] These objections were overcome by Nyers, who towards the end of this debate gave his blessing to the document.

Nyers's backing, while crucial to the preservation of the party, was delivered in a manner which left reformers less than pleased. Speaking in a manner described by one observer as 'vintage Kádár', Nyers called

52. Gubcsi, *4 nap, amely megrengette az országot*: 77–82.
53. For the entire text of the manifesto, see *Népszabadság*, 8 October 1989: 2.
54. On this point, see the text of the speech by Peoples' Democratic Platform spokesman János Gönci in *Kongresszus '89*: 98–9.
55. *Kongresszus '89*, no. 27 (morning, 8 October 1989): 3–4.

for party unity in support of a new Hungarian socialist party, appealing openly to conservatives to stay the course. At the same time, Nyers warned state officials such as Pozsgay, Németh and Horn not to use this transformation to liberate themselves from their subservience to the MSZMP, becoming an 'independent expert government' beyond the dictates of a new socialist party.[56]

With these statements Nyers was able to rally a majority of delegates in support of the document - in essence, placing almost everyone on the side of 'reform' by implying that in reality the party would continue much as before. Only Berecz and his Solidarity platform still voiced strong opposition to the dissolution of the MSZMP, Grósz having given up the struggle against what appeared to be inevitable. A vote was called. By a large majority, with only 159 opposed and 39 abstaining, the congress manifesto was approved on 8 October, at 8:24 p.m, and a new party, *Magyar Szocialista Párt* - the Hungarian Socialist Party (MSZP) - was finally established.

'HE WHO IS WITH US IS ALSO AGAINST US': TURMOIL WITHIN THE REFORM ALLIANCE

Had a major victory been won? This was the question a number of Reform Alliance delegates began to ask as what was now the opening session of the first MSZP congress convened on the Sunday. The conservative lines had been breached; the MSZMP had been overthrown. Grósz himself refused to join the new MSZP, and Berecz's Solidarity platform had dissolved in the wake of its defeat.[57] But despite these obvious successes there began to spread among the platform the sense that too much had been compromised for the sake of unity, and that as a result they had been 'overly victorious', achieving their aims in

56. Tőkés, 'Beyond the Party Congress': 6, and idem, *Hungary's Negotiated Revolution*: 353–4. See also the text of Nyers's speech in *Kongresszus '89*: 155–8.

57. Berecz in fact stated that he intended to remain within the MSZMP, that is, to resurrect the old party, notwithstanding the fact that he had also voted for its dissolution. For the former general-secretary's reaction to events, see Károly Grósz, 'Nyugdíjas leszek, de reformkommunista maradok [I shall retire, but remain a reform communist]', *Népszabadság*, 8 October 1989: 2, and 'Grósz Károly meg fogja találni a maga pártját [Károly Grósz will find his own party]', *Magyar Nemzet*, 9 October 1989: 3.

form, but not in content. As several observers noted, instead of the conclusive showdown between party reformers and conservatives, in the end 'it turned out that everyone was a reformer', and as a result of compromises no real break had occurred. Everyone had won, and so everyone had lost.[58]

Many began to regret that the decision on a new party name had preceded those of the new party statutes and leadership, since victories on these points could have better facilitated the isolation or expulsion of the conservative faction.[59] This was reinforced by the realization that although more than 150 delegates had voted against the dissolution of the MSZMP, and therefore technically did not adhere to the tenets of the new party, most of these delegates had not left the congress, nor had they been expelled, but rather remained to influence the continuing formation of the new party. A sarcastic joke, paraphrasing Kádár's famous slogan, began to spread among the Reform Alliance ranks: 'he who is with us is also against us'.[60]

When Reform Alliance delegates met in session that afternoon, the displeasure over the course of events had reached a breaking-point. The morning's debate over the MSZP's new basic statutes had gone on much as it had on the first day of the congress. The old conservative positions had not fallen away, but rather had been strengthened by their continuing migration into the Peoples' Democratic Platform (which had grown by another 70 members from the day before). Again the idea of a 'clean break' with the congress began to re-emerge within the Reform Alliance, with some members demanding a vote for or against the compromise that had been hammered out so far. Imre Keserű went so far as to state that 'the bloody-handed murderers have left, but the party has still not freed itself of the rats', causing an uproar inside and out of the platform meeting.[61]

58. Bihari, 'A múltat végleg eltörölni': 5; Kéri and Petschnig, 'Ez a név lesz a végső', part I: 6; Ágh, 'Öt fontos nap': 15–18.

59. *Népszabadság*, 9 October 1989: 4; see also József Géczi, 'Négy nap kongresszus = négy év illegalitásban [Four days at the congress = four years working illegally]', interview by István Bőle, *Délmagyarország*, 11 October 1989: 3.

60. Kéri and Petschnig, 'Ez a név lesz a végső', part I: 6, and part II: 7, n. 1; see also István Győrffy, 'Négy történelmi nap pillanataiból [From the moments of four historical days]', *Zalai Hírlap*, 14 October 1989: 6.

61. *Népszabadság*, 9 October 1989: 4.

Pozsgay attempted to assuage the agitated delegates. He agreed that there had to be limits to compromise, but also warned them not to expect an ideal 'all or nothing' victory which would exclude everyone but themselves. What would have happened, Pozsgay asked, if Martin Luther had decided not to accept anyone who had been Roman Catholic? In addition, he raised the fear that a split within the party would affect parliament and government as well, paralysing those institutions and the process of democratic reform.[62] Already that day a new set of rumours had spread that a number of cabinet members had stepped down from office in order to provoke a government crisis, which the Prime Minister had to publicly refute.[63] But despite these deterrents, in the end the organizational limitations of the reform circles were still the most potent impediment.

Would splitting off from the party not simply be playing into the hands of party conservatives, who would then be free to halt the process of party reform? The vast majority of the Reform Alliance was not made up of radical reform circle members, but of more moderate or merely opportunistic delegates. How many would support the formation of a new party? Indeed, would MSZMP members - and the populace in general - support a new party made up largely of unknown intellectuals? Was the platform willing to run the risk of shattering the entire left-wing movement?[64] Given the lack of preparation and consensus on party split, Horn and other Reform Alliance delegates reconciled themselves to no more compromises on the remaining central points of contention: party cells in the workplace, the future of the Workers' Guard, party property and the question of who would fill leadership positions. This would form their final stand over the future of the MSZP.[65]

62. Ibid.; Győrffy, 'Négy történelmi nap pillanataiból': 6.
63. Ibid.: 1.
64. Ágh, 'Öt fontos nap': 17–18; see also the interviews with two Reform Alliance delegates on the congress: György Kerényi, 'Kerényi György szolgálni akar [György Kerényi wants to serve]', interview by Imre Goór; and László Bruszel, 'Új zakó - de kiről vették a méretet? [A new coat - but from whom did they take the measurements?]', interview by Fábián Józsa, *Bács-kapocs*, 17 October 1989: 3.
65. *Népszabadság*, 9 October 1989: 4; 'Kongresszusi napló': 7.

FURTHER SETBACKS AND THE THREAT OF A PARTY SPLIT

This set of Reform Alliance demands was soon put to the test, and with discouraging results. During the course of the day, congress delegates had debated and voted upon various proposed sections of the party statutes. However, by far the most divisive issue which remained was that of party cells in the workplace, which the reform circles and Reform Alliance had consistently opposed. Just prior to the vote on this issue, left until the very end of the day, Nyers gave a short address. Nyers implored the delegates to support the retention of the party cells in workplace, arguing (incorrectly) that even under Horthy's dictatorship in the 1930s the Social Democratic party was allowed to have party organizations in the factories.[66]

By an overwhelming majority congress delegates voted to retain cells in the workplace, with only 107 votes against - including Pozsgay, Horn, Németh and the 'hard core' of the Reform Alliance, the actual reform circle delegates. That so many Reform Alliance members had themselves voted in favour of workplace cells pointed out clearly how few members subscribed fully to the tenets on which the platform was based. This lack of unity did not bode well for coordinated action on the remaining crucial issues. The Reform Alliance was in full retreat.

By the last day of the congress the party was again veering towards a split. This time, however, it was openly being considered by reform leaders such as Pozsgay and Németh who had been urging patience up until now. It was clear that as a result the compromise programme that created the new MSZP, the method of executive election - by competing closed lists - was no longer suitable. The use of closed electoral lists had been promoted specifically to force an early split of the MSZMP, blocking compromise between internal party factions. But elections had been pushed to the end of the congress, preventing the divorce that the Reform Alliance had envisaged. Now, given that the Reform Alliance had reconciled themselves to a new party under

66. Kimmel, *Kongresszus '89*: 217–18. Nyers had confused the fact that there had been legal unions in the factories, and that these were strongly allied to the Social Democratic party. However, party cells themselves did not function at the workplace. Győrffy, 'Negy történelmi nap pillanataiból': 6.

compromised conditions, competing party lists would serve only to polarize the delegates, setting them and the party leadership against one another and threatening what gains had been achieved.

Discussions began again behind closed doors and among the party leaders and platform negotiators. Representatives from the Peoples' Democratic Platform, the Reform Alliance, the Agriculture, Youth and Countryside Platforms set about to hammer out a single compromise list for the presidium which the platforms as well as the four party leaders could accept. A wide range of party members, including even those expelled from the MSZMP, such as Mihály Bihari and László Lengyel, came under consideration.[67] Finding acceptable candidates was not easy. The Reform Alliance and Peoples' Democratic Platform quickly came into sharp conflict, in particular over the nomination of Foreign Minister Horn, who many conservatives reviled as a champion of bourgeois political values and saw as a much easier target than the more prominent Németh or Pozsgay.[68] To make matters worse, this personal opposition apparently had the backing of Nyers.

Nyers also refused a proposal from Pozsgay, Horn and Németh that he, as the only leader acceptable to the majority of congress delegates, remain party president, while the other three form a collective vice-presidency below him. Nyers resisted, fearing that such a body would leave him effectively encircled by reformers.[69] Nyers even continued to press for the leadership to include Berecz and Grósz, something no one was willing to accept.[70]

By late morning these conflicts had led to a stalemate. Word spread that Horn, Németh and Pozsgay were debating leaving the party altogether, possibly taking the reform circle delegates with them.[71] For Nyers this was an especially worrying prospect, which was tied to his earlier warnings against the formation of an 'independent expert government'. Both Pozsgay and Horn were cabinet members, and Németh

67. For details, see Attila Ágh, 'Kongresszusról utólag [After the congress]', interview by Gábor Rejtő, *Világ*, 19 October 1989: 18–19; 'Kongresszusi napló': 9–10. For the original Reform Alliance list, see Kéri and Petschnig, 'Ez a név lesz a végső', part I: 7.

68. 'Kongresszusi napló': 9.

69. Tőkés, 'Beyond the Party Congress': 6; Bihari, 'Az állampárt végórái': 105.

70. Győrffy, 'Négy történelmi nap': 6; see also Zoltan D. Barany, 'The Hungarian Socialist Party: A Case of Political Miscalculation', *RFER* (22 December 1989): 2.

71. Tőkés, 'Beyond the Party Congress': 6.

remained prime minister. Since his election to the party presidency Nyers had given up his state ministerial position. The withdrawal of these three reformers from the MSZP would not only split the party, but would leave the MSZP without control over the government, possibly setting off a conflict within parliament and endangering the reform process.

With widespread fears of this conflict now dominating the congress, Reform Alliance member Iván Vitányi called on the four to bring their debate into the open and address the delegates. The congress went into closed session as the party leaders emerged to voice their judgement of the current situation. By this time, delegates had become so tense after days of bitter debate and little sleep, and party factions so heterogeneous, that there was within all platforms widespread apprehension that a split at this point would in fact not 'correct' the internal conflicts of the MSZP but rather prompt its total disintegration. Similarly, while the reform leaders mulled over their break from the party, it was evident that they were unprepared to make good on their threat to break away from the MSZP. Just as the Reform Alliance had realized that they lacked the support necessary to form an independent party, so Pozsgay, Németh and Horn could not be certain how many would follow them out. Unable to force each other's hand, and fearing the consequences of their intransigence, the party leadership backed away from the edge. Nyers and the Peoples' Democratic Platform relented on Horn's inclusion in the presidency, and Pozsgay, Horn and Németh withdrew their demand for vice-presidential posts. The time for a party split, if there had been one, had already passed. Instead, the four agreed to find a middle ground on the composition of the new party leadership.[72]

A COMPROMISE OUTCOME AND AN UNCERTAIN VICTORY

The crisis past, negotiators formed an electoral list based primarily on neutral party figures not clearly allied to one faction or another, and therefore more palatable, if not specifically loved by anyone in

72. Pozsgay, *1989*: 172; M. Bihari, 'Az állampárt végórái': 103–6; Benkő, Kerekes and Patkós, *A születés szépséges kínjai*, 38–44. For the speeches of the four party leaders during the closed session see Kimmel, *Kongresszus '89*: 228–34.

particular. After five hours of closed-door discussion, congress delegates reconvened that night and were presented with their one party presidential nominee – Nyers – and one list for the presidium. Pozsgay was officially designated as the party's candidate for the new office of national president.

The majority of nominees were relatively unknown, only some 10 out of 24 being recognized political figures. Eleven nominees represented the Reform Alliance, including Pozsgay, Németh, Horn, Kosa and Géczi. The Peoples' Democratic Platform made up another five. The majority of the remaining eight had remained unaligned with any platform (including Csongrád county party secretary Vastagh).[73] Many delegates were by now particularly angry that they had been effectively removed from any real electoral role. By having earlier accepted the proposal of election by closed lists, since now only one list was being forwarded they had little influence on the selection of the leadership. The congress had been reduced to 'rubber-stamping' a list assembled by a handful of platform representative and party leaders.[74]

Despite these reservations delegates had few other options, and the nominations were accepted by an overwhelming majority of the congress. Few, however, were happy with the results. The party had shaken off the conservative old guard, but the new leadership was no more unified than it had been before the congress. On all sides there was the dominant feeling that too much had been compromised for the sake of party unity, although it was unclear what other option could have been followed without fragmenting the party. This frustration was compounded by the fact that most delegates felt that they had been left out of the decision-making process, even 'betrayed' by their own negotiators. In the end many on all sides felt that they had been the losers in the congress struggle.[75]

Among many reform circle delegates there was an additional sense of bitterness as well. As a number of interview subjects mentioned, the congress made reform circle delegates realize that they were mere amateurs in the face of professional politicians from the central apparatus, unprepared and thus easily outflanked. Many felt that too much effort

73. Bihari, 'Az állampárt végórái': 11.

74. Kéri and Petschnig, 'Ez a név lesz a végső', part II: 9–10; M. Bihari, 'Az állampárt végórái': 105–6; Kimmel, *Végjáték a fehér házban*: 162–4.

75. Kimmel, *Végjáték a fehér házban*: 169.

had been spent on dismantling the old party, and too little attention paid to how a new party should be constructed in its place.[76] Reformers were bound by negative shared values, by what they *did not* want, but in the end taking a unified stand on what the new party should represent was a far more contentious question.[77]

This sense of a pyrrhic victory was reinforced by the final decisions taken by the congress, where the final proposals of the Reform Alliance regarding the MSZP's position on the Hungarian Revolution, the future of the Workers' Guard, and the nationalization of MSZMP assets were rejected in favour of more ambiguous declarations. An attempt by some reform circle delegates to reopen the issue of eliminating party cells in the workplace was also rejected by the congress.[78]

OBSTACLES TO THE NEW PARTY

No matter what reservations reform circle and Reform Alliance members may have had, their basic goal had been achieved: the old order had been overthrown. But a new party would not arise by default; it would have to be built from the ground up. Reflecting the ambiguous outcome of the party congress, in the weeks to follow the shape of the new political system in general and the form and role of the MSZP within it remained uncertain.

Initially the prospects for the new socialist party seemed bright. Surveys taken in late October and November indicated that the public had certain reservations as to how far the MSZP had broken with the past, but nevertheless regarded the new party in a largely positive light. Popular support for the new MSZP was the largest of any party, apparently even re-capturing support taken by the MDF (whose support during the same period declined). The majority of those sampled

76. See also the interview with reform circle delegate Gyula Gráner in Gubcsi, *4 nap, amely megrengette az országot*: 176, and Erzsébet Sulyok, 'Antipolitikus sorok, reformkörben [Anti-political ranks in the reform circles]', *Szegedi Egyetem*, 16 October 1989: 1.
77. Lengyel, *Micsoda év!*: 80–81.
78. *Népszabadság*, 11 October 1989: 5; see also Reform Alliance delegate Béla Mandik, 'A küzdelem igazából most kezdődik [The struggle now begins]', *Vas Népe*, 12 October 1989: 3.

saw the MSZP as likely to win the majority of votes in the next election.[79]

MSZP leaders, including Nyers, spoke confidently that they expected to lose only half of their old members, leaving them with a base of nearly 400,000 - vastly outnumbering the membership of all other parties put together.[80] Forthcoming direct presidential elections, scheduled for November and prior to those for parliament, were also certain to bring a victory for Pozsgay, who remained one of the most popular and well-known politicians in the nation. His victory would help the party in its bid for parliamentary power.

But this optimism was short-lived. By November the fortunes of the MSZP began to decline rapidly, which can be traced to several factors both inside and outside the new party. Inside the MSZP, party members from its predecessor were given until the end of October to re-register with the new party. As mentioned earlier, this process consisted of no more than simply signing a statement of one's compliance to the new party statutes. Yet despite this lack of restrictions, few chose to join.

From the predictions of a membership in the hundreds of thousands, the MSZP was forced to extend the registration deadline due to the lack of members: by early November the party had attracted only some 15,000, primarily former members of the party apparatus.[81] This was particularly embarrassing given the unexpected resurrection of the MSZMP itself by some party hardliners (including Grósz and Berecz), who claimed that the party had never in fact been dissolved and that it had more than 100,000 members.[82]

In terms of formal organization, prospects were not much brighter. In most parts of the country, the MSZMP's basic cells were neither maintaining their link to the old party, nor reorganizing into new party units of the MSZP, but simply dissolving; the rank and file was drifting

79. 'A közvélemény 1989-ben', in Kurtán, Sándor and Vass, *Magyarország Politikai Évkönyve 1990*: 448–9, 460–3.
80. See, for example, the interview with MSZP presidium member Csaba Vass, 'Küzdenünk kell a hitelsségünkért [We must fight for our credibility]', *Világ*, 26 October 1989: 21–2; Rezső Nyers, 'Az MSZP várja tagjait az MSZMP-ből és azon kívülről is [The MSZP expects members from the MSZMP and outside it as well]', *Népszabadság*, 14 October 1989: 14.
81. Zoltan D. Barany, 'The Hungarian Socialist Party: A Case of Political Miscalculation', *RFER* (22 December 1989): 1–2.
82. Judith Pataki, 'Hungarian Socialist Workers' Party To Hold Congress', *RFER* (22 December 1989): 1–5.

away. Even in some of the most 'red' sectors of Hungary, such as the industrial areas of Budapest, entire party organizations in many large industrial complexes simply vanished.[83]

Where some semblance of local party leadership was maintained, in many cases it was led by old party cadres who hoped to maintain their privileges in the new order. This repelled a large number of reform-orientated former MSZMP members, who at their own level could see no difference between the old party and the new. For those rank-and-file members whose past membership had been more opportunistic, incentives to join the MSZP were also minimal. Given the radical transition of the party from ruling apparatus to incumbent political party, the MSZP had surrendered the tools which had sustained its predecessor: the *nomenklatura*, control over resources, guarantees of security, access. What remained was only the stigma of association with the past. Why then join?

THE END OF THE REFORM CIRCLE MOVEMENT

As for the reform circles themselves, for the vast majority of members the goal of the movement had been achieved, for better or worse. The majority appear to have drifted away from the party, no longer interested in political struggles and dissatisfied with the compromise formation of the MSZP. Within the core of activists, those original founders of the movement, members remained politically active as well as strongly divided on what had in fact been achieved. Some reform circle activists attempted to transform their organizations into local MSZP cells at the territorial level or integrated them into the new city and county party apparatus.[84] The Reform Alliance (as well as the Peoples' Democratic Platform) also attempted to institutionalize its platform within the new party, continuing the battle for the ideological soul of the MSZP.[85] Other reform circle members, angry with the congress

83. 'Vándorkommunisták [Wandering communists]', *Világ*, 16 November 1989: 18–19.

84. For one example, see 'Reformkörből pártalapszervezet [From reform circle to basic party organization]', *Somogyi Néplap*, 2 November 1989: 2.

85. For details on the reformation of the Reform Alliance within the MSZP, see *Népszabadság*, 20 November 1989: 8; with regard to the Peoples' Democratic Platform see Szigeti, *Balra, ki a zűrzavarból!*: 132–73; see also the interview with

outcome, remained uncertain as to what their future relationship with the MSZP should be. Almost immediately following the party congress a number of notable reform circle figures strongly condemned the congress outcome, some refusing to join the new party as a result. There still remained the hope that the original goals of the reform circles could still be realized, if not within the MSZP, then by means of another organization.[86]

This dissent within the movement culminated in a third and final reform circle conference, held in Nagykanizsa on 11 November 1989. Although having the tacit support of the Reform Alliance, the conference was in fact initiated by the local reform circle, intended primarily as a meeting of discontented reform circle radicals who were seeking to resolve their anger over the compromised MSZP. The conference was to address directly the future of the reform circle movement: whether to remain within the party, form an independent movement, or found their own political party.[87]

The local reform circle was anticipating that the participants would split off. One possible outcome of this split under consideration by the Nagykanizsa organizers would be that the members would merge with the new *Fuggetlen Szociáldemokrata Párt* – the Independent Social Democratic Party (by this time the Hungarian Social Democratic Party's internal rifts had become so great that they resulted in the split of the party). Independent Social Democratic leaders had been hoping that as a result of the inconclusive outcome of the MSZMP–MSZP party congress reform circle members would join them, giving a boost to their strife-torn party.[88]

Ferenc Baja (Reform Alliance) and László Iklódi (Peoples' Democratic Platform), 'Hogyan tovább, MSZP? [Where to now, MSZP?]', *Kelet-Magyarország*, 14 October 1989: 3.

86. See, for example, the interview with Imre Keserű, 'Az MSZMP utolsó kongresszusának visszhangja [The echo of the last MSZMP congress]', *Szegedi Egyetem*, 16 October 1989: 3; see also the exchange between Imre Keserű and József Géczi, 'Folytatódik a kötélhúzás [The tug-of-war continues]', interview by Ervin Tamás and István Tanács, *Népszabadság*, 10 November 1989: 6.

87. Invitation to the third reform circle conference, Nagykanizsa reform circle, unpublished document, dated 25 October 1989; see also the interviews with Nagykanizsa reform circle member Attila Izsák and Zala county MSZP Coordinating Council President László Vári, 'Hárc a fehér báránnyal [Fight with the white lamb]', interview by László Rab, *Népszabadság*, 3 November 1989, 6.

88. See, for example, the interview with Independent Social Democratic leader György

But as with the reform circle conferences that had preceded it, the meeting in Nagykanizsa was inconclusive.[89] Although approximately 200 participants were present, they were no longer delegates, representing thousands of other members, but rather the remnants of a movement which had already lost momentum and dissolved. Despite the exhortations of some conference organizers for a party split, the majority of participants, including many of the most radical reform circle figures, opposed any new form of organization. As one participant noted, the arguments upon which the reform circles had been built were in the present political context no longer relevant – the movement had outlived its purpose, and could not expect to build a real membership base as an independent organization.

Concurring with this view, a majority argued that their efforts were now best concentrated on influencing the MSZP. A short concluding statement was drafted, reflecting the views for and against a party split, with the general agreement that work must continue on rebuilding a left-wing movement within Hungary. A subsequent conference scheduled for December never came about.

NATIONAL ELECTIONS AND THE MSZP IN DEFEAT

Outside the party, the dissolution of the MSZMP and its rebirth as a western-style competitive political party intensified the campaign for the forthcoming national elections. Opposition parties discarded what few restraints they had exercised earlier in the pursuit of popular support. The failure to reach a unified agreement during roundtable talks in September led the SZDSZ and FIDESZ to launch a petition to bring to national referendum those issues which the Reform Alliance had lost: (1) whether the assets of the MSZMP (now under the control of the MSZP) should be accounted for (and, presumably, nationalized); (2) whether the Workers' Guardshould be disbanded; (3) whether party

Ruttner, 'Borúraború [After rain, more clouds]', *Magyarország*, 20 October 1989: 6.

89. For details, see László Rab, 'Nem a folyóson kell politizálni [We must not politicize in the corridors]', *Népszabadság*, 13 October 1989: 1, 4; see also 'Nem történt szakadás Nagykanizsán, a reformkörök III. országos találkozóján [A split did not occur at the third reform circle national conference in Nagykanizsa]', *Zalai Hírlap*, 13 November 1989: 1–2.

organizations should be banned from the workplace; and (4) whether presidential elections should be held in advance of those for parliament.

Although parliament acceded to the first three demands prior to the referendum, the petition received more than the necessary signatures, and all four issues went to a national vote in late November. The MSZP, which had a direct stake in early presidential elections above all else, campaigned for a no vote on point four alone, while the MDF for various reasons urged the population to boycott the elections as whole. Despite these attempts, all four questions in the referendum - the first national democratic vote since the imposition of socialism - were passed, although on the matter of presidential elections by less than one per cent.[90]

The referendum was crucial for the political prospects of the MSZP, and not only with regard to Pozsgay's presidential aspirations. As a result of this early national plebiscite, the hostility between rival opposition parties, discussed in the last chapter, intensified, and the MSZP found itself caught in the crossfire. Given the MDF's stance on the referendum, the SZDSZ was able to give weight to its charge that the MDF was a party of communist fellow-travellers, seeking to abet their new MSZP allies (at this time many still expected that elections would bring an MSZP–MDF coalition government).

This was a highly effective tactic. The SZDSZ was able to portray itself as the party unwilling to surrender the fate of the nation to the crypto-communists, and its popularity subsequently began to rise.[91] Under this attack the MDF was obliged to intensify its own countercharges that the SZDSZ were in fact the real communist force.[92] This consequently became the central issue of opposition party struggles until the 1990 parliamentary elections: who is the more implacable foe of communism, liberals or nationalists?

Not surprisingly, the MSZP were hardest hit by this tactic, continuously under attack and unable to respond effectively to charges that

90. For details, see O'Neil, 'Hungary: Political Transition and Executive Conflict': 205–7.

91. Csizmadia, 'Utak a pártosodáshoz': 21–4; see also the retrospective of the campaign by SZDSZ founding member Péter Kelemen, 'Liberálisok, baloldal - ki mire emlékszik? [Liberals, the left wing - who remembers what?] *Magyar Hírlap*, 18 February 1992: 7.

92. Ibid. A notable example of this was the second congress of the MDF on 20–22 October, when party head Zoltán Bíró was replaced by József Antall.

they were no more than the remnants of that group which had led the nation to economic ruin.[93] The party was also seriously wounded by revelations by the SZDSZ and FIDESZ that the Ministry of Interior still had opposition parties under surveillance, reinforcing accusations that the MSZP was no different from its predecessor. A final problem was that while the MSZP struggled to define its new ideology in a competitive political setting, various parties were able to appropriate parts of its socialist and social-democratic ideology, whittling away at its potential voting base. Although the population retained a strongly social-democratic orientation,[94] opposition propaganda and tactics thus played a not insubstantial role in turning an uncertain population away from the Socialists. This is a general irony of any slow transition, in that as it unfolds, the greater public openness and ability to criticize the status quo only serves to undermine the liberalizing regime, rather than to legitimize it.

But perhaps the greatest damage done to the MSZP was that which it had inflicted on itself. The great achievement of the last party congress was to destroy the myth of the monolithic party, encompassing all social interests and embodying total competency. By late 1989 few had much faith in the MSZMP, eroded by the declining economic situation, intra-party struggles, and the open criticism of state socialism that had resulted from these developments. Yet this hostility towards the MSZMP did not translate directly into opposition support or support for capitalism as a whole. A large portion of the public continued to view radical change as a threat to the status quo, and remained hostile

93. Just before the elections, the Hungarian Public Opinion Research Institute conducted an analysis of public criticism by the various political parties. This showed that while the MSZP employed the second least amount of criticism towards the other parties, it was by far the greatest target of such attacks: cited in Rudolf L. Tőkés, *A pozstkommunizmusból a demokráciába* [From post-communism to democracy] (Budapest: Konrad Adenauer Alapitvány, 1990): 44–5. For a general analysis of the role of anticommunism in the 1990 elections, see József Bayer, 'Antikommunizmus Magyarországon, 1990 [Anticommunism in Hungary, 1990]', in Kurtán, Sándor and Vass, *Magyarország Politikai Évkönyve 1991*: 242–8.

94. This point has been documented by a number of researchers; see in particular Bruszt and Simon, 'Politikai orientációk Magyarországon': 67–71; Kolosi et al., 'The Making of Political Fields in Post-Communist Transition: Dynamics of Class and Party in Hungarian Politics, 1989-90': 132–62; and Guy Lázár, 'Kell-e szociáldemokrácia? [Must there be social democracy?]', *Mozgó Világ* (October 1990): 27–32.

to the re-emergence of class divisions and apprehensive of the turbulence that political and economic transition would inevitably bring.[95]

This was the last appeal of the MSZMP, a known quantity as opposed to an uncertain and risky change of power. But with the dissolution of the MSZMP and its rebirth as a Western-style socialist party the option of sticking with the status quo disappeared, forcing the population to choose between a new set of political unknowns. In this situation the MSZP faced the worst of both worlds, associated with the failures of the recent past and shorn of the centralized power of their predecessor. The first open multiparty elections for parliament were held in March and April 1990, on the basis of a combination of single-member districts, county and national lists.[96] One interesting aspect of the elections in Hungary was the low turnout in comparison to other elections in Eastern Europe in 1989 and 1990: 63 per cent and 46 per cent in the two respective rounds, compared with rates of 80 per cent and above in most of the region. While this has been attributed to the legacy of political paternalism, another answer lies in the fact that the reformist posture and slow unravelling of the party-state prevented the kind of catalyst for popular mobilization that was seen elsewhere in Eastern Europe.[97] Far from its original predictions, the MSZP took fourth place in the elections, behind the MDF, SZDSZ, and the FGKP (*Független Kisgazda-, Földmunkás- és Polgári Párt*, or Independent

95. See, for example, the findings of Bruszt and Simon, which indicate that in November 1989 the majority of those questioned still favoured the retention of industry in state or workers' hands: *A lecsendesített többség*: 126, Table 10.
96. For detailed information on the outcome of the elections see György Szoboszlai (ed.), *Parlamenti választások 1990* [Parliamentary elections 1990] (Budapest: MTA Társadalomtudományi Intézet, 1990); an analysis of the Hungarian electoral system can be found in John R. Hibbing and Samuel Patterson, 'A Democratic Legislature in the Making: The Historic Hungarian Elections of 1990', *Comparative Political Studies* **24**, (January 1992): 430–54. For a comparison of the 1990 elections with voter demographics prior to the communist take-over, see András Körösényi, 'Revival of the Past or a New Beginning? The Nature of Post-Communist Politics', in Bozóki, Körösényi and Schöpflin, *Post-Communist Transition*: 111–31.
97. For a discussion of the political culture in the Hungarian elections and the political transition as a whole see János Simon, 'Post-paternalist Political Culture in Hungary: Relationship Between Citizens and Politics During and After the "Melancholic Revolution" (1989–1991)', *Communist and Post-Communist Studies* **26** (June 1993), esp. 228–32.

Smallholders), netting some half-million votes (about 11 per cent of the total) and 33 out of 386 total seats.

What voter support existed for the MSZP reflected continuing contradictions within the party as a new organization with its roots in the authoritarian past. Like the party membership itself, support bifurcated into two distinct groups: a younger (under fifty) cohort of intelligentsia – the social base of the reform circles – alongside a group of voters over sixty years of age. The MSZP's support among the youth was poorer than any parliamentary party with the exception of the KDNP (*Kereszténydemokrata Néppárt*, or Christian Democrats).[98]

Reflecting the general scepticism that had developed towards the MSZP among the populace – one survey indicated that the greatest determining factor in voter support for a given candidate was whether he or she had been a member of the MSZMP[99] – the socialists did particularly badly in single-member mandates, where they relied on the former *nomenklatura* for nearly half of their candidates (although a number of independent intellectuals, including reform circle figures, also stood for office).[100] Of all the MSZP seats gained in parliament, only one candidate – President of Parliament Mátyás Szűrös – was elected in a single-member district; Prime Minister Németh also won an individual mandate, but ran as an independent rather than as a candidate of the MSZP. Pozsgay, once seen as the great champion of reform, himself came in third place in his district behind FIDESZ and MDF candidates, and made it into parliament only on the basis of the

98. László Bruszt and János Simon, 'A "választások éve" a közvélemény-kutatások tükrében [The 'year of elections' in the reflection of public opinion research]', in Sándor Kurtán, Péter Sándor and László Vass (eds), *Magyarország Politikai Évkönyve 1991* (Budapest: Ökonómia Alapítvány and Economix, 1991): 632, Table 31; see also the demographic breakdown of the MSZP in Attila Ágh, 'Organizational Change in the Hungarian Socialist Party', paper originally presented at the ECPR Conference, Madrid, April 1994; Hungarian Center for Democracy Studies Foundation, Budapest Papers on Democratic Transition no. 76 (1994): 31–2.

99. Ágnes Bokor, 'A közvélemény a rendszerváltás folyamatában [Public opinion in the course of the transition]', in Rudolf Andorka, Tamás Kolosi and György Vukovich (eds), *Társadalmi Riport 1990* [Social Report 1990] (Budapest: TÁRKI, 1990): 616.

100. Ágnes Vajda and E. János Farkas, 'Az 1990-es magyar parlamenti választások képviselőjelöltjei társadalmi jellemzői [Social characteristics of the candidates for the 1990 Hungarian parliamentary elections]', in Kurtán, Sándor and Vass, *Magyarország Politikai Évkönyve 1991*: 94–5.

party list. As for candidates from the ranks of the reform circles, lacking prominence within the MSZP or the public at large, not one was able to win a seat in the new parliament. A coalition government composed of the MDF, and the smaller FGKP and KDNP was formed, and the MSZP went into opposition. The era of socialist rule was officially over.

EPILOGUE: A POLITICAL RESURRECTION

With the failure of the reform circles to create the kind of socialist party they had envisaged, it was perhaps not surprising that the MSZP did so poorly in parliamentary elections, unable to form a clear electoral base and define their relationship to the past. Their overwhelming rejection by the population was a serious blow to the party, especially given their earlier expectations for a central role in a democratic Hungary. Many initial MSZP supporters drifted away from the party, particularly former party *apparatchiki* who found no advantage in a party which could not provide them with the benefits enjoyed before. Several important party leaders also soon left the MSZP, seeing their future prospects elsewhere than in a compromised ex-communist party.

Unhappy with the compromise outcome he had been instrumental in forging, Imre Pozsgay left the MSZP in late 1990 to found his own party, hoping to recreate the kind of mass populist base he had earlier envisaged. However, like his earlier organizational attempts the effort was half-hearted and unsuccessful, failing to attract any significant public support.[101] Following his independent candidacy for parliament, Miklós Németh continued his disassociation from the MSZP, stepping down from his position in the party presidium and in 1991 from parliament entirely to take a job with the European Bank for

101. For details, see the copy of Pozsgay's resignation letter to the MSZP and the founding declaration of his new National Democratic Federation in Pozsgay, *1989*: 244–50. It is interesting to note that Pozsgay's co-founder in this party was Zoltán Bíró, former president of the MDF. The National Democratic Federation remained peripheral in Hungarian political life, and did not win any seats in the 1994 parliamentary elections (including Pozsgay). It finally dissolved itself in January 1996. In retrospect, Pozsgay has expressed regret that he sought to maintain party unity at the last MSZMP congress and did not split off from the party with reformist delegates; see Pozsgay, 'Itt semmi, valóban semmi nem változik': 21.

Reconstruction and Development in London. Several observers outside the party argued that there was no longer a future for the MSZP in Hungarian political life, while internal party struggles, both personal and ideological, continued.[102]

But while this crisis within the party may have been a baptism by fire, in the end it worked to the benefit of the MSZP. First, the disastrous showing of the MSZP in elections not only helped shed the party of undesirable 'careerist' members, but also provided ammunition to the reformist wing of the party, which was able to blame their defeat on the congress compromise and the ambiguous, quasi-Marxist party platform that had resulted (that is, the Peoples' Democratic Platform and its supporters). Second, although the loss of two of the best-known leaders of the party may have reduced the MSZP's prominence, this turnover also helped facilitate the rise of party figures whose connection to the MSZMP's past was less direct, putting more distance between the new socialist party and the old communist order.

Strengthened by these developments, after serious internal struggles the next MSZP congress - held in two sessions in May and November 1990 - brought a clear victory for the radical reformers within the party. Nyers stepped down from his post as party president and presidium member, and was replaced by Horn, whose nomination to the presidium had been bitterly opposed just one year earlier. The presidium itself, whose large size was in part a mechanism for compromise at the first congress, was reduced in size by almost half and subjected to an almost complete turnover. Only four members were re-elected, all originally from the Reform Alliance (Géczi, Horn, Kosa and Vitányi), while the remaining seats were filled by new representatives. The presidium became dominated by Reform Alliance and reform circle figures (eight out of thirteen), while the representation of those linked

102. For both sides of the debate on this issue see the series of articles on 'the death of the left' in the journal *Kritika*: 'Bucsú a baloldaltól [Farewell to the left]' (April 1989): 10–16; the roundtable discussion of Attila Ágh, István Eörsi, Tamás Krausz and Mária Ludassy, 'Vita a baloldalról [Debate on the left]' (February 1990): 11–16; László Lengyel, 'Elégia a baloldalról [Elegy to the left]' (March 1990): 18–19; and György Litván, 'Kitől búcsúzzunk? [Whom do we bid farewell?]', (April 1990): 19–20. See also the analysis by MDF parliamentary delegate József Debreczeni, *Népszabadság*, 13 May 1992, cited in Alfred A. Reisch, 'Hungarian Socialist Party Looks Ahead', *Radio Free Europe/Radio Liberty Research Report* (10 July 1992): 22.

to the Peoples' Democratic Platform shrank to one. In the area of party ideology, references to the party's connection to the international workers' movement, Marxism and communism were removed from the basic statutes of the party, to be replaced by a statement of commitment to 'the principles and values of the Socialist International' and 'national, left-wing values'.

Overall the congress was widely viewed as a victory for the party wing associated with the Reform Alliance, and 'a watershed in the separation of the MSZP from the former communist party'.[103] Outside of the party ideological and leadership structure, from 1990 to 1992 some six of the party's parliamentary faction stepped down, to be replaced by younger reformist party intellectuals (including one former reform circle leader, József Géczi). These moves unmistakably turned the MSZP in a social democratic direction, freeing the party from what Bihari had called its 'conglomerate captivity'.[104]

From 1991 until 1994 the MSZP continued to strengthen its social-democratic base, forming a more unified party leadership. Platforms within the party, both on the left and right, were not successfully institutionalized. The Peoples' Democratic Platform, having lost most of its political power after the 1990 party congress, faded away. The Reform Alliance also eventually disappeared, having lost a motivating objective. By the end of 1990 it had achieved many of its original goals, if not in the manner originally expected.[105]

103. Barnabas Racz, 'The Socialist-left Opposition in Post-Communist Hungary', *Europe–Asia Studies* **45** (1993): 651; see also the excellent overview in Vass, 'A Magyar Szocialista Párt': 150–53. Other analyses of the organizational and ideological development of the MSZP include Tamás Fricz, 'Párttagoltság és polgárosodás [Party stratification and *embourgeoisement*]', in Ágnes Heller, Ferenc Fehér, András Bozóki and Tamás Fricz, *Polgárosodás, civil társadalom és demokrácia* [*Embourgeoisement*, civil society and democracy] (Budapest: MTA Politikai Tudományok Intézete, 1992): 39–40; and Ágh, 'Organizational Change in the Hungarian Socialist Party'.

104. M. Bihari, 'Az állampárt végórái': 116.

105. From late 1989 onwards a number of platforms sprang up within the party, but none of them developed any organizational power or stability. By 1991 the Reform Alliance was no longer registered as a platform within the party, while the Peoples' Democratic Platform had been rechristened the *Baloldali tömörülés*, or 'Left-wing grouping'. What did develop in the place of platforms were a number of 'sections' (*tagozat*), each concerned with relatively narrow and specific interest groups within the party (agriculture, intellectuals, press, pensioners, and so on). Outside the MSZP, however, there remained the independent *'Baloldali alternatíva' egyesülés*

The MSZP also began the long process of slowly rebuilding its public image, primarily through its activity in parliament. While antagonism between coalition and opposition parties intensified, the MSZP took advantage of its outcast position, keeping apart from the political fray and taking a critical but moderate position on a limited number of issues.[106] One ironic contribution to this policy stemmed from the party's historical burden, in that the MSZP was able to portray itself as possessing well-qualified experts with strong experience in the state apparatus.[107]

By 1994 it was clear that these tactics had paid off far better than anyone expected. Despite the results of several mid-term parliamentary by-elections where the MSZP did well, either winning the mandate or coming in second, expectations for the party were modest, anticipating a limited increase in support in the next national elections.[108] However, as the popularity of the MDF coalition government waned in 1992 and 1993, hurt by its inconsistent economic policies and the widespread impression that it was attempting to consolidate political power by less than democratic methods, public support began to shift. But support did not move towards the liberal camp of FIDESZ and the SZDSZ as expected; rather, the public began to turn towards the MSZP. The population, increasingly weary of the costs of economic transition, found the MSZP's social market ideology, based on its image of political experience and technocratic expertise, more attractive than the opposition promise of more radical reform.[109]

('"Left-wing alternative" association', or *BAL* for short) whose leadership overlapped with the original leaders of the Peoples' Democratic Platform. See József Farkásfalvi (ed.), *Politikai kalauz 1991* [Political guidebook 1991] (Budapest: Mediant, 1991): 51–3, 221.

106. Racz, 'The Socialist-left Opposition in Post-Communist Hungary': 660–63; for a selection of the MSZP position statements on various issues see *Van jobb út! Szocialisták gazdaságról, társadalomról, politikáról 1990–1992* [There is a better way! The Socialists on the economy, society, and politics 1990–1992] (Budapest: Magyar Szocialista Part Országos Elnöksége, 1992), and *'Időben': A Magyar Szocialista Párt III. kongresszusának dokumentumai* ['In time': Documents from the Hungarian Socialist Party third congress] (Budapest: MSZP Országos Elnökség, 1992).

107. Ibid.: 654–63.

108. Ibid.: 663–6. In mid-1992 Horn was himself hoping for about 15 per cent of the popular vote in 1994: Reisch, 'Hungarian Socialist Party Looks Ahead': 24.

109. For a brief overview of Hungarian politics from 1990 to 1994, see Patrick H. O'Neil, 'Hungary's Hesistant Transition', *Current History* (March 1996): 135–9.

Parliamentary elections in May 1994 consequently led to an overwhelming victory for the MSZP that no one would have predicted just one year before. Repeating their low-key campaign strategy, the socialists won 149 seats in single-member districts (as opposed to one in 1990) and another 60 on national and territorial lists: in total over 54 per cent of the seats in parliament, enough to govern alone. Seeking to broaden their base of support and avoid the stigma of 'one-party' rule, a coalition was quickly forged with the SZDSZ, giving the new government a more liberal-orientated appearance. Horn became the new prime minister.[110] This change in fortune did not extend as dramatically to former members of the reform circles. Most having left the party or active political life after 1989, only a handful of figures from the movement re-emerged as new parliamentarians in 1994, and only one, Ferenc Baja, rose to a position of any power in the new cabinet (as environment minister). Their objective long since achieved, reform circle activists proved less successful at playing a dominant role in a democratic organization than at undermining an authoritarian one.

The startling electoral turnabout and victory of the MSZP can in large part be attributed to voter dissatisfaction with the previous coalition government. However, the fact that the populace chose to give their vote overwhelmingly to the MSZP is a testament to the success of that party in raising itself out of the ruins of state socialism to find its own distinct political voice. The goal of the MSZP to portray itself as a moderate, Western-style social-democratic party after several long years in the political 'ghetto' was finally achieved.

In this accomplishment a great debt is owed to the reform circles. As one of the founders of the first Szeged reform circle, József Géczi, had already concluded in 1990, the reform circles were in fact victorious in their defeat. Unable to realize their objectives as swiftly or conclusively as they had hoped, in the end they were instrumental in bringing about the destruction of the old order, so that a democratic system and a modern socialist party within it could be built in its place.[111]

110. For details, see Judith Pataki, 'Hungary's New Parliament Inaugurated', *Radio Free Europe/Radio Liberty Research Report* (22 July 1994): 7–11.

111. József Géczi, 'Jöttünk, láttunk, buktunk ... bukva győztünk? [We came, we saw, we failed ... in failure were we victorious?]', *Népszabadság*, 23 June 1990: 17.

PART III

Conclusions

6. Institutional Order and the Path of Political Change: Hungary and Eastern Europe

THE HUNGARIAN TRANSITION REASSESSED

The rise and impact of the reform circle movement is indicative of the particular institutional path taken by Hungarian state socialism after 1956. A system of rule, violently opposed by the population, eventually sought compromise through a policy of formal and informal co-optation, defusing hostility through the ideology of reform socialism. At the informal level, the party appealed to the domestic technical and institutional environment by promoting limited economic and political reforms and social liberalization. The party touted the rationalization of the means of control, and incorporated or tolerated Western institutional forms and technical knowledge. A process of formal co-optation also developed as a means of incorporating potentially antagonistic social segments, this most clearly seen in their targeting of the white-collar and intelligentsia sectors.

But such actions did not represent a transformation of the party-state's institutional core. This remained buffered from environmental and rank-and-file pressures through selective leadership recruitment. The MSZMP sought domestic legitimacy by appealing to the demands of Hungarian society while remaining loyal to the Soviet model, attempting to reconcile the needs of the two different environments. The policies of the MSZMP were in fact quite successful in atomizing society, turning the populace away from organized opposition by providing relatively broad personal freedoms and the opportunity for personal gain. A clear enemy for society to rally against was eliminated by making the majority of the populace beneficiaries of current order.

However, the contradictions of this dual system eventually came to the fore by the 1980s, in terms of both economic and political stagnation. The party was unable to respond to the challenge provided by this domestic crisis and the beginnings of Soviet institutional change. The MSZMP had for decades relied on the standard institutional routines of neutralizing opposition via co-optation and limited change; yet such policies would not solve the acute technical or institutional problems endemic to state socialism. The only real solution, radical organizational transformation, was difficult to accept, as it went against the fundamental institutional tenets upon which the party had been built.

As the party became paralysed at its centre, the practices of formal co-optation showed their own inherent dangers as the reform circle movement developed from the party intelligentsia rank and file. Forming from within the party structure itself, the reform circles emerged as an anti-institutional, horizontal challenge to the vertically-based power of the MSZMP, eroding leadership authority and the party's ability to maintain the status quo or dictate the manner of political change. This rending of party unity in turn helped to pave the way for civil pluralization, by providing a greater opportunity for oppositional collective action without fear of reprisal and by undermining remaining public confidence in the party. Without this slow revolt from within, it is imaginable that the Grósz regime would have continued forward with its half-hearted reforms, fostering increasing tension in the county which might eventually have exploded in a public outburst - whether in the form of a 'velvet' uprising, as in the GDR and Czechoslovakia, or a more violent reaction not unknown in Hungary.

How does the Hungarian case broaden our understanding of political transitions in Eastern Europe? Put simply, it shows that the manner in which party-states are institutionalized matters greatly in understanding their failure, as well as the inadequacy of existing approaches in understanding the nature and decline of state socialism. Dominant characterizations of state socialism have typically characterized these systems as monolithic, homogeneous entities, machines blindly following Marxist–Leninist programming or blunt instruments in the hands of a few political leaders who alone dictated the course of the nation. In contrast, events in Hungary point to the importance of how socialist political institutions developed over time - linking to the broader external environment, seeking to co-opt certain social forces and transforming in the process.

Institutionalization generated differentiated patterns of organizational strengths and weaknesses, strongly influencing the downfall of socialism as a whole as well as those variations found within it. The particular nature of Hungarian 'goulash communism', its inadvertent creation of adversaries within and their ability to eventually pull down the ruling élite, indicates that dramatic political change in Eastern Europe stemmed not only from the actions of those at the top, or systemic weaknesses generic to each state. Rather, the very different patterns of rule which developed across the region dramatically influenced kinds of political action, the formation of oppositional activity, the opportunities for collective action and the consequent reaction of party leaders. While state socialism as a specific political form carried with it institutional characteristics that were central to its sudden, profound and widespread collapse, the institutional variations between these states led to radically different political outcomes. Socialism in Eastern Europe must therefore be reinterpreted not only in terms of its inability to engender organizational change, something unexpected but consistent with institutional analysis, but also of how political activity differed so dramatically in each East European case, something obscured by the façade of organizational similarities within the bloc.

These conclusions take on wider implications. Rather than reject process- or structural-based models of political change, institutional analysis gives us a means by which we can integrate the two fields of research, connecting larger economic or social conditions with the intricacies of individual actors and choice. The institutional order, itself shaped by the environment around it, provides a set of conditions which help create the norms, motivations, opportunities and resources of political actors, influencing the path that the eventual transition may take. These parameters both enable and constrain, creating certain contingencies while reducing the likelihood of others. It is in fact here argued that the kinds of transition modalities which exist, such as those outlined by Philippe Schmitter and Terry Karl – imposition (coercive, élite dominant), pact (negotiated, élite dominant), reform (negotiated, mass ascendant), and revolution (coercive, mass ascendant) – can be better understood not if we ascribe them to chance but rather if we link their forms back to the institutional matrix from where they emerged.[1]

1. Schmitter and Karl, 'The Types of Democracy': 59–61.

This conclusion parallels the findings of Linz and Stepan, specifically their assertion that 'the characteristics of the previous nondemocratic regime have profound implications for the transition *paths* available and the *tasks* different countries face when they begin their struggles to develop consolidated democracies'.[2]

In using this approach, analysis of the institutional framework should take into account not only the degree to which the autocratic order has become institutionalized (and is thus willing or able to accept or initiate change), but, equally important, the manner in which that system has become institutionalized – the way in which it has positioned itself in relationship to the particular contours of the institutional and technical environment. In the case of Eastern Europe, the way in which domestic institutionalization manifested itself varied widely from country to country, creating unique fault lines in each case. Consequently, although all were subject to collapse under intense political stress, their different weaknesses led to radically different kinds of structural failure.

One caveat is necessary in that it must be stressed that this argument is meant to ascribe institutions with probabilistic, as opposed to deterministic, functions. As stated in the beginning of this study, the goal is not to supplant other approaches to political transitions, but rather to show how the incorporation of an institutional approach into these other forms of analysis can increase their utility. This can help to broaden our understanding of authoritarian collapse, not only in framing the different modalities and causal mechanisms of transitions which may exist, but also in giving us a better sense of the linkage between the death of authoritarian rule and the prospects for the (re-) institutionalization of democracy. Although it assumes many of the contextual peculiarities in a given case, institutional analysis cannot anticipate the effects of individuals, international forces, synergism or random events, which may overcome existing constraints and send a transition down an unforeseen path.

2. Linz and Stepan, *Problems of Democratic Transition and Consolidation*: 55 (emphasis in original).

VARIATIONS IN INSTITUTIONALIZATION AND POLITICAL TRANSITION IN EASTERN EUROPE

To place these conclusions in comparative perspective, in contrast to the Hungarian case the different institutional paths taken by other East European party-states over the last few decades eventually led to widely different transition outcomes. Poland most closely resembled Hungary in its attempts to pacify a hostile population by legitimizing the party-state as a modernizing and conciliatory force. However, poor economic decisions meant that these policies quickly backfired, leading to social and internal party unrest and setting in motion a negotiated transition which was frozen by martial law.[3] With this act the party lost what popular legitimacy it had gained.

The period which followed can be described as one of party de-institutionalization, whereby communist rule was held in place not by legitimizing structures but rather by coercion (a highly unstable form of control), while opposition institutions grew in force and deepened their links to society. When semi-free elections finally did come about in 1989 - despite the fact that they were predicated on constitutional changes to provide institutional advantages for the communists - the party was annihilated at the polls.[4] In this sense, the Polish roundtable agreements initiated in 1989 were the second phase of a transition begun nearly a decade earlier.

Elsewhere in East-Central Europe, attempts to institutionalize the party at the domestic level were much more limited and narrow, with the dominant concern being loyalty to Soviet institutional forms. Attempts at domestic institutionalization were halted in 1968 in Czechoslovakia, while in East Germany a specific form of technocratic rationality and co-optation was developed to validate party rule. In both cases, coercion became a basic method of control (rather than a last resort, as in Poland or Hungary). When in 1989 the Soviet Union eliminated its demands for institutional compliance, both the East German and Czechoslovak systems were so profoundly institutionalized in terms of their conformity to the Soviet model that they were

3. Jean Woodall, *The Socialist Corporation and Technocratic Power* (Cambridge: Cambridge University Press, 1982).
4. For details, see Bartolmiej Kaminski, *The Collapse of State Socialism: The Case of Poland* (Princeton, NJ: Princeton University Press, 1991).

incapable of responding to the Soviet directive to reform. Both parties reacted in the only way they could, ignoring changes elsewhere in the bloc until demonstration effects and popular mobilization forced them finally to capitulate to mass protest. This sudden collapse paved the way for the rapid re-incorporation of East Germany into West (lacking credible domestic institutions, East Germans saw their future in an institutional *anschluss*[5]) while in Czechoslovakia opposition forces immediately gained the upper hand, avoiding the need to make any major concessions to the communist party.

Finally, unlike in Czechoslovakia and East Germany, the Balkan states exhibited a much higher degree of domestic institutionalization, although of a kind far different from that found in Hungary. Institutional patterns reflected the existing social environment, conforming to and reinforcing entrenched patterns of clientelistic, nepotistic and tributary rule whose origins stretch back centuries. These were complemented by coupling the party to nationalistic tendencies, redefining the party as the defender of the people against ancient imperial threats (Hungarians, Turks) rather than class enemies.[6] Such developments were facilitated by the low levels of economic development in the Balkans, which stunted the development of earlier autonomous institutions that could have effectively limited the scope of autocratic rule (for example, independent political or social organizations, a strong market sector – the elements of civil society). The absence of such obstacles abetted the accrual and centralization of political power, reinforcing the norm of a dirigist role for the state.

Transitions in both nations have subsequently been indeterminate in their outcomes, lacking an institutional base upon which to build and having to struggle against strong undemocratic patterns. The transition in Bulgaria is noted less for its mass action than for the palace coup and the subsequent strength of a socialist party whose transformation into a truly democratic organization has been less clear. Utilizing paternalistic and nationalistic dogma, the Socialists won a clear parliamentary

5. Sigrid Meuschel, 'The End of "East German Socialism"', *Telos* 82 (Winter 1989–90): 3–26; see also Daniel V. Friedheim, 'Accelerating Collapse: The East German Road from Liberalization to Power-Sharing and its Legacy', in Shain and Linz, *Between States*: 160–78.
6. See Katherine Verdery, *National Ideology under Socialism: Identity and Cultural Politics in Ceauşescu's Romania* (Berkeley, CA: University of California Press, 1991).

victory in 1990. Even though that government eventually lost much of its popularity, during the 1991 elections the Socialists polled behind the opposition Union of Democratic Forces by less than two per cent. In the immediate years that followed, the Socialists have continued to play a powerful role in Bulgarian politics, commanding a great deal of rural support in particular and hindering comprehensive institutional change.[7]

Events have been even less clear in Romania, where extreme oppression fuelled by the megalomania of Ceauşescu finally resulted in his violent overthrow. However, given the historical lack of autonomous organized opposition and the total oppression of independent thought and action, the eventual outcome of the uprising was a 'coup by revolution', where power was acquired by the hegemonic National Salvation Front, dominated by former *apparatchiki*. The Front followed the path of its ruling predecessor, retaining if not cultivating many of the centralized, undemocratic institutions and environmental connections of the previous order (such as a strong domestic security apparatus to control dissent, anti-market and xenophobic ideologies), and stifling the development of new autonomous organizations and technical forms (for example, an independent media or extensive privatization) that could help turn the social environment more in the direction of liberal democracy.[8] Despite the eventual parliamentary and presidential victory of the democratic opposition in 1996, a real transition to democracy in Romania remains a challenge, rather than something already achieved.

INSTITUTIONAL EFFECTS AND POST-TRANSITION CONSOLIDATION

Variations in the form and eventual decline of state socialism in Eastern Europe and the new political systems which have followed lead to a

7. See Georgi Karasimeonov, 'The Post-Communist Party Panorama: The Case of Bulgaria' (unpublished paper, 1992); Luan Troxel, 'Socialist Persistence in the Bulgarian Elections of 1990–1991', *East European Quarterly* **XXVI** (January 1993): 407–30.
8. See Sabrina Ramet, 'Balkan Pluralism and its Enemies', *Orbis* **36** (Fall 1992): 547–64; see also Daniel N. Nelson (ed.), *Romania After Tyranny* (Boulder, CO: Westview Press, 1992).

second issue, that of the influence of institutions in the post-transition period. Just as it is here argued that transitions unfold within the context provided by existing political institutions, so by way of extension it follows that institutions also affect political outcomes that follow in the post-transition period. By way of contrast, it has been argued by some scholars of Eastern Europe that the current post-communist period, as a 'truly transformational' epoch, has brought about the wholesale disintegration of the old system, whereby 'formal institutions, along with norms, conventions, and informal as well as formal rules are in the process of withering away and yet being generated. The structure of the situation, in short, is that there is not much.'[9] To some extent this is true. After all, it has been the argument of this study that the institutionalization process tends to create organizational rigidity, making these structures more susceptible to sudden collapse – as in the case of Eastern Europe.

However, the rejection of institutional analysis in the consolidation period is mistaken, for two reasons. First, this assumption underestimates the 'ripple effect' of causality which emanates from those institutions which have collapsed, generating path-dependent trajectories in their wake. Second, equally neglected as an important causal factor are state and economic institutions which survive the transition period.

With regard to the first point, institutions continue to play a central role in part because the very process of institutional collapse shapes the context in which new institutions form – in essence a reformulation of Marx's argument that history is made under circumstances transmitted from the past. Just as the transition process is in part a result of the given institutional matrix, so the outcomes influenced by that matrix in turn affect the reinstitutionalization of political rule. What political resources are open to the various actors, which policies and ideologies become dominant in post-transition struggles and who is politically victorious as a result are affected by how the transition unfolds and the institutional legacies left by the means of exit of the previous order. Schmitter and Karl have reached a similar conclusion, arguing that 'the mode of transition from autocracy has a significant impact on the

9. Bunce and Csanádi, 'Uncertainty in the Transition: Post-Communism in Hungary': 262–3; see also Herbert Kitchelt, 'The Formation of Party Systems in East Central Europe', paper presented at the annual meeting of the American Political Science Association, Washington, DC, 1991.

possibility of a democratic outcome and, where that was possible, in the kind of democracy that would subsequently emerge'.[10] Yossi Shain and Juan Linz have also drawn similar conclusions in their analysis of interim governments during periods of political transition.[11]

PATH-DEPENDENCY AND REINSTITUTIONALIZATION

One area in which the effect of transition forms on political formation is apparent is in the area of party organization and development. As seen in previous chapters, the internal crisis within the MSZMP and the changing international climate emboldened party reformers to prepare for democratic change. But the incremental fragmentation of the party-state strongly affected the opposition as well, as it removed the necessity for the opposition to unify into a single, mass-based 'front' movement, as was prominent elsewhere in the region (the MDF, as a vague socialist/populist movement, stands out as a failed attempt in this regard). Lacking a monolith against which to unite, opposition currents developed into various distinct organized groups, while pre-communist political parties also quickly re-emerged – all attempting to locate and mobilize their own potential constituencies.

One outcome of this transition form is that following Seymour Martin Lipset and Stein Rokkan's 'freezing thesis', an institutionalized party spectrum emerged much earlier in Hungary than elsewhere in the region, whose cleavage patterns show a remarkable similarity to those found in the immediate post-war period.[12] Accordingly, following the first set of founding elections fragmentation among the Hungarian

10. Schmitter and Karl, 'The Types of Democracy': 58–9; see also Nancy Bermeo, 'Redemocratization and Transition Elections: A Comparison of Spain and Portugal', *Comparative Politics* **19** (January 1987): 213–31.
11. Shain and Yossi, *Between States*, chaps 1–3; see also James W. McGuire, 'Interim Government and Democratic Consolidation: Argentina in Comparative Perspective', in idem: 179–210.
12. Seymour Martin Lipset and Stein Rokkan, 'Cleavage Structures, Party Systems, and Voter Alignments: An Introduction', in Seymour Martin Lipset and Stein Rokkan (eds), *Party Systems and Voter Alignments* (New York: The Free Press, 1967): 1–64; for the application of this argument in the Hungarian case see Körösényi, 'Revival of the Past or a New Beginning?'.

parliamentary parties has been much more limited than elsewhere in the region. Despite internal squabbling, the MDF-dominated coalition remained intact for the entire length of its four-year term (the longest by far of any government in the region) and 1994 elections returned to parliament only those six political parties that entered in 1990.[13]

In comparison to developments in Hungary, in the rest of Eastern Europe the freezing of party cleavages has come much later, as mass-based opposition parties fragmented or disintegrated entirely upon gaining power. One can hypothesize that this drawn-out process of party institutionalization has impaired the initial ability of many East European parliaments to build stable ruling coalitions necessary to support governments or enact comprehensive reform. At a minimum, the early institutionalization of the Hungarian party system has meant that that country has had one less obstacle to face in this regard. Such factors alone will not determine the long-term success or failure of post-communist governments in enacting reform. However, it underscores the argument made elsewhere with regard to other cases of political transition in Western Europe and Latin America that institutional variations do affect the formation and institutionalization of a new party spectrum, influencing the distribution and consolidation of political resources and thus shaping the party spectrum and their policies in the post-transition period.[14]

In the area of electoral provisions and constitutional formation as well, several scholars have found that transition modality also seems to be an important factor in the kinds of institutional changes that have emerged in this area. As Arend Lijphart has noted, the institutional outcomes of these transitions clearly reflect 'the logic of the democratization process itself'.[15] This is important, in that, concurring with Lipset and Rokkan's arguments, Lijphart concludes from his study that in the case of both party systems and constitutional structures in Eastern

13. It should also be noted, however, that the Hungarian parliament is based on a German-style 'constructive vote of no confidence', which makes the removal of a government much more difficult. This does not account for the organizational stability of parliamentary parties, however.
14. Bermeo, 'Redemocratization and Transition Elections': 213; Barbara Geddes, 'A Comparative Perspective on the Leninist Legacy in Eastern Europe', *Comparative Political Studies* **28** (July 1995): 239–74.
15. Arend Lijphart, 'Democratization and Constitutional Choices in Czecho-Slovakia, Hungary, and Poland, 1989–1991', in Szoboszlai, *Flying Blind*: 109.

Europe the particular configurations now becoming institutionalized will leave these countries with political systems dictated more by the exigencies of the transition than by objective considerations *per se.*[16]

In the Hungarian case, an important consequence of the incremental process of the transition and the dispersal of political power is that early negotiations for political reform, intended as a means for the MSZMP to reinstitutionalize itself, were successfully routed and became instead a forum for constitutional change. As Péter Paczolay notes, 'while constitutions usually create the legal framework *after* previous social and political changes, in Hungary the reverse happened: a constitutional change was declared first, and the shaping of a new political social and economic system began later'.[17] While there were widespread expectations that following the victory of opposition parties in 1990 the constitution would be completely rewritten, the inability of the MSZMP to bias the constitution in their favour has undermined much of the momentum for such action. Thus, a reformed variant of the old socialist constitution remains in force. Despite calls for a wholly new document and a sufficient margin of parliamentary votes held by the government coalition to effect such a change, the constitution's institutionalized status becomes more apparent each day.[18]

This can again be contrasted with other transitions in the region. In several cases, the rapid dissolution of communist rule prevented the old order from enacting institutional mechanisms that would have re-institutionalized their power (such as Czechoslovakia and East Germany), while elsewhere the opposition's inability to summarily bring down the party allowed for the creation of biased institutions

16. Lijphart, 'Democratization and Constitutional Choices': 99–113. However, in subsequent work Lijphart seems to move away from this view, stressing more the 'immediate context' in affecting the saliency of particular institutional legacies: Crawford and Lijphart, 'Explaining Political and Economic Change': 194–7.

17. Péter Paczolay, 'Constitutional Transition and Legal Continuity', *Connecticut Journal of International Law* **8** (Spring 1993): 565 (emphasis in original). One interesting side-effect of this development has been that in part as a result of the debates which derive from the existence of constitutional continuity from the previous era, Hungary has developed an extremely strong constitutional court to actively settle these disputes. In fact, it has even been suggested that the Hungarian constitutional court has become one of the most powerful in the world: Jon Elster, 'On Majoritarianism and Rights', *East European Constitutional Review* **1** (Fall 1992): 22.

18. Paczolay, 'Constitutional Transition and Legal Continuity': 566–7.

(initially intended to favour the communists) which have since influenced the patterns of political authority in the post-communist era (Poland, Bulgaria, Albania). Such variations are worth further study, in that, following Przeworski's observations, transition by extrication leaves institutional legacies that necessitate or invite subsequent change, making the existing political structure more unstable.[19]

Such considerations are further compounded by the problem that post-communist forces may equally be tempted towards institutionalizing their own power once they have assumed political control. Where constitutions have not been reformed as a precursor to open elections, this provides the opening for the new dominant party to rationalize the rewriting of that document, biasing it in their own favour (as has been the case in Romania). Where constitutions have in fact been altered to provide extrication mechanisms for the previous order, this can also in the end provide a set of structures which a victorious opposition may wield to their own advantage. Or, as with the case of unreformed constitutions, it can provide the excuse for subsequent changes which may institutionalize a new set of political advantages. While Przeworski's rational-choice approach avoids drawing a link between these outcomes and the institutional nature of the previous autocratic system, it is here argued that the causal relationship is strong.

One particular area where this differentiation in constitutional reform has been particularly noticeable is in the dispersal of executive power, parliamentary versus presidential systems. As this author and others such as Lijphart and Jon Elster have argued, these institutional outcomes appear as much the outcome of the particular transition process as the rational expression of specific interests themselves.[20] As Elster notes, in the course of the formation of executive institutions 'things rarely worked out as intended' – reflecting the institutional emphasis on unintended outcomes.[21]

In Poland, for example, the weak institutionalization of the communist party led to their roundtable demands for a strong presidency, as a means by which their power could be reinvested in the state structure. Although the communists soon lost power, this extrication legacy was

19. Przeworski, *Democracy and the Market*: 79–83.
20. Lipjhart, 'Democratization and Constitutional Choices': 105–7; O'Neil, 'Hungary: Political Transition and Executive Conflict'; Jon Elster, 'Bargaining over the Presidency', *East European Constitutional Review* **2–3** (Fall 1993/Winter 1994): 95–8.
21. Elster, 'Bargaining over the Presidency': 95.

not dismantled by the opposition, who were just as interested in using a strong presidency to consolidate their own political power. The result has thus been the formation of a relatively powerful semi-presidential system in the post-communist era. In Hungary, the communist party similarly set in motion the creation of a powerful presidential office that it hoped to control. However, given the disintegration of the MSZMP during roundtable negotiations and before elections, opposition forces were able to blunt this manoeuvre, leading to the creation of a presidential office with rather ambiguous powers that have since been a source of controversy. Quite apart from these cases, in Czechoslovakia the rapid transition eliminated any opportunity for the communist party to vest its power in a presidential office. A presidential structure was revived from existing constitutional provisions, but its role has been demarcated more clearly than in the other two cases. This reflects the process of institutional change in Czechoslovakia following democratic elections, rather than being a precondition for them.

These same processes can be seen in the area of electoral reform. In Hungary the inability of any one side to monopolize power led to the creation of an extremely complicated mixed proportional and majoritarian electoral system that was intended to minimize major losses by either the ruling party (which expected to do well in single-member districts where it could field many well-known candidates) or the smaller opposition forces (which counted on proportional representation as the best means to gain support and remove the communists from power).[22] This is quite the opposite from Czechoslovakia, where the abrupt transition and the temporary hegemony of opposition power eliminated the need for any constitutional guarantees as a condition for communist extrication. Consequently, the new parliament enacted an electoral system more proportionally representative than that found in Hungary.[23]

Finally, among the various conditions for open elections in Poland were certain electoral guarantees for the communists, in particular a majoritarian system for electing both houses of parliament. Because of this distinct extrication legacy, it increased the subsequent likelihood

22. Hibbing and Patterson, 'A Democratic Legislature in the Making': 431–2; see also Jack Bielasiak, 'Regime Transition, Founding Elections, and Political Fields in Post-Communist States', unpublished paper, Indiana University, 1991: 11.
23. Lijphart, 'Democratization and Constitutional Choices': 105.

that the post-transition parliament would seek to rewrite the electoral law in order to remove this concession to the old order. In 1991, parliament in fact took just such an action, moving to the opposite end in the enactment of a highly proportional system for the larger and more powerful chamber of parliament, the Sejm.[24]

The new highly proportional system, however, with its lack of a minimum threshold for representation, helped exacerbate the already serious parliamentary fragmentation and impede the process of political consolidation. Such problems necessitated another set of electoral modifications prior to the third set of parliamentary elections in 1993. Electoral mechanisms have been slower to institutionalize.

We have attempted to show the impact that institutional structure can have on the political transitions that emerge, arguing that the given institutional matrix shapes the form of political collapse, which in turn generates particular conditions and sets in motion a process of path dependency. Our second institutional component is equally important – that of institutional persistence, the retention of pre-transition political institutions into the post-transition period.

While transitions may involve the collapse of given institutionalized political orders, the actual state, para-statal and economic machinery of these systems – bureaucracies, staffs, industrial organization, regulatory and supervisory routines – are much more resistant to de-institutionalization than the ruling order itself. Parties, leaders and ideologies may become bankrupt, losing the confidence of society, but the fact that these systems end in political *transitions* indicates that the institutions of rule are not destroyed, as often occurs in civil war or revolution, but rather transferred from one ruling order to another. Organizational reform may be enacted, governmental and economic patterns may alter, but large sections of the state and economic institutional core are likely to remain intact – for better or worse.

This is evident in Eastern Europe, where although the single-party system of control has collapsed, the institutional matrix of state structures was left much intact. Rather than withering away, these organizations have become the only certain reference points in the post-communist order, central tools in the formation of new policies and a source of political conflict. While there is no doubt that these

24. This was ironically also backed by the ex-communists, who had done much worse in single-member districts than they had originally imagined.

institutions are now more subject to radical change or dismantlement than under state socialism, the wholesale remaking of their organizational forms is unlikely.

In fact, as Joachim Jens Hesse notes with regard to public administration, even in the more developed states of East–Central Europe 'it might come as a surprise that the extensive array of government departments and national offices, which form the core of the central machinery of the national government, has not been subject to comprehensive reform since 1989.[25] In many cases parliamentary parties lack the political power or administrative capital to enact comprehensive organizational change, hoping instead to reform existing institutions rather than to replace them. These remaining political institutions have a strong influence on post-communist consolidation, for as a new institutional matrix is formed it will be built in large part from the remnants of the old order. Institutional precedents continue the process of cooptation and isomorphism; political transitions, then, appear as more of a turning-point in institutional history than one of sudden discontinuity.

In the case of Hungary, this element of state institutional continuity initially resulted in the creation of an almost conspiratorial 'elite transplacement' argument that in fact what has occurred is not so much a political transition but rather a change in the political élite at the top.[26] This argument can in fact be extended across much of Eastern Europe. However, what is particularly striking is the fact that unlike in the rest of Eastern Europe, where institutional inertia plays a strong role in blunting organizational change, in Hungary widespread administrative reform appears much less necessary to begin with.

This is a direct result of the legacy of the Kádárist liberalization and its 'intellectualization' of state organs under socialism, where technical experts were recruited into the state sector as a way to implement

25. Joachim Jens Hesse, 'From Transformation to Modernization: Administrative Change in Central and Eastern Europe', *Public Administration* **71** (Spring/Summer 1993): 225; see also Eric M. Rice, 'Public Administration in Post-Socialist Eastern Europe', *Public Administration Review* **52** (March/April 1992): 116–24; and Theo A.J. Toonen, 'Analysing Institutional Change and Administrative Transformation: A Comparative View', *Public Administration* **71** (Spring/Summer 1993), esp. 159–66.

26. As this relates to the Hungarian case in particular: see Tőkés, 'Hungary's New Political Elites', and Erzsébet Szalai, 'A hatalom metamorfózisa? [The metamorphosis of power?]', *Valóság* **6** (1991): 3–6.

reform and block their rise through the party ranks – as we discussed in Chapter 2. The effect of these institutional patterns has been that in comparison to other post-communist states, following the transition Hungary enjoyed a relatively high level of competency among its existing staff, who had been involved since the 1960s in studying and implementing the legal and administrative mechanisms needed for a market economy.[27]

The weaker influence of the cadre system within the Hungarian state *apparatus* has also meant that the need or desire to purge civil servants because of their close association with the previous regime has been negligible in comparison to Poland and Czechoslovakia, where intelligentsia co-optation was much lower.[28] As one observer of Hungarian politics has noted, the result has been that the 'national spring cleaning', promised by the ruling MDF in its 1990 campaign, in the final analysis became little more than a 'light house dusting'.[29]

Several authors have in fact argued that as a result of this particular institutional legacy administrative modernization and the framework for a market economy were in the early years of the transition much more advanced in Hungary than in either Poland or the Czech Republic.[30] However, this would seem to contradict what appears to be more successful economic reform in the last two cases than in Hungary (though this may have been changing, at least in the case of the Czech Republic).[31] To return to an earlier point, while institutional configurations may create certain political opportunities just as they do restraints, this in no way guarantees that political actors will successfully translate these opportunities into good policy.

Returning to our two main themes, the vacuum created by the collapse of the ruling order and the persistence of other institutions which the post-transition order must face will have a powerful effect on the

27. Gábor Szabó, 'Administrative Transition in a Post-Communist Society: The Case of Hungary', *Public Administration* 71 (Spring/Summer 1993): 90–92.
28. Toonen, 'Analysing Institutional Change and Administrative Transformation': 165.
29. Tőkés, 'Hungary's New Political Elites': 259.
30. Toonen, 'Analysing Institutional Change and Administrative Transformation': 163–4; Szabó, 'Administrative Transformation in a Post-Communist Society'; Hesse, 'From Transformation to Modernization': 227.
31. Paul Marer, 'Hungary During 1988–1994: A Political Economy Perspective', in *East–Central European Economies in Transition: Study Papers Submitted to the Joint Economic Committee, Congress of the United States* (Washington, DC: US Government Printing Office, 1994): 480–505.

trajectory of these political systems. How the new political landscape forms is tied to the system which preceded it. And, as new political actors 'settle into the trenches', they will confront existing norms and structures which will influence their behaviour and the policies that follow.[32] It is still too early to tell how these variations in institutional change will affect the success or failure of political and economic transformation in these countries.

However, beyond the terms of success or failure, the continued interaction of institutions and institutional change will also be crucial in the particular *kind* of state, societal and economic relations which develop in the region as a whole and from country to country. We have seen that at the constitutional and party organizational levels, institutions have had an important impact in this regard. They also play a significant role in those sectors where entirely new institutions are being constructed.

One important example where the previous institutional matrix continues to affect current policy is that of marketization and privatization. In his study of privatization strategies in East–Central Europe, David Stark has noted the wide variation in the policies pursued from country to country, ranging from citizen grants and voucher systems to spontaneous privatization or the direct auctioning of state economic assets to the highest bidder.

Rather than being the result of élite bargaining, random forces or objective policy formation, Stark found that the distinct differences in each form of privatization policy in the region could be best explained by variations in institutional patterns under the previous order and the impact they have had on transitions and the subsequent consolidation of democratic rule. As he concludes, 'these diverse paths of extrication, and the preceding differences in social structure and political organization that brought them about, have had the consequence that the current political institutions and forms of interest intermediation between state and society differ significantly'.[33] Similarly, László Bruszt has pointed to the importance of system variation in the region in the post-transition

32. Philippe C. Schmitter (with Terry Lynn Karl), 'The Conceptual Travails of Transitologists and Consolidologists: How Far to the East Should They Attempt to Go?', *Slavic Review* **53** (Spring/Summer 1994): 176.

33. David Stark, 'Path Dependence and Privatization Strategies in East Central Europe', *East European Politics and Societies* **6** (Winter 1992): 48–9; see also G. Szabó, 'Administrative Transition in a Post-Communist Society'.

possibilities for carrying out painful economic restructuring without jeopardizing social peace.[34]

The effect of institutional configuration in influencing the differing paths taken to privatization and marketization are important, for they will not only influence the relative success of these economies but, as Stark points out, they will also affect the particular kind of economy that results from economic transformation. In short, as Bruszt and Stark have observed elsewhere with regard to political transition and the post-transition order, 'the differences in how the pieces fell apart have consequences for how political and economic institutions can be reconstructed in the current period'.[35]

CONCLUSION

During the process of continuing transition in Eastern Europe and elsewhere, state and societal patterns and structures will not be reconstituted from whole cloth. Rather, they will in part be fashioned from the remnants of the old order, informed by the legacies of institutions which have persevered or collapsed. Some of these legacies may easily be overcome by new leaders, parties and programmes; other legacies are much more entrenched, and not so easily erased.[36] How civil society, market economies and state power develop over the long term requires us to understand the institutional framework of the past, and in what ways it persists into the present period.

The use of institutional analysis into this study of the Hungarian political transition has been intended to serve as a heuristic device, elucidating how undemocratic orders develop with reference to their

34. László Bruszt, 'Transformative Politics: Social Costs and Social Peace in East Central Europe', *East European Politics and Societies* **6** (Winter 1992): 55–75.
35. László Bruszt and David Stark, 'Remaking the Political Field in Hungary: From the Politics of Confrontation to the Politics of Competition', *Journal of International Affairs* **45** (Summer 1991): 19, n. 11.
36. Stephen Hanson disaggregates the institutional legacy of state socialism into its ideological, political, socioeconomic and cultural components, arguing that each has its own particular ability or inability to persist into the present; such frameworks are useful in narrowing our research on post-communist change: 'The Leninist Legacy and Institutional Change', *Comparative Political Studies* **28** (July 1995): 306–14.

wider environment, which they seek to manipulate, reorder, adapt to, or ignore. We draw the conclusion that the kind of institutionalization which results will affect the manner of autocratic rule, as well as its inevitable decline and the prospects for subsequent democratization. This gives us a set of parameters in which undemocratic systems can be analysed, while allowing for the importance of individual, regional or historical factors in each case. Ideally, such an approach can be a means by which area studies and general theory reinforce each other, rather than a source of conflict (as has become the case in East European studies since 1989).[37] Another important point is that while institutionalization can strongly affect politics as a constraining and enabling force, it alone will not dictate the form of transition or the political consolidation which follows. The role of chance, individuals, unforeseen domestic or international developments can have a tremendous impact, overriding institutional forces and turning history in a radically different direction. Nor can institutional analysis predict *when* a transition is more or less likely to occur.

Keeping in mind these caveats, by integrating our studies of 'transitology' and 'consolidology' with an institutional approach, we can complement our current understanding of the impact of micro- and macro-level forces surrounding political transitions. This can help derive a more theoretical view of the topic without sacrificing the unique aspects of the circumstances under consideration. In doing so, we allow for the broader forces of theory to merge with the more inexplicable aspects of time and place.

37. The best example of this debate can be found in the exchange between Terry Lynn Karl, Philippe Schmitter and Valerie Bunce: see Valerie Bunce, 'Should Transitologists Be Grounded?', *Slavic Review* **54** (Spring 1995): 111–27; and Terry Lynn Karl and Philippe C. Schmitter, 'From an Iron Curtain to a Paper Curtain: Grounding Transitologists or Students of Postcommunism?', *Slavic Review* **54** (Winter 1995): 965–87.

Appendix 1

A Note on Primary Sources

This study, which has its origins in an earlier doctoral dissertation, is based upon research carried out in Hungary in 1991 and from September 1992 to June 1993. Analysis is based fundamentally on primary sources, in particular approximately two hundred unpublished documents produced by various reform circles. A significant number of these documents were provided by József Géczi, Member of Parliament for the Socialist Party and co-founder of the first reform circle in Szeged. This personal archive consists of documents which both Géczi and others collected throughout the course of the movement. Additional documents were also made available to the author by other interview subjects.

These documents primarily take the form of position papers which analyse the current political situation in Hungary, suggest various forms of institutional reform, map out potential strategies at the local and national level, or form short manifestos meant for internal party circulation in order to broaden the base of support. Administrative documents and communications make up a much smaller portion of the papers. During the course of the study particular documents are cited on occasion, although more general observations or arguments derive from a qualitative assessment and synthesis of these materials from given points in time.

A second major source of information were interviews. Open-ended interviews were conducted with the most prominent reform circle figures, numbering about thirty in total, with each interview lasting approximately one to two hours. Interviews were targeted for those regions with the most active reform circles, covering half of the total counties in Hungary. These interviews were capped by a concluding roundtable discussion with close to twenty reform circle participants, some of whom had not previously been interviewed. This took place within the context of a public presentation by the author of his initial findings, sponsored by the Europrogress Association, Budapest on 11 June 1993.

These discussions with reform circle participants were complemented by interviews with a half-dozen prominent social scientists in Hungary, who were actively involved in the internal reform dialogue within the upper ranks of the MSZMP. A last major source of interviews were those conducted with three of the four members of the party's ruling Presidium in 1989: former Ministers of State Imre Pozsgay and Rezső Nyers, and former General Secretary Károly Grósz. These interviews were conducted in an open-ended format, lasting one to two hours apiece.

A final important primary source utilized was Central Committee and Politburo documents and transcripts, now administered by the Hungarian National Archives, which permitted a restricted investigation of this material. Verbatim transcripts of Central Committee meetings were provided and are cited in this study. Other material included documents from these meetings and those of the Politburo, as well as summaries of particular Politburo sessions. Analyses of verbatim transcripts of Politburo sessions were not, however, permitted.

Secondary research material was derived largely from national and provincial newspapers and magazines (including independent publications as well as those under jurisdiction of party and government organs) and both published and unpublished studies of the Hungarian transition.

Appendix 2

List of Abbreviations

AJTE	*Attila József Tudományos Egyetem* József Attila Scientific University
EKA	*Ellenzéki Kerekasztal* Opposition Roundtable
FIDESZ	*Fiatal Demokraták Szövetsége* Alliance of Young Democrats
FKGP	*Független Kisgazda- Földmunkás és Polgári Párt* Independent Smallholders' Party
HNF	*Hazafias Népfront* Patriotic Peoples' Front
KDNP	*Kereszténydemokrata Néppárt* Christian Democratic Party
MDF	*Magyar Demokrata Fórum* Hungarian Democratic Forum
MDP	*Magyar Dolgozók Pártja* Hungarian Workers' Party
MSZDP	*Magyarországi Szociáldemokrata Párt* Hungarian Social Democratic Party
MSZMP	*Magyar Szocialista Munkáspárt* Hungarian Socialist Workers' Party
MSZP	*Magyar Szocialista Párt* Hungarian Socialist Party
OKT	*Országos Koordinációs Tanács* Reform Circle National Coordinating Council
PIB	*Politikai Intéző Bizottság* Political Executive Committee (successor to the Politburo)
PZPR	*Polska Zjednoczona Partia Rabotnicza* Polish United Workers' Party

SZDSZ	*Szabad Demokraták Szövetsége* Alliance of Free Democrats
TTI	*Társadalomtudományi Intézet* Social Science Institute

Select Bibliography

I. THEORETICAL WORKS

Almond, Gabriel, *A Discipline Divided: Schools and Sects in Political Science*. Newbury Park, CA: Sage, 1990.

Bermeo, Nancy, 'Redemocratization and Transition Elections: A Comparison of Spain and Portugal'. *Comparative Politics* **19** (January 1987): 213–31.

Calhoun, Craig, Marshall W. Meyer and W. Richard Scott (eds), *Structures of Power and Constraint: Papers in Honor of Peter M. Blau*. Cambridge: Cambridge University Press, 1990.

Cardoso, Fernando Henrique, 'The Characterization of Authoritarian Regimes', in David Collier (ed.), *The New Authoritarianism in Latin America*. Princeton: Princeton University Press, 1979: 33–57.

Cook, Karen Schweers and Margaret Levi (eds), *The Limits of Rationality*. Chicago: University of Chicago Press, 1990.

Dahl, Robert A., *Polyarchy: Participation and Contestation*. New Haven, CT: Yale University Press, 1971.

——, *Democracy and its Critics*. New Haven, CT: Yale University Press, 1989.

Dahrendorf, Ralf, *Class and Class Conflict in Modern Society*. Stanford, CA: Stanford University Press, 1959.

DiMaggio, Paul J. and Walter W. Powell, 'The Iron Cage Revisited: Institutional Isomorphism and Collective Rationality in Organizational Fields', in Powell and DiMaggio, 1991: 63–82.

DiPalma, Guiseppe, *To Craft Democracies: An Essay on Democratic Transitions*. Berkeley, CA: University of California Press, 1990.

Douglas, Mary, *How Institutions Think*. Syracuse, NY: Syracuse University Press, 1986.

Etzioni, Amitai, *A Comparative Analysis of Complex Organizations*. New York: The Free Press, 1975.

Friedrich, Carl and Zbigniew Brzezinski, *Totalitarian Dictatorship and Autocracy*. Cambridge: Cambridge University Press, 1956.

Gamson, William, *Power and Discontent*. Homewood, IL: Dorsey, 1968.

Gella, Aleksander (ed.), *The Intelligentsia and the Intellectuals*. London: Sage, 1976.

Giddens, Anthony, *The Class Structure of Advanced Societies*. New York: Harper & Row, 1975.

Gottman, Jean, *Center and Periphery: Spatial Variation in Politics*. Beverly Hills, CA: Sage, 1980.

Gouldner, Alvin, *Patterns of Industrial Bureaucracy*. Glencoe, IL: Free Press, 1957.

——, 'Cosmopolitans and Locals: Toward an Analysis of Latent Social Roles–I'. *Administrative Science Quarterly* **2** (December 1957): 281–306.

——, 'Organizational Analysis', in Robert K. Merton, Leonard Broom and Leonard S. Cottrell, Jr (eds), *Sociology Today*. New York: Basic Books, 1959: 400–28.

——, *The Future of the Intellectuals and the Rise of the New Class*. New York: Seabury Press, 1979.

Heberle, Rudolph, *Social Movements: An Introduction to Political Sociology*. New York: Appleton, 1951.

Heper, Metin, 'Transitions to Democracy Reconsidered: A Historical Perspective', in Dankwart Rustow (ed.), *Comparative Political Dynamics: Global Research Perspectives*. New York: Harper-Collins, 1991: 192–210.

Higley, John and Richard Gunther (eds), *Elites and Democratic Consolidation in Latin America and Southern Europe*. Cambridge: Cambridge University Press, 1992.

Hirschman, Albert O., *Exit, Voice, and Loyalty*. Cambridge, MA: Harvard University Press, 1970.

Huntington, Samuel P., *Political Order in Developing Societies*. New Haven, CT: Yale University Press, 1968.

——, 'Will More Countries Become Democratic?'. *Political Science Quarterly* **99** (Summer 1984): 193–218.

——, *The Third Wave*. Norman, OK: University of Oklahoma Press, 1991.

—— and Clement C. Moore (eds), *Authoritarian Politics in Modern Society*. New York: Basic Books, 1970.

Ikenberry, John C., 'Conclusion: An Institutional Approach to American Foreign Economic Policy', in John C. Ikenberry, David A. Lake and Michael Mastanduno (eds), *The State and American Foreign Economic Policy*. Ithaca, NY: Cornell University Press, 1991: 219-43.

Janos, Andrew C., *Politics and Paradigms*. Stanford, CA: Stanford University Press, 1986.

Jepperson, Ronald L., 'Institutions, Institutional Effects, and Institionalism', in Powell and DiMaggio, 1991: 143–63.

—— and John W. Meyer., 'The Public Order and the Construction of Formal Organizations', in Powell and DiMaggio, 1991: 204–31.

Krasner, Stephen D., 'Approaches to the State: Alternative Conceptions and Historical Dynamics'. *Comparative Politics* **16** (January 1984): 226–30.

Lammers, Cornelius J., 'Strikes and Mutinies: A Comparative Study of Organizational Conflicts between Rulers and Ruled'. *Administration Science Quarterly* **14** (December 1969): 558–72.

Linz, Juan, 'Totalitarian and Authoritarian Regimes', in Fred I. Greenstein and Nelson Polsby (eds), *Handbook of Political Science*. Reading, MA: Addison-Wesley, 1975, vol. 3: 175–411.

—— and Alfred Stepan, *The Breakdown of Democratic Regimes*, 4 vols. Baltimore, MD: Johns Hopkins University Press, 1978.

——, *Problems of Democratic Transition and Consolidation*. Baltimore, MD: Johns Hopkins University Press, 1996.

Lipset, Seymour Martin, 'Some Social Requisites of Democracy: Economic Development and Political Legitimacy'. *American Political Science Review* **53** (March 1959): 69–105.

——, *Political Man: The Social Bases of Politics*. Garden City, NY: Anchor Books and Doubleday, 1960.

——, 'Revolt against Modernity', in Per Torsvik (ed.), *Mobilization, Center-Periphery Structures and Nation-Building*. Bergen: Universitetsforlaget, 1981: 431–500.

March, James G. (ed.), *Handbook of Organizations*. Chicago, IL: Rand-McNally, 1965.

—— and Johan P. Olsen, *Ambiguity and Choice in Organizations*. Bergen: Universitetsforlaget, 1976.

——, 'The New Institutionalism: Organizational Factors in Political Life'. *American Political Science Review* **78** (September 1984): 734–49.

——, *Rediscovering Insitutions: The Organizational Basis of Politics*. New York: The Free Press, 1989.

Marx, Karl, 'The Eighteenth Brumaire of Louis Bonaparte', in Robert C. Tucker (ed.), *The Marx–Engels Reader*. New York: W.W. Norton, 1972: 436–525.

Meyer, John W. and Brian Rowan, 'Institutionalized Organization: Formal Structure as Myth and Ceremony', in Meyer and Scott, 1983: 21–44.

Meyer, John W. and W. Richard Scott (with the assistance of Brian Rowan and Terrence Deal), *Organizational Environments: Ritual and Rationality*. Beverly Hills, CA: Sage, 1983.

——, 'Centralization and the Legitimacy Problems of Local Government', in Meyer and Scott, 1983: 199–215.

Michels, Robert, *Political Parties* (Glencoe, IL: The Free Press, 1949 [1915]).

Moore, Barrington, *Social Origins of Dictatorship and Democracy: Lord and Peasant in the Making of the Modern World*. Boston, MA: Beacon Press, 1966.

O'Donnell, Guillermo, Phillippe C. Schmitter and Lawrence Whitehead (eds), *Transitions from Authoritarian Rule*, 4 vols. Baltimore, MA: Johns Hopkins University Press, 1986.

Parsons, Talcott, 'Communism and the West: The Sociology of the Conflict', in Amitai Etzioni and Eva Etzioni (eds), *Social Change: Sources, Patterns, and Consequences*. New York: Basic Books, 1964: 390–99.

Perrow, Charles, *Complex Organizations: A Critical Essay*. New York: McGraw-Hill, 1986.

Polsby, Nelson, 'The Institutionalization of the U.S. House of Representatives'. *American Political Science Review* **62** (March 1968): 144–68.

Pondy, Louis R., 'Varieties of Organizational Conflict'. *Administrative Science Quarterly* **14** (December 1969): 499–505.

Powell, Walter W. and Paul J. DiMaggio (eds), *The New Institutionalism in Organizational Analysis*. Chicago, IL: University of Chicago Press, 1991.

——, 'Introduction', in Powell and DiMaggio, 1991:1–40.

Przeworski, Adam, *Democracy and the Market: Political and Economic Reforms in Eastern Europe and Latin America*. Chicago, IL: University of Chicago Press, 1991.

Pye, Lucian W., 'Political Science and the Crisis of Authoritarianism'. *American Political Science Review* **84** (March 1990): 3-19.

Rustow, Dankwart, 'Transitions to Democracy: Toward a Dynamic Model'. *Comparative Politics* **2** (April 1970): 337-63.

Sartori, Giovanni, 'Totalitarianism, Model Mania, and Learning from Error'. *Journal of Theoretical Politics* **5** (January 1993): 5-22.

Schmitter, Philippe C. and Terry Karl, 'The Types of Democracy Emerging in Southern and Eastern Europe and South and Central America', in Volten, 1992: 42-68.

Schmitter, Philippe C. with Terry Lynn Karl, 'The Conceptual Travails of Transitologists and Consolidologists: How Far to the East Should They Attempt to Go?'. *Slavic Review* **53** (Spring/Summer 1994): 173-85.

Scott, W. Richard, 'Unpacking Institutional Arguments', in Powell and DiMaggio, 1991: 164-82.

——, *Organizations: Rational, Natural and Open*. Englewood Cliffs, NJ: Prentice Hall, 1992.

Selznick, Philip, *Leadership in Administration*. Evanston, IL: Row, Peterson, 1957.

——, *The Organizational Weapon*. Glencoe, IL: The Free Press, 1960.

——, 'Foundations of the Theory of Organization', in Amitai Etzioni (ed.) *Complex Organizations*. New York: Holt, Rinehart & Winston, 1961: 18-31.

——, *TVA and the Grass Roots*. Berkeley, CA: University of California Press, 1980 [1949].

Shain, Yossi and Juan J. Linz (eds), *Between States: Interim Governments in Democratic Transitions*. Cambridge: Cambridge University Press, 1995.

Shepsle, Kenneth, 'The Institutional Foundations of Committee Power'. *American Political Science Review* **81** (1987): 85-104.

——, 'Studying Institutions: Some Lessons from the Rational Choice Approach'. *Journal of Theoretical Politics* **1** (1989): 131-47.

Shills, Edward, *Center and Periphery: Essays in Macrosociology*. Selected papers of Edward Shills, vol. 2. Chicago, IL: University of Chicago Press, 1975.

Simon, Herbert A., *Administrative Behavior*. New York: Macmillan, 1945.

Skocpol, Theda, *States and Social Revolutions*. Cambridge: Cambridge University Press, 1979.

——, 'Bringing the State Back In: Current Research', in Peter B. Evans, Dietrich Reuschemeyer and Theda Skocpol (eds), *Bringing the State Back In*. Cambridge: Cambridge University Press, 1985, 3–43.

Stepan, Alfred, 'Paths toward Redemocratization', in O'Donnell, Schmitter and Whitehead, 1986: 64–84.

Tarrow, Sidney, *Between Center and Periphery*. New Haven, CT: Yale University Press, 1977.

Thompson, James D., *Organizations in Action*. New York: McGraw-Hill, 1967.

Valenzuela, J. Samuel, *Modernization and Bureaucratic Authoritarianism: Studies in South American Politics*, Institute of International Studies, Politics and Modernization Series, no. 9. Berkeley, CA: Institute of International Studies, 1973.

Weber, Max, *The Theory of Social and Economic Organization*, ed. and trans. A.M. Henderson and Talcott Parsons. New York: The Free Press, 1947.

Wiarda, Howard J., 'Comparative Politics Past and Present', in Howard J. Wiarda (ed.), *New Directions in Comparative Politics*. Boulder, CO: Westview Press, 1985: 3–25.

Wilson, James Q., *Political Organizations*. New York: Basic Books, 1973.

Zald, Mayer N., *Organizational Change: The Political Economy of the YMCA*. Chicago, IL: University of Chicago Press, 1970.

—— and John D. McCarthy, 'Epilogue: An Agenda for Research', in Mayer N. Zald and John D. McCarthy (ed.), *The Dynamics of Social Movements*. Cambridge, MA: Winthrop, 1979: 238–46.

Zucker, Lynne G. (ed.), *Institutional Patterns and Organization*. Cambridge, MA: Ballinger, 1988.

II. STUDIES OF EASTERN EUROPE AND THE SOVIET UNION

Ash, Timothy Garton, *The Uses of Adversity*. New York: Vintage, 1990.

Baylis, Thomas A., *The Technical Intelligentsia and the East German Elite*. Berkeley, CA: University of California Press, 1974.

Beck, Carl, 'Bureaucracy and Political Development in Eastern Europe', in Joseph LaPalombara (ed.), *Bureaucracy and Political Development*. Princeton, NJ: Princeton University Press, 1967: 268–300.

Bermeo, Nancy (ed.), *Liberalization and Democratization: Change in the Soviet Union and Eastern Europe*. Baltimore, MD: Johns Hopkins University Press, 1992.

Bielasiak, Jack, 'Lateral and Vertical Elite Differentiation in European Communist States'. *Studies in Comparative Communism* **11** (Spring/Summer 1978): 121–41.

——, 'Regime Transition, Founding Elections, and Political Fields in Eastern Europe', unpublished paper, Indiana University, 1991.

Bruszt, László, 'Transformative Politics: Social Costs and Social Peace in East Central Europe'. *East European Politics and Societies* **6** (Winter 1992): 55–75.

Childs, David, Thomas A. Baylis and Marlyn Reuschemeyer (eds), *East Germany in Comparative Perspective*. New York: Routledge, 1989.

Chirot, Daniel, 'The Corporatist Model and Socialism: Notes on Romanian Development'. *Theory and Society* **9** (March 1980): 363–79.

Comisso, Ellen, 'Introduction: State Structures, Political Processes, and Collective Choice in CMEA States'. *International Organization* **40** (Spring 1986): 196–238.

——, 'Where Have We Been and Where Are We Going? Analyzing Post-Socialist Politics in the 1990s', in William Crotty (ed.), *Political Science: Looking to the Future*, vol. 2, *Comparative Politics, Policy and International Relations*. Evanston, IL: Northwestern University Press, 1991: 77–122.

Crawford, Beverly and Arend Lijphart, 'Explaining Political and Economic Change in Post Communist Eastern Europe: Old Legacies,

New Institutions, Hegemonic Norms, and International Pressures'. *Comparative Political Studies* **28** (July 1995): 171–99.

Croan, Melvin, 'Is Mexico the Future of Eastern Europe: Institutional Adaptability and Political Change in Comparative Perspective', in Huntington and Moore, 1970: 451–83.

Djilas, Milovan, *The New Class*. New York: Praeger, 1957.

Fleron, Frederic J., 'Cooptation as a Mechanism of Adaptation to Change'. *Polity* **2** (Winter 1969): 177–201.

Geddes, Barbara, 'A Comparative Perspective on the Leninist Legacy in Eastern Europe'. *Comparative Political Studies* **28** (July 1995): 239–74.

Gitelman, Zvi, 'The Limits of Organization and Enthusiasm: The Double Failure of the Solidarity Movement and the Polish United Workers' Party', in Kay Lawson and Peter H. Merkl (eds), *When Parties Fail*. Princeton, NJ: Princeton University Press, 1988: 421–46.

Hahn, Werner, *Democracy in a Communist Party*. New York: Columbia University Press, 1987.

Hanson, Stephen E., 'The Leninist Legacy and Institutional Change'. *Comparative Political Studies* **28** (July 1995): 306–14.

Hesse, Joachim Jens, 'From Transformation to Modernization: Administrative Change in Central and Eastern Europe'. *Public Administration* **71** (Spring/Summer 1993): 219–57.

Hodges, Donald C., *The Bureaucratization of Socialism*. Amherst, MA: University of Massachusetts Press, 1981.

Holmes, Leslie (ed.), *The Withering Away of the State?* London: Sage, 1981.

Hough, Jerry F., *The Soviet Prefects: The Local Party Organs in Industrial Decision-making*. Cambridge, MA: Harvard University Press, 1969.

——, *The Soviet Union and Social Science Theory*. Cambridge, MA: Harvard University Press, 1977.

Ionescu, Ghita, *The Politics of the European Communist States*. New York: Praeger, 1967.

Janos, Andrew C., 'Group Politics in Communist Society: A Second Look at the Pluralistic Model', in Huntington and Moore, 1970: 437–50.

——, (ed.), *Authoritarian Politics in Communist Europe: Uniformity and Diversity in One-Party States*. Institute of International Studies

Research Series no. 28. Berkeley, CA: Institute of International Studies, 1976.

——, 'Social Science, Communism, and the Dynamics of Political Change', in Bermeo, 1992: 81–112.

Johnson, Chalmers (ed.), *Change in Communist Systems*. Palo Alto, CA: Stanford University Press, 1970.

Jowitt, Kenneth, 'Weber, Trotsky and Holmes on the Study of Leninist Regimes'. *Journal of International Affairs* **45** (Summer 1991): 31–49.

——, *New World Disorder: The Leninist Extinction*. Berkeley, CA: University of California Press, 1992.

Kaminski, Bartolmiej, *The Collapse of State Socialism: The Case of Poland*. Princeton, NJ: Princeton University Press, 1991.

Kautsky, John H., 'Comparative Communism versus Comparative Politics'. *Studies in Comparative Communism* **6** (Spring–Summer 1973): 135–70.

Kennedy, Michael D., *Professionals, Power, and Solidarity in Poland*. Cambridge: Cambridge University Press, 1991.

Lane, David, *The Socialist Industrial State*. Boulder, CO: Westview Press, 1976.

Lipjhart, Arend, 'Democratization and Constitutional Choices in Czecho-Slovakia, Hungary, and Poland, 1989–1991', in Szoboszlai, *Flying Blind*: 99–113.

Lovenduski, Joni and Jean Woodall, *Politics and Society in Eastern Europe*. Bloomington, IN: Indiana University Press, 1987.

Nee, Victor and David Stark (eds), *Remaking the Economic Institutions of Socialism: China and Eastern Europe*. Stanford, CA: Stanford University Press, 1989.

Perry, Albert, *The New Class Divided*. New York: Macmillan, 1966.

Rakovski, Marc [pseud. of János Kis and György Bence], *Toward an East European Marxism*. London: Allison & Busby, 1978.

Rigby, T.H., 'Politics in the Mono-organizational Society', in Janos, 1976: 31–80.

—— and Ferenc Fehér (eds), *Political Legitimation in Communist States*. London: Macmillan, 1982.

Skilling, H. Gordon and Franklyn Griffiths (eds), *Interest Groups in Soviet Politics*. Princeton, NJ: Princeton University Press, 1971.

Stansizkis, Jadwiga, *The Dynamics of the Breakthrough in Eastern Europe*. Berkeley, CA: University of California Press, 1991.

Stark, David, 'Path Dependence and Privatization Strategies in East Central Europe'. *East European Politics and Societies* **6** (Winter 1992): 17–54.

—— and Victor Nee, 'Toward an Institutional Analysis of State Socialism', in Nee and Stark, 1989: 1–31.

Szelényi, Iván, *Urban Inequalities Under State Socialism*. Oxford: Oxford University Press, 1983.

——, 'The Prospects and Limits of the East European New Class Project: An Auto-critical Reflection on *The Intellectuals on the Road to Class Power*'. *Politics and Society* **15** (1986–87): 103–44.

—— and György Konrád, *The Intellectuals on the Road to Class Power*. New York: Harcourt, Brace, Jovanovich, 1979.

——, 'Intellectuals and Domination in Post-Communist Societies', in Iván Szelényi, *A poszt-kommunista átmenet társadalmi konfliktusai* [The social conflicts of the post-communist transition]. Budapest: MTA Politikai Tudományok Intézete, 1992: 59–75.

Szoboszlai, György (ed.), *Democracy and Political Transformation: Theories and East–Central European Realities*. Budapest: Hungarian Political Science Association, 1991.

—— (ed.), *Flying Blind: Emerging Democracies in East–Central Europe*. Budapest: Hungarian Political Science Association, 1992.

Toonen, Theo A.J., 'Analysing Institutional Change and Administrative Transformation: A Comparative View'. *Public Administration* **71** (Spring/Summer 1993): 151–68.

Triska, Jan F. and Paul M. Cocks (eds), *Political Development in Eastern Europe*. New York: Praeger, 1977.

Ulam, Adam, *The Unfinished Revolution*. New York: Random House, 1960.

Volten, Peter M.E. (ed.), *Bound to Change: Consolidating Democracy in East Central Europe*. New York: Institute for East–West Studies, 1992.

Weydenthal, Jan B. de, *The Communists of Poland*. Stanford, CA: Hoover Institution Press, 1986.

Wiatr, Jerzy (ed.), *Studies in the Polish Political System*. Warsaw: Ossolineum, 1967.

Woodall, Jean, *The Socialist Corporation and Technocratic Power*. Cambridge: Cambridge University Press, 1982.

III. SPECIFIC MATERIAL RELATING TO HUNGARY

A modellváltás anatómiája [The anatomy of the change of model]. Budapest: TTI, 1989.

Ács, Zoltán, *Kizárt a párt* [Expelled from the party]. n.p.: Primo Kiadó, n.d.

Ágh, Attila, 'A félfordulat éve [The year of the half-turn]', in Kurtán, Sándor and Vass, 1989: 23-34.

——, *A Századvég Gyermekei* [The children of the end of the century]. Budapest: Közgazdasági és Jogi Könyvkiadó, 1990.

——, 'The Emergence of the "Science of Democracy" and its Impact on the Democratic Transition'. *Aula* **XIII** (1991): 96-111.

——, 'Organizational Change in the Hungarian Socialist Party'. Paper originally presented at the ECPR Conference, Madrid, April 1994; Hungarian Center for Democracy Studies Foundation, Budapest Papers on Democratic Transition no. 76 (1994).

Andorka, Rudolf, Tamás Kolosi and György Vukovich (eds), *Társadalmi Riport 1990* [Social Report 1990]. Budapest: TÁRKI, 1990.

——, *Társadalmi Riport 1992*. Budapest: TARKI, 1992.

Antal, László, Lajos Bokros, László Lengyel and György Matolcsy, 'Fordulát és reform [Turnabout and reform]'. *Medvetánc*, special issue (1987): 5-129.

Batt, Judy, *Economic Reform and Political Change in Eastern Europe*. New York: St. Martin's Press, 1988.

Benkő, Judit, György Kerekes and János Patkós, *A születés szépséges kínjai, avagy a rendhagyó híradás az MSZMP kongresszusról 1989 Október 6-9*. [The beautiful agony of birth, or irregular information concerning the 6-9 October 1989 MSZMP congress]. Budapest: Kossuth, n.d.

Berend, Iván T., 'Magyarország 1988 [Hungary 1988]', in Kurtán, Sándor and Vass, 1989: 45-52.

——, *The Hungarian Economic Reforms 1953-1988*. Cambridge: Cambridge University Press, 1990.

Bihari, Mihály, *Demokratikus út a szabadsághoz* [Democratic road to freedom]. Budapest: Gondolat, 1990.

—— (ed.), *A többpártrendszer kialakulása Magyarországon 1985-*

1991 [The formation of multiparty system in Hungary, 1985–91]. Budapest: Kossuth, 1992.

Bogár, László, *Kitörési kísérleteink* [Our attempts to break out]. Budapest: Közgazdasági és Jogi Könyvkiadó, 1989.

Bőhm, Antal, 'A helyi hatalom és a lakosság részvétel esélyei [Local power and the chances for community participation]'. *Tér és társadalom* **1** (1987): 17–30.

—— and László Pál (eds), *Helyi Társadalom* [Local society], 5 vols. Budapest: TTI, 1983–87.

Borsányi, György and János Kende, *The History of the Working Class Movement in Hungary*. Budapest: Corvina, 1988.

Bozóki, András, 'Post-Communist Transition: Political Tendencies in Hungary', in Bozóki, Körösényi and Schöpflin, 1992: 13–29.

——, 'Hungary's Road to Systemic Change: The Opposition Roundtable'. *East European Politics and Society* **7** (Spring 1993): 276–308.

——, András Körösényi and George Schöpflin (eds), *Post-Communist Transition: Emerging Pluralism in Hungary*. London: Pinter, 1992.

Bruszt, László, '"Without Us but For Us"? Political Orientation in Hungary in the Period of Late Paternalism'. *Social Research* **55** (Spring/Summer 1988): 43–76.

——, '1989: The Negotiated Revolution in Hungary', in Bozóki, Körösényi and Schöpflin, 1992, 45–59.

—— and János Simon, *A lecsendesített többség* [The appeased majority]. Budapest: TTI, 1990: 33–74.

Bruszt, László and David Stark, 'Remaking the Political Field in Hungary: From the Politics of Confrontation to the Politics of Competition'. *Journal of International Affairs* **45** (Summer 1991): 201–45.

Bunce, Valerie and Mária Csanádi, 'Uncertainty in the Transition: Post-Communism in Hungary'. *East European Politics and Societies* **7** (Spring 1993): 240–75.

Burawoy, Michael and János Lukács, *The Radiant Past: Ideology and Reality in Hungary's Road to Capitalism*. Chicago, IL: University of Chicago Press, 1992.

Csanádi, Mária, 'The Diary of Decline: A Case-study of the Disintegration of the Party in One District in Hungary'. *Soviet Studies* **43** (1991): 1085–99.

Demszky, Gábor (ed.), *Szamizdat '81–89: Válogatás a Hírmondó című folyóiratból* [Samizdat 1981–89: Selections from the periodical *Hírmondó*]. Budapest: AB, 1990.

Dus, Ágnes (ed.), *A Pártélet Kisszótára* [A mini-dictionary of party life]. Budapest: Kossuth, 1984.

El nem égetett dokumentok [Unburned documents]. Budapest: Szabad Tér Kiadó, 1990.

Erényi, Tibor and Sándor Rákosi (eds), *Legyőzhetetlen erő: a magyar kommunista mozgalom szervezeti fejlődésének 50 éve* [Undefeatable strength: fifty years in the development of the Hungarian communist movement]. Budapest: Kossuth, 1974.

Faragó, Béla, 'Mi történik Magyarországon? [What is happening in Hungary?]'. *Századvég* **1–2** (1989): 5–17.

Farkasfalvi, József (ed.), *Politikai kalauz 1991* [Political guidebook 1991]. Budapest: Mediant, 1991.

Fehér, Ferenc, 'Kádárism as applied Khrushchevism', in Robert F. Miller and Ferenc Fehér (eds), *Khrushchev and the Communist World*. London: Croon Helm, 1984: 221–9.

Fellegi, Tamás L., 'Regime Transformation and the Mid-Level Bureaucratic Forces in Hungary', in Volten, 1992: 119–50.

Földes, György, 'Többpártrendszer (1956–1957) [Multiparty Democracy, 1956–57]'. *Társadalmi Szemle* **XLIV** (1989): 66–71.

Gazsó, Ferenc, 'Cadre Bureaucracy and the Intelligentsia'. *Journal of Communist Studies* **8** (September 1992): 76–90.

Gergely, András A., *A pártállam varázstalanítása* [The disenchantment of the party-state]. Budapest: TTI, 1992.

Gombár, Csaba, 'A helyi hatalomról [On local power]', in *Magyar Politikatudományi Társaság Évkönyv 1984: Ideológia és demokrácia* [Hungarian Political Science Association Yearbook 1984: Ideology and democracy]. Budapest: Magyar Politikatudományi Társaság, 1984): 191–4.

Grothusen, Klaus-Detlev (ed.), *Hungary*. Handbook on South Eastern Europe, vol. V. Göttingen: Vanderhoeck & Ruprecht, 1987.

Gubcsi, Lajos, *4 nap, amely megrengette az országot* [Four days that shook the nation]. Eger: Agria, 1989.

Gyurkó, László, 'A magyar szocializmus válsága [The crisis of Hungarian socialism]'. *Valóság*, no. 3 (March 1988): 12–25.

Hankiss, Elemér, *East European Alternatives*. Oxford: Clarendon, 1990.

Haraszti, Miklós, *The Velvet Prison*. New York: Basic Books, 1987.

Heller, Ágnes, Ferenc Fehér, András Bozóki and Tamás Fricz, *Polgárosodás, civil társadalom és demokrácia* [*Embourgeoisement*, civil society and democracy]. Budapest: MTA Politikai Tudományok Intézete, 1992.

Hibbing, John R. and Samuel Patterson, 'A Democratic Legislature in the Making: The Historic Hungarian Elections of 1990'. *Comparative Political Studies* **24** (January 1992): 430–54.

Hoensch, Jörg K., *A History of Modern Hungary*. London: Longman, 1988.

Horváth, Agnes and Árpád Szakolczai, *The Dissolution of Communist Power: The Case of Hungary*. London: Routledge, 1992.

Huszár, Tibor (ed.), *A magyar értelmiség a '80-as években* [The Hungarian intelligentsia in the 1980s]. Budapest: Kossuth, 1986.

——, *Mit ér a szellem, ha …* [What is the value of the mind, if …]. Budapest: Szabad Tér Kiadó, 1990.

Kemény, István, 'The Unregistered Economy in Hungary'. *Soviet Studies* **XXXIV** (July 1982): 349–66.

——, 'Programok és ellenmondások [Programmes and contradictions]'. *Magyar Füzetek*, nos 19–20 (1988): 53–77.

——, *Szociológiai írások* [Sociological writings]. Szeged: Replika Könyvek, 1992.

Kende, Péter, 'A szocialista államrend válsága Magyarországon [The crisis of the socialist state in Hungary]'. *Magyar Füzetek* (Paris), nos 19–20 (1988): 5–29.

Kerekes, György and Zsuzsa Varsádi (eds), *Reformkörök és reformalapszervezetek budapesti tanácskozása* [Reform circles and reform cells Budapest conference]. Budapest: Kossuth, n.d. [1989].

Kéri, László, *Politikai folyamatok szocializációs metszetben* [Political processes in segmented socialization]. Budapest: TTI, 1989.

——, *Between Two Systems: Seven Studies on the Hungarian Political Changes*. Budapest: Institute for Political Science, Hungarian Academy of Sciences, 1992.

Kiállni a politikáért, tenni az orszagért! Grósz Károly beszéde a Budapesti pártaktíván, 1988. November 29. [Fight for the political, act for the nation! Károly Grosz's speech to Budapest party activists, 29 November 1988]. Budapest: Kossuth, 1988.

Kimmel, Emil, *Végjáték a fehér házban* [Endgame in the white house]. n.p.: Tibor Drucker, 1990.

—— (ed.), *Kongresszus '89: rövidett, szerkesztett jegyzőkönyv az 1989 október 6–9 között tartott kongresszus anyagából* [Congress '89: abbreviated, edited transcripts of the material of the 6–9 October 1989 congress]. Budapest: Kossuth, 1990.

Kis, János, 'Az 1956–57-es restauráció [The 1956–57 restoration]'. *Medvetánc*, nos 2–3 (1988): 229–77.

Kolosi, Tamás, 'Jegyzetlapok 1989 nyarán [Notes in the summer of 1989]'. *Valóság*, no. 10 (October 1989): 1–9.

—— and Ágnes Bokor, 'A párttagság és a társadalmi rétegződés [Party membership and social stratification]', in *A társadalmi struktúra, az életmód és a tudat alakulása Magyarországon* [Social structure and the formation of lifestyle and consciousness in Hungary]. Budapest: TTI, 1985: 77–111.

Kolosi, Tamás and Edward Lipinski, *Equality and Inequality Under Socialism*. Beverly Hills, CA: Sage, 1983.

Körösényi, András, 'Vázlat a magyar értelmiség szellemi–politikai tagoltságáról [Outline of the intellectual–political articulation of the Hungarian intelligentsia]'. *Magyar Politikatudományi Társaság Évkönyv 1987: Válság és reform* [Hungarian Political Science Association Yearbook 1987: Crisis and reform]. Budapest: MPT, 1987, 43–58.

Kovács, Mária M. and Antal Örkény, *Káderek* [Cadres]. Budapest: ELTE Szociológiai és Szociálpolitikai Intézet és Továbbképző Központ, 1991.

Kovrig, Bennett, *Communism in Hungary: From Kun to Kádár*. Stanford, CA: Hoover Institution Press, 1979.

——, 'Hungary: The Deceptive Hybrid', *East European Politics and Societies* **1** (Winter 1987): 113–34.

Kurtán, Sándor, Péter Sándor and László Vass (eds), *Magyarország Politikai Évkönyve 1988* [Political Yearbook of Hungary 1988]. Budapest: Reform, 1989.

——, *Magyarország politikai évkönyve 1990* Budapest: AULA-OMIKK, 1990.

——, *Magyarország politikai évkönyve 1991*. Budapest: Ökonómia Alapítvány-Economix Rt, 1991.

——, *Magyarország politikai évkönyve 1992*. Budapest: Demokrácia Kutatások Magyar Központja Alapítvány-Economix Rt, 1992.

——, *Magyarország politikai évkönyve 1993* Budapest: Demokrácia Kutatások Magyar Központja Alapítvány-Economix Rt, 1993.

Lakitelek 1987: a magyarság esélyei [Lakitelek 1987: The chances of Hungariandom]. Budapest: Püski Kiadó and Antológia Kiadó, 1991.

Lel-Tár: Új társadalmi szervezetek katalógusa I [Inventory: Catalogue of new social organizations], vol I. Budapest: Pszichoteam, 1988.

Lendvai, Paul, *Hungary: The Art of Survival*. London: I.B. Tauris, 1988.

Lengyel, László, 'Reformdiktatúra vagy bürokratikus authoritarianizmus [Reform dictatorship or bureaucratic authoritarianism]'. *Valóság*, no. 5 (May 1989): 61–7.

——, 'Ezerkilencszáznyolcvannyolc [Nineteen hundred and eighty eight]', in Kurtán, Sándor and Vass, 1989: 81–9.

——, *Végkifejlet* [Final denouement]. Budapest: Közgazdasági és Jogi Könyvkiadó, 1989.

——, *Micsoda év!* [What a year!]. Budapest: Szépirodalmi Könyvkiadó, 1991.

Litván, György (ed.), *The Hungarian Revolution of 1956: Reform, Revolt and Repression, 1953–1956*. London: Longman, 1996.

Lomax, Bill, *Hungary 1956*. London: Allen & Busby, 1976.

McDonald, Jason, 'Transition to Utopia: A Reinterpretation of Economic Ideas and Politics in Hungary, 1984–1990'. *East European Politics and Societies* **7** (Spring 1993): 203–39.

Molnár, Miklós, *From Béla Kun to János Kádár: Seventy Years of Hungarian Communism*. New York: Berg and St. Martin's Press, 1990.

Németh, József, *Értelmiség és konszolidáció, 1956–1962* [Intelligentsia and consolidation, 1956–62]. Budapest: Kossuth, 1988.

Nyírő, András (ed.), *Segédkönyv a politikai bizottság tanulmányozásához* [Resource guide to the study of the Politburo]. Budapest: Interart, n.d.

O'Neil, Patrick H., 'Revolution from Within: The Hungarian Socialist Workers' Party "Reform Circles" and the Transition from Socialism'. PhD dissertation, Indiana University, 1994.

——, 'Revolution from Within: Institutional Analysis, Transitions from Authoritarianism, and the Case of Hungary'. *World Politics* **48** (July 1996): 579–603.

——, 'Hungary: Political Transition and Executive Conflict: The Balance or Fragmentation of Power?', in Ray Taras (ed.), *Post-*

Communist Presidents. Cambridge: Cambridge University Press, 1997: 195–224.

Örkény, Antal, 'Social Mobility and the New Elite in Hungary', in Rudolph Andorka and Miklós Hadas (eds), *Social Structure, Stratification, and Mobility in Central and Eastern Europe* (Papers presented at the Inter-University Center of Postgraduate Studies, Dubrovnik, Yugoslavia, 14–17 April 1989). Budapest: Budapest University of Economic Sciences, n.d., 255–68.

Ormos, Mária, 'A konszolidáció problémiai (1956–57) [The Problems of Consolidation, 1956–57]'. *Társadalmi Szemle* **XLIV** (1989): 48–65.

Pokol, Béla, 'Alternatív utak a politikai rendszer reformjára [Alternative roads to the reform of the political system]'. *Valóság*, no. 12 (December 1986): 32–45.

Pozsgay, Imre, *Októberi kérdések* [October questions]. n.p.: Eötvös Kiadó and Püski Kiadó, 1988.

——, *Egy év után, választás előtt* [After a year, before elections]. Budapest: Püski, 1990.

——, *1989: Politikus-pálya a pártállamban és a rendszerváltásban* [1989: A politician's track within the party-state and the transition]. Budapest: Püski, 1993.

Racz, Barnabas, 'The Socialist-left Opposition in Post-Communist Hungary'. *Europe–Asia Studies* **45** (1993): 647–70.

Ratkai, Árpád, 'Az állampárt utolsó évei Csongrádban [The last years of the party-state in Csongrád]'. Unpublished paper, n.d.

Richter, Anna, *Ellenzéki Kerekasztal* [Opposition Roundtable]. Budapest: Ötlet, 1990.

Robinson, William F., *The Pattern of Reform in Hungary*. New York: Praeger, 1973.

Róna-Tas, Ákos, 'The Second Economy in Hungary: The Social Origins of the End of State Socialism'. PhD dissertation, University of Michigan, 1990.

Schlett, István, 'Közelítések a politikai rendszer reformjához [Approaches to the reform of the political system]'. *Társadalmi Szemle* **XLII** (1987): 41–53.

Schöpflin, George, 'Opposition and Para-Opposition: Critical Currents in Hungary, 1968–78', in Rudolf L. Tőkés (ed.), *Opposition in*

Eastern Europe. Baltimore, MD: Johns Hopkins University Press, 1979: 142-86.

——, Rudolf L.Tőkés and Iván Völgyes, 'Leadership Change and Crisis in Hungary'. *Problems of Communism* **37** (September-October 1988): 23-46.

Shawcross, William, *Crime and Compromise: Janos Kadar and the Politics of Hungary Since Revolution*. New York: Dutton, 1974.

Statisztikai adatok a káderállományról [Statistical data on cadre positions]. Budapest: MSZMP KB Párt- és Tömegszervezetek Osztálya, 1983.

Stumpf, István, 'Pártosodás '89 [Party development 1989]', in Kurtán, Sándor and Vass, 1989: 386-98.

Swain, Nigel, *Hungary: The Rise and Fall of Feasible Socialism*. London: Verso, 1992.

Szabó, Gábor, 'Administrative Transition in a Post-Communist Society: The Case of Hungary'. *Public Administration* **71** (Spring/Summer 1993): 89-103.

Szakadát, István and Gábor Kelemen, 'Career Types and Mobilization Channels in the Hungarian Communist Party, 1945-1990'. *Journal of Communist Studies* **8** (September 1992): 46-61.

Szelényi, Iván, *A vidéki értelmiség helyzete* [The state of the rural intelligentsia], 7 vols. Budapest: TTI, 1971-73.

——, *Socialist Entrepreneurs*. Madison, WI: University of Wisconsin Press, 1988.

Szelényi, Szonja. 'Social Inequality and Party Membership: Patterns of Recruitment into the Hungarian Socialist Workers' Party'. *American Sociological Review* **52** (October 1987): 559-73.

Szenes, Iván, *A Kommunista Párt Újjászervezése Magyarországon 1956-57* [The Reorganization of the Communist Party in Hungary, 1956-57]. Budapest: Kossuth, 1976.

Szószék: Alternatív krónika '88 [Pulpit: Alternative chronicle 1988]. n.p.: n.d.

Telekes, Annamária and János Rechnitzner, 'A "vidék" a mozgások évében [The 'countryside' in the year of movement]'. *Valóság*, no. 9 (September 1989): 97-108.

Tőkés, Rudolf L., 'The Science of Politics in Hungary in the 1980s: People, Ideas, and Contradictions'. *Südosteuropa* **37**, (1988): 8-32.

——, *A posztkommunizmusból a demokráciába* [From post-communism to democracy]. Budapest: Konrad Adenauer Alapítvány, 1990.

——, *Hungary's Negotiated Revolution: Economic Reform, Social Change, and Political Succession, 1957–1990.* Cambridge: Cambridge University Press, 1996.

——, 'Hungary's New Political Elites: Adaptation and Change, 1989-1990', in Szoboszlai, 1991: 226-86.

Toma, Peter. *Socialist Authority: The Hungarian Experience.* New York: Praeger, 1988.

Torkos, Veronika, Zoltán Kárpáti and András Vágvölgyi, *Középvárosok a mérlegen* [Intermediate cities in the balance]. Budapest, MTA Politikai Tudományok Intézete, 1992.

'Történelmi utunk [Our historical road]', *Társadalmi Szemle* **XLIV**, special issue (February 1989): 1-79.

Új Márciusi Front 1988 [New March Front, 1988], Budapest: Múzsák, 1989.

Vass, László (ed.), *Reform-műhely* [Reform workshop]. Budapest, Kossuth, 1989.

Völgyes, Iván, *Hungary: A Nation of Contradictions.* Boulder, CO: Westview, 1982.

——, 'Leadership Drift in Hungary: Empirical Observations on a Normative Concept'. *Studies in Comparative Communism* **XXII** (Spring 1989): 23-41.

Index

Academy of Sciences 34
Ács, Zoltán 40, 90
Aczél, György 60
Adeen, Alf 20
administrative reform 50–51
Ágh, Attila 56, 57, 59, 65, 152, 163, 164, 169, 170, 175, 180, 182, 193, 195, 196
Albania 212
Alliance of Free Democrats *see* Szabad Demokraták Szövetsége (SZDSZ)
alliance policy
of MSZMP 36–41
Alliance of Young Democrats *see* Fiatal Demokraták Szövetsége (FIDESZ)
Almond, Gabriel 4, 13
Anderle, Ádám 92, 96, 101
Annus, József 90
Antal, László 59–60
Antall, József 190
anti-Semitism 47, 61, 62, 125
Arato, Andrew 41
Ash, Timothy Garton 37, 39, 51
Åslund, Anders 38
Attila József Scientific University (AJTE) 87, 90, 91, 92, 93, 96
Austria 134, 160
authoritarian transition *see* transition process
authority
forms of 42–3

Bahro, Rudolf 42, 47
Baja, Ferenc 188, 198
balance of power 132, 138–4
see also decentralization
Balázs, István 81
Baló, György 50
Balogh, Andrea 117
Baloldali alternatíva (BAL) 196–7
Baloldali tömörülés 196
Bánlaky, Pál 83
Barany, Zoltan D. 139, 149, 182, 186
Bárdi, Ida 110
Batt, Judy 38
Bayer, József 191
Baylis, Thomas A. 47
Bence, György 48, 49, 83
Benedek, István Gabor 104
Benkő, Judit 170, 171, 172, 173, 183
Benkő, Péter 36
Berecz, János 64, 98, 111, 139, 171, 178, 186
Berend, Iván 50, 65
Bermeo, Nancy 3, 209, 210
Bielasiak, Jack 45, 53, 213
Biermann, Wolfgang 47
Bierstedt, Robert 12
Bihari, László 165
Bihari, Mihály 60, 61, 63, 64, 69, 170,176, 179, 182, 183, 184, 196
Bilecz, Endre 83, 111
Biró, Ferenc 169
Biró, Zoltán 61, 63, 135, 136, 140, 190
Biszku, Béla 49
Black, Cyril E. 4
Bogár, László 56, 80
Böhm, Antal 78
Bokor, Agnes 50, 193
Bokros, Lajos 59
Bőle, István 148, 179
Borsányi, György 29
Bossányi, Katalin 110
Bozóki, András 74, 117, 123

Braham, Randolph L. 62
bribery *see* corruption
Brown, J.F. 63
Brúszel, László 119, 180
Bruszt, László xv, 51, 103, 126, 146, 191, 192, 193, 217–18
Budapest xiv, 77, 80, 118, 124, 125, 130, 133, 137, 145
Budapest congress (1989) 145, 149, 150–57, 170–85
 compromise agreements 175–8
 delegate election 161–6
 delegates 171
 discussions 172–8
 outcome 178–80
the Budapest School 41, 49
Bulgaria xii, 48, 206–7, 212
Bunce, Valerie 14, 208, 219
Burawoy, Michael 8

Ceauşescu, Nicolae 48, 68, 207
censorship 51, 88, 96, 99
 self-censorship 39
Central Statistical Office 117
centre–periphery theory 84–6
Childs, David 47
China 20, 160
Chirot, Daniel 48, 71
Christian Democratic Party *see* Kereszténydemokrata Néppárt (KDNP)
circulation of élites 55
 see also intelligentsia class
class structure 55–6, 72, 129, 191–2
clientelism 80–81
coalition governments 190, 194, 197–8, 210
coercion
 government by 33
cohort groups 74
Coleman, James S. 4
Comisso, Ellen 14
communist parties 87
 anti-communism 191
 Eurocommunism 92
 intelligentsia as members of 34, 40, 45, 50, 52–5, 66, 74–83, 88, 193, 215–16
 national communism 23
 non-party groups 61–3, 67–8, 130, 135, 171–2, 182
 rationalization of 44–6
 see also party leadership
 reformist movements
 specific parties
 state socialism
Congress '89 *see* Budapest congress (1989)
consensual government 36–7
Conservative Platform for the MSZMP *see* Platform az MSZMP-ért
constitutional continuity 211
controlled pluralism 52
convergence theory 44
Cook, Karen Schweers 14
co-optation 17–19, 20, 24, 28, 40, 201
co-optation policies
 of MSZMP 35–41, 50, 52–3, 71, 108
corruption 80–81, 88–9, 105
the countryside *see* rural areas
county party organizations 79–81, 88–92, 93–7, 161–2
 conference (1988) 96–7, 100
 reform circles in 72–92, 93–7, 98, 100–101, 104–8
Crawford, Beverly 14
Croan, Melvin 44
Csaba, Gombár 109
Csanádi, Mária 14, 81, 208
Császár, László Nagy 109
Cseri, István 153
Csizmadia, Ervin 49, 140, 141
Csongrád (county)
 reform circle in 86–9, 92, 93–7, 98, 100–101, 104, 107, 108, 113, 138, 142
Csonka, István 88
Czechoslovakia xii, 46, 61, 79, 134, 149, 160, 205–6, 211–12, 213, 216

Dahl, Robert A. 3
Debreczeni, József 195
decentralization
 of party authority 106, 115–16, 131–2
 see also balance of power
decision-making 78

delegate election
for party congresses 161-6, 168
democratic transition *see* transition process
democratization *see* modernization process
demonstrations and mass meetings 68, 69, 86, 91
depoliticization *see* alliance policy
Devcsics, Miklós 161-2
DiMaggio, Paul J. 12
DiPalma, Giuseppe 3, 6
dissidents xiii, 59, 62, 84-5, 107
see also intelligentsia class
opposition groups
Djilas, Milovan 22
Dolecskó, Kornélia 133
domestic institutionalization 22-4, 46-52, 74-5, 204
Domokos, László 90
dualism *see* institutional dualism
Dus, Ágnes 17, 95

East Germany xii, 32, 47, 160, 205-6, 211-12
Eastern Europe
electoral systems 192, 205
foreign debts 56
intelligentsia class 42-9
institutionalization in 205-7
reformist movements 62-3, 84-6
Soviet Union and 63, 205-7
state socialism in 22-4, 41, 77, 79
transition process 201-19
see also individual countries
economic conditions 36-7, 47, 55-7, 68, 87, 116, 206
economic forces
emborgeoisement hypothesis 8, 105
in transition process 5, 8, 55-6, 66, 214
reform movement and 55-6, 66
economic reforms 37-8, 50, 67, 129
New Economic Mechanism 38, 49, 50, 56-7
economic structures
development of 4
see also institutional structure
educational standards 39-40, 53-4, 58, 66, 105, 164
educational institutions 66, 87, 90-92, 94
see also students and young people
electoral reform 213-14
electoral systems xv, 66, 67, 89, 103, 121, 123, 129, 140, 158, 159, 210-11
in Eastern Europe 192, 205
local elections 146-51, 166
national elections (1990) 189-94
numbers voting 192
parliamentary elections (1994) 198
presidential elections 184, 186, 189-90
élites *see* intelligentsia class
political élites
Ellenzéki Kerekasztal (EKA) 123, 125-6, 132-3, 134, 158
Elster, Jon 211, 212
embourgeoisement hypothesis 8, 105
environmental factors
in institutional theory xvi, xvii-xviii, 16-17, 18-19, 21, 22-3, 36
Eörsi, István 51, 195
Erdei, Ferenc 78
Erényi, Tibor 35
Eurocommunism 92
see also communist parties
Evans, Peter 12-13
external institutionalization 19-24
extrication
transition by 212-13

fascism 47
factionalism 85, 92, 95, 97, 104
platform freedom 104, 106, 111, 112, 119, 120, 128, 130, 152, 176
see also reformist movements
Faragó, Béla 99, 103
Farkas, János 193
Farkásfalvi, József 197
Fehér, Ferenc 33, 36, 49
Fejti, György 132-3, 147-8, 165
Fellegi, Tamás L. 8
Ferenc Münnich Society 123

Fiatal Demokraták Szövetsége (FIDESZ) 62, 67, 94, 98, 103, 140, 141-2, 158, 189, 191, 193, 197
Financial Research Institute *see* Pénzügykutatási Intézet
Fleron, Frederic J. 45, 53
Földes, György 32
force
  government by 31, 32, 33, 87, 96-7, 139
Fordulat és reform (Turnabout and Reform) (Pénzügykutatási Intézet) 59, 63
foreign debts 56
Fricz, Tamás 196
Friedheim, Daniel V. 206
Független Kisgazda-, Földmunkás-és Polgári Párt (FGKP) 192-3, 194
Független Szociáldemokrata Párt 188

Gábor, László 127
Gamson, William 83
Gazsó, Ferenc 53-4, 66, 78, 135
Géczi, József 73, 90, 93, 101, 110, 112-13, 119, 127-8, 179, 184, 188, 195, 196, 198
Geddes, Barbara 210
Geréb, Sándor 34
Gergely, András A. 80, 105
Gerő, Ernő 29-30
Giddens, Anthony 44
Gierek, Edward 47-8
Gombár, Csaba 40, 61, 78
Gönci, János 177
Goór, Imre 180
Gorbachev, Mikhail 38, 57, 58, 62-3, 64, 66
Gosztonyi, Peter 64
Gottman, Jean 84
Gouldner, Alvin 19, 21, 42, 43, 58-9
government
  by coalition 190, 194, 197-8, 210
  by coercion 33
  by consent 36-7
  by force 31, 32, 33, 87, 96-7, 139
  see also state socialism
Gráner, Gyula 119, 146-7, 185
Grósz, Károly xii, xiv, 57-8, 63-6, 68-70, 75-6, 80, 92, 95-103, 106, 108-23, 129, 133-4, 142-3, 159, 160-62, 167, 174-5, 178, 186
Group of 25 91-2, 96, 100-101
  see also reform circles
Gubcsi, Lajos 170, 172, 177
Gunther, Richard 3
Gyenes, Antal 139
Győrffy, István 166, 179, 180, 181, 182
Győri, Imre 88
Gyurkó, László 57

Haggard, Stephan 3
Hahn, Werner 85
Hajdu, Pal 34
Halász, Miklós 88-9
Hálozet 62
Hankiss, Elemér xiii, 36-7, 39, 56, 69, 81
Hanson, Stephen 218
Haraszti, Miklos 37, 51
Harz, Wanda 81
Havemann, Robert 42, 47
Hazafias Népfront (HNF) 60, 61, 101, 117
Heberle, Rudolph 74
Hegedüs, András 39, 49
Hegedüs, István 138
Held, David 3
Heller, Ágnes 49, 52
Heper, Metin 7
Hesse, Joachin Jens 215, 216
Hibbing, John R. 192, 213
Higley, John 3
Hirschman, Albert O. 82, 111
Hodges, Donald C. 43
Hoensch, Jörg K. 39, 349, 87
Holmes, Leslie 47
horizontal organizations 85, 91, 93-5, 106, 108, 110, 115
Horn, Gyula 144, 160, 167, 172, 182-3, 184, 195, 197
Horthy, Miklós 87
Horváth, Ágnes 81
Horváth, István 144
Horváth, Jenő 170
Horváth, József K. 98, 110
Hovanyecz, László 81

human rights xiv
Hungarian Democratic Forum *see* Magyar Demokrata Fórum (MDF)
Hungarian nation (magyarság) concept 61, 83
Hungarian Public Opinion Research Institute 191
Hungarian revolution (1956) 27, 30–31, 73, 99–100, 127, 133, 185
Hungarian Social Democratic Party *see* Magyarországi Szociáldemokrata Párt (MSZDP)
Hungarian Socialist Party *see* Magyar Szocialista Párt (MSZP)
Hungarian Socialist Workers' Party *see* Magyar Szocialista Munkáspárt (MSZMP)
Hungarian Workers' Party *see* Magyar Dolgozók Pártja (MDP)
Huntington, Samuel P. 3, 5
Huszár, Tibor 34, 41, 78, 83

ideology *see* political ideology
Ifjúságért Platform 171, 172, 174, 176, 182
Ikenberry, John C. 13
Iklódi, László 188
inclusion process 44
Independent Smallholders' Party *see* Független Kisgazda-, Földmunkás- es Polgári Párt (FGKP)
Independent Social Democratic Party *see* Független Szociáldemokrata Párt
industrial development 87, 105
inflexibility
  of institutions 12–13, 18–19
information provision and transmission 38–9, 83, 90, 100, 135
  see also journalism and publishing
institutional continuity 214–16
institutional development 72–7, 202–3
institutional dualism 37, 39
institutional reform xvii–xviii, 18, 22, 23–4, 60, 62, 66–8, 131
institutional structure
  characteristics of 11–12
  economic structures 4
  effects of 203
  flexibility xvii
  hierachical 43
  horizontal 85, 91, 93–5, 106, 108, 110, 115
  importance of 106
  institutional function 204
  instrumentality xvii
  means-ends relationships xvii, 18
  political 31–2
  relationships within xvii
  revolutionary institutions 43
  self-replicating 11–12
  of state socialism xvi–xviii, 13–15, 19–24, 27, 43–7, 80–81, 201–19
institutional theory xvi, 10–13
  application of 13–15, 107, 209–19
  cooptation 17–19, 20, 24, 28, 35–41, 50, 52–3, 71, 108, 201
  environmental factors xvi, xvii–xviii, 16–17, 18–19, 21, 22–3, 36
  inflexibility 12–13, 18–19
  legitimacy xvi, 17–18, 24, 31–2, 47, 51–2, 205
  new institutionalism 10, 16–19
  of post-transition period 207–9
  stability xvi, 18
  of transition process 201–19
institutionalization 12–13, 15, 18, 204, 205–7
  deinstitutionalization 205
  domestic 22–4, 46–52, 74–5, 204
  external 19–24
  political 20, 23
  reinstitutionalization 209–18
intelligentsia class xvii, xviii, 41–55, 72–3, 87
  anti-intelligentsia movements 21–2, 28–9, 33–4, 43–4, 46–51, 64
  as a blocked class 43–4, 58–9
  circulation of elites 55
  in Eastern Europe 42–9
  liberalization of 38–41
  as the New Class 41–2, 43
  as party members 34, 40, 45, 50, 52–5, 66, 74–83, 88, 193, 215–16
  political elites 6–8, 45, 75–6

in political structure 43, 53–5, 66, 75–83, 88, 215–16
populists 61–2
in rural areas xiv, 61–2, 76–86
technical 24, 41–2, 43, 47, 53, 57–8, 60, 65, 66, 67, 75–6, 116
as a threat 34, 43–4, 46, 49
see also reform circles
reformist movements
interest groups 171–2, 182
Izsák, Attila 188

János, Andrew C. 4
Jasinka, Aleksandra 81
Jassó, Mihály 111, 119, 132
Jepperson, Ronald L. 14
jews *see* antisemitism
journalism and publishing 39, 51, 59, 61, 64, 88–90, 93, 97, 99, 101, 104, 107, 109, 117, 148, 150
censorship 51, 88, 96, 99
samizdat 59, 61, 90
self-censorship 39
Jowitt, Ken 14, 15, 44

Kádár, János xii, 28, 30, 31–7, 40–41, 49, 50, 58, 62–3, 64, 66, 72, 73, 75–6, 81–2, 128
Kaminski, Bartolmiej 205
Kamm, Henry 123
Karasimeonov, Georgi 207
Karl, Terry Lynn 15, 203, 208–9, 217, 219
Kárpáti, Zoltán 105
Kaufman, Robert 3
Kecskemét meeting (1989) 109–14, 115, 121, 125, 168–9
Kékesi, Katalin 116, 163–4, 170
Keleman, Péter 190
Kelemen, Gébor 80
Kemény, István 55, 59
Kende, János 29
Kende, Péter 57
Kenedi, János 140, 141
Kennedy, Michael D. 48
Kerekes, György 151, 152, 154, 155, 156, 170, 171, 172, 173, 183
Kerényi, György 73, 105, 119, 128, 180
Kereszténydemokrata Néppárt (KDNP) 193, 194
Kéri, László 41, 57, 64, 72–3, 74, 170, 179, 182, 184
Keserű, Imre 96, 113, 179, 188
Kesselman, M. 13
Khrushchev, Nikita 29, 31, 33, 34, 36
Kimmel, Emil 100, 111, 143, 144, 170, 173, 174, 175, 181, 183, 184
Király, Zoltán 63, 64, 89–90
Kis, János 32, 35, 48, 49, 59, 83
Kiss, István 146–7
Kiss, József 33
Kitchelt, Herbert 208
Kloss, Andor 61, 165
Kolakowski, Leszek 42
Kolankiewicz, George 85
Kolosi, Tamás 39–40, 50, 58, 141, 191
Komócsin, Mihály 88, 89–90
Komócsin, Zoltán 49
Könczöl, Csaba 90
Konrád, György 8, 42, 76, 82
Körösényi, András 74, 192, 209
Kósa, Ferenc 167, 184, 195
Kőszeg, Ferenc K. 59
Kovács, Imre Attila 91
Kovács, Jenű 104, 122
Kovács, László 110
Kovács, Mária M. 28
Kováts, Flórian 138
Kovrig, Bennett 28, 29, 31, 34, 36, 37, 81
Kozák, Gyula 57
Krasner, Stephen D. 13
Krausz, Tamás 174, 195
Krisch, Henry 47
Kukorelli, István 89
Kulin, Ferenc 51
Kuroń, Jacek 42
Kurtán, Sandór 65, 67, 135, 143, 146, 186, 191
Kurucz, Péter 109

Lakitelek meeting (1987) 61–2, 63, 140
Lammers, Cornelius J. 75
Lane, David 43
Láng, Zsusza 145, 149, 151

late paternalism 51–2
Lázár, Guy 191
legal structure 123
legitimacy
 of institutions xvi, 17–18, 24, 31–2, 47, 51–2, 205
Lengyel, András György 127
Lengyel, László 37, 40, 58, 59, 60, 61, 62, 63, 64, 69, 72, 75, 86, 98, 116, 126, 160, 182, 185, 195
Lenin, Vladimir Ilyich 20, 104, 128
Lendvai, Paul 37
Levi, Margaret 14
life expectancy 56
Lijphart, Arend 14, 210–11, 212, 213
Linz, Juan J. 3–4, 9, 204, 209
Lipinski, Edward 39–40
Lipset, Seymour Martin 3, 4, 5, 84, 209, 210
Litván, György 28, 31, 32, 33, 195
living standards 36–7, 38, 55, 56, 72, 77, 87
local elections 146–51, 166
 see also electoral system
local politics 78
Lökös, Zoltán 97, 109
Lomax, Bill 28
Lovászi, József 93, 101, 110, 119, 130, 131, 132, 151–2
Lovenduski, Joni 85
Ludassy, Mária 195
Lugosi, Győző 125, 130
Lukács, György 30–31, 41
Lukács, János 8

McCarthy, John D. 107
McDonald, Jason 8–9, 40, 59, 67
McGuire, James W. 209
Magyar Demokrata Fórum (MDF) 67, 94, 98, 103, 134–5, 140–41, 146–7, 166, 190, 192–4, 197, 210
Magyar Dolgozók Pártja (MDP) 29–31
Magyar Szocialista Munkáspárt (MSZMP) 31, 35–6, 49
 alliance policy 36–41
 assessment of 201–2, 209–11, 213
 collapse of xii–xv, xviii, 57, 113–14
 cooptation policies 35–41, 50, 52–3, 71, 108
 counter-reform movements 49–52, 63–7, 68, 73–4, 78–81, 98–9, 115–57, 158–78, 210–11, 213
 county party organizations 79–81, 88–92, 93–7, 161–2
 declarations and documents 49, 158–9
 dissolution 174–8
 economic policies 38, 49, 50, 56–7
 final congress (1989) 158, 161–6
 intelligentsia class and 34, 40, 43, 45, 50, 52–5, 66, 74–83, 88, 193, 215–16
 Intelligentsia Committee 34
 internal dissent xiii–xv, xviii, 7–8, 55–70, 71–114, 115–57, 158–98
 leadership 65–6, 80–81, 88–9, 91, 96, 105, 106, 107, 111, 113, 167–8, 173, 179, 180, 182, 184, 186, 194–5, 196
 legitimacy of 51–2
 manifesto 158–9
 membership 32, 34, 40, 52, 53–5, 65–6, 72–7, 79–80, 95, 105–6, 180, 186
 organization 80, 99
 Party Conference (1988) 64–7, 91, 92
 party conferences 122–3, 133–4
 Party Congress (1985) 56–7
 party congresses 121, 129, 132, 133, 136–7, 145, 149–50, 158, 161–6
 party discipline xiv, 34
 purges 29, 35, 46, 47, 49, 52, 63, 90, 107, 108, 216
 reform conference/workshop 68–9, 92, 98, 108–13, 115
 Reformszövetség and 179–85, 187–9, 195–6
 in rural areas 76–86
 split in 98–103
 see also Magyar Szocialista Párt (MSZP)
  Platform az MSZMP-ért
  reform circles
Magyar Szocialista Párt (MSZP)
 as compromise party 178–80, 181

congresses 178–85, 195–6
consolidation of 196–8
executive elections 181–5
foundation xiv–xv, 174, 178
internal dissent 194–8
leadership 167, 179, 180, 182, 184, 186, 194–5, 196
manifesto 158–9, 177–8
membership 186–7, 193, 194
in national elections (1990) 189–94
obstacles faced by 185–7, 190–94
organization 186–7, 191–2
in parliamentary elections (1994) 198
public opinion of 185–6, 197–8
Reformszovetseg and 179–85, 187–9, 195–6
statutes 179
SZDSZ and 198
Magyarországi Szociáldemokrata Párt (MSZDP) 126, 188
Mandik, Béla 185
Mannheim, Karl 16
Mao Zedong (Tse-Tung) 20, 41
March, James G. 11, 13
Marer, Paul 38, 216
the market economy 8, 38, 55–6, 58, 67, 113, 129, 131, 216, 217
see also modernization process
Markus, György 49
Markus, Mária 49
martial law 31, 48, 205
Marx, Karl xviii, 16, 90, 128
neo-Marxism 41, 45, 73–4, 75, 139
Marxist Unity Platform *see* Marxista Egység Platform
Marxista Egység Platform 139
Matolcsy, György 59–60
the media 39, 51, 101, 104
see also journalism and publishing
Mélykuti, Attila 116, 127, 130
Mester, Ákos 116, 175
Mészáros, Balázs 169
Meuschel, Sigrid 206
Meyer, John W. 21, 84
Michels, Robert 16, 43
military issues 149, 160, 175
domestic security 98, 156
state socialism and xi
Workers' Guard 33, 68, 98–9, 107, 122–3, 149, 156, 175, 180, 185, 189–90
Ministry of Culture 117
Ministry of the Interior 118, 191
modernization process xi, xiv, 4, 129, 131
institutional reform xvii, 18, 22, 23–4, 60, 62, 66–7, 131
market economy and 8, 38, 55–6, 58, 67, 113, 129, 131, 216, 217
parliamentary government 113, 192
reactions to xvii–xviii
see also transition process
Modzelewski, Karol 42
Moe, Terry M. 13–14
Molnár, Miklós 28
Molnár, Tivadar 110
Monor meeting (1985) 61
Mónus, Imre 61
Mosca, Gaetano 16
Movement for a Democratic Hungary *see* Mozgalom a Demokratikus Magyarországért
Mozgalom a Demokratikus Magyarországért 135–6, 138, 169
multiparty system *see* political pluralism

Nádor, István 87
Nagy, Imre 29, 30, 31, 32, 33, 35, 68, 99–100, 132, 133, 134, 141, 142
Nagy, Mihály 153
Nagykanizsa conference (1989) 188–9
Narojek, Winicjusz 81
national communism 23
National Coordinating Council *see* Országos Koodinációs Tanács (OKT)
National Democratic Federation 194
national elections (1990) 189–94
see also electoral systems
nationalism 206
nationalization 28
nation-building 44
Nee, Victor 8, 14, 15
Nelson, Daniel N. 207
Németh, József 33–4, 102

Németh, Miklós 69, 116, 118, 134, 141, 142–3, 154–5, 167, 172, 181, 182–3, 184, 193, 194–5
neo-Marxism 41, 45, 73–4, 75, 139
neo-Stalinism 64
Népi Demokratikus Platform 139, 171, 174, 175, 176, 179, 182, 183, 184, 187, 195, 196–7
Network of Independent Initiatives *see* Hálozat
New Economic Mechanism (NEM) 38, 49, 50, 56–7
new institutionalism 10, 16–19
  see also institutional theory
the New Left
  in Europe 41
New March Front 64
newspapers *see* journalism and publishing
nomenklatura system 28, 50–51, 53–4, 79, 123, 164–5, 193
Nyers, Rezső 37–8, 50–51, 63–4, 66, 69, 76, 99, 101–2, 109–10, 112, 18, 127, 131, 135, 142–5, 154–6, 167–8, 174, 177–8, 181–3, 186, 195
Nyírő, András 49, 50, 54, 80, 88

O'Donnell, Guillermo 3, 6
Odorics, Ferenc 88
Olász, Sándor 90
Olsen, Johan P. 11, 13
Oltay, Edith 156, 158
O'Neil, Patrick H. 136, 158, 190, 197, 212
opposition groups
  dissidents xiii, 59, 62, 84–5, 107
  within ruling parties xiii–xv, xviii, 43–6, 47, 49–52
  see also reform circles
Opposition Roundtable *see* Ellenzéki Kerekasztal (EKA)
Orban, Viktor 141–2
organizational structure *see* institutional structure
Örkeny, Antal 28
Ormos, Mária 32–3
Országos Koordinácios Tanács (OKT) 156–7, 159, 165, 167, 168, 169

Összefogás az MSZMP Megújításért 139, 171, 178

Paczolay, Peter 211
Pál, László 78
Palkó, Sándor 97
paramilitary forces *see* Workers' Guard
parliamentary elections (1994) 198
  see also electoral systems
parliamentary government 113, 192
  see also modernization process
Parsons, Talcott 42–3
party bureaucracy 43–4, 45
party cells
  in the workplace 177, 180, 181, 189–90
party discipline xiv, 34
party leadership 65–6, 80–81, 88–9, 91, 96, 105, 106, 107, 111, 113, 167–8, 173, 179, 180, 182, 184, 186, 194–5, 196
party membership 32, 34, 40, 52, 53–5, 65–6, 72–7, 79–80, 95, 105–6, 180, 186
  revolt by 89–92
party property 129, 180, 185, 189–90
party unity 20–21, 108–14, 174–5, 189–94
Pataki, Judith 68, 127, 133, 142, 146, 161, 166, 186, 198
path-dependency theory 209–18
Patkós, János 170, 171, 172, 173, 183
Patriotic Peoples' Front *see* Hazafias Népfront (HNF)
patronage 81–2
Patterson, Samuel 192, 213
Pénzügykutatási Intézet 40, 59, 63
Peoples' Democratic Platform *see* Népi Demokratikus Platform
Perrow, Charles 42
Petrovszki, István 115, 120–21
Petschnig, Mária Zita 170, 179, 182, 184
platform freedom 104, 106, 111, 112, 119, 120, 128, 130, 152, 176
  see also factionalism
Platform az MSZMP-ért 171
pluralism *see* political pluralism
Pogány, Sára 143

Pogonyi, Lajos 148, 150
Pokol, Béla 59
Poland xii, 47–8, 79, 81, 85, 93, 110, 116, 135, 139, 160, 205, 212–14, 216
police forces 88, 100–101, 118
Polish United Workers' Party (PZPR) 85
political crises 180
political elites 45, 75–6
in transition process 6–8
see also intelligentsia class
Political Executive Committee (of MSZMP) *see* Politikai Intéző Bizottság (PIB)
political generations 74
political ideology 21, 41–2, 44–5, 53, 65, 191, 196
political institutionalization 20, 23
see also Magyar Szocialista Munkáspárt (MSZMP)
political institutions 31–2
political pluralism 53, 65, 66, 90, 91, 95–7, 98–9, 101, 102–3, 117, 123, 131, 152, 158
Politikai Intéző Bizottság (PIB) (of MSZMP) 144, 147–8, 151, 165
Pondy, Louis R. 75
populist intellectuals 61–2
see also intelligentsia class
Porro, Jeffrey D. 52
Powell, Walter W. 12, 22
Pozsgay, Imre xv, 49, 58, 60–64, 66, 68–9, 76, 91, 98–103, 108–18, 125–43, 154–8, 167, 169, 172, 174–5, 180–84, 190, 193–4
Pravda, Alex 63, 160
presidential elections 184, 186, 189–90
see also electoral system
press freedom *see* censorship
Pridham, Geoffrey 4
process approach
to transition process 4, 6–10, 203
proletarianization 34
Przeworski, Adam 3, 6, 212
public opinion 51, 103, 134, 135, 185–6, 191–2
publishing *see* journalism and publishing
purges 29, 35, 46, 47, 49, 52, 63, 90, 107, 108, 216
Pye, Lucian W. 6

qualifications *see* educational standards

Ráb, László 148, 188, 189
Racz, Barnabas 196, 197
Radio Budapest 100
Radio Free Europe 51–2
Radnóti, Sándor 51
Raffay, Ernő 88, 146
Rajk, László 29, 30
Rákosi, Matyas 29, 31, 38
Rakosi, Sándor 35, 73, 75
Rakovski, Marc (pseud) *see* Bence, György
Rakowski, Mieczysław 110
Ramet, Sabrina 207
rational-choice theory 13, 43–4
Rátkai, Árpád 87, 90, 91–2, 96
Rechnitzner, János xv, 86, 91
Reform Alliance *see* Reformszövetség
reform cell concept 93–5
reform circles (reformkörök)
attempts to pacify 120–23
autonomy 169–70
Budapest congress (1989) 145, 149, 150–57, 161–6, 170–85
coordination between 114, 117–57
in county parties 72–92, 93–7, 98, 100–101, 104–8
in Csongrád 86–9, 92, 93–7, 98, 100–101, 104, 107, 108, 113, 138, 142
declarations and documents 106–7, 113, 118, 121, 130–32, 155–6, 189
dissolution 187–9, 194
effectiveness 117, 123–6, 130
influence 104–8, 133
internal dissent 124–6, 137–42, 145, 151–4, 187–9
in local elections 146–51
membership 105, 107, 138
Nagykanizsa conference (1989) 188–9
national support for 164–7
objectives 106–8, 119–20, 121, 124, 127–9, 131–2, 136–7, 141, 148–9, 152–7, 168–9

OKT 156–7, 159, 165, 167, 168, 169
opposition to 95–7, 107, 115–26
organization 105, 117–18, 126, 138, 145–6, 157–8
origins 72–92, 121
at party congress (1989) 159, 161–4
reformist groups and 108–14, 118, 141
spread of 104–8, 117–18, 149–50
Szeged conference (1989) 117, 118–19, 123, 125–6, 127–32, 133, 137, 138, 141
in transition process xii–xv, xvi, xviii, 7–8, 158–78
see also intelligentsia class
opposition groups
Reformszövetség
reformist movements
counter-reform 49–52, 63–7, 68, 73–4, 79–81, 98–9, 115–57, 158–78, 210–11, 213
economic forces and 55–6, 66
reform circles and 108–14, 118, 141
in rural areas xiv, 61–2, 76–83, 86, 104–8, 115–18, 125, 145
state socialism and 43–6, 47, 49–52, 55–70, 138–42
in urban areas 49, 61–2, 125
see also intelligentsia class
Reformszövetség 168, 175, 185
alliances 176–8
autonomy 169–70
at Budapest congress (1989) 171
electoral votes 172
foundation 167
internal dissent 181–3, 184–5
membership 172
MSZP and 179–85, 187–9, 195–6
objectives 168–9, 172–3, 174, 179–80, 181
see also reform circles
refugees 160
regional politics 84–6
see also rural areas
Reisch, Alfred 62, 68, 69, 99, 100, 122, 135, 137, 139, 142, 143, 151, 197
Rejtő, Gábor 182
Rekvényi, László 118, 170
Rueschemeyer, D. 13
Révai, József 32
Révész, Mihály 119
revolutionary institutions 43
see also institutional structure
Ribánski, Robert 138–9
Rice, Eric M. 215
Richta, Radovan 42
Richter, Anna 123
Rimoczi, Károly 163–4
Ripp, Zoltán 33
Robinson, William F. 37, 38, 50
Rokkan, Stein 209, 210
Romania xii, 48, 68, 69, 71, 160, 206, 207, 212
Róna-Tás, Ákos 8
Rostow, W.W. 4
routinization
of orders 44
Rowan, Brian 21
Rupnik, Jacques 46
rural areas
opposition politics in xiv, 61–2, 76–83, 86, 104–8, 115–18, 125, 145
relations with the centre 76–86
see also reform circles
Rustow, Dankwart 9
Ruttner, György 188–9

Sajó, Péter 163
samizdat publications 59, 61, 90
see also journalism and publishing
Sándor, Péter 65, 67, 135, 143, 146, 186, 191
Schapiro, Leonard 104
Schlett, István 37, 59
Schmitter, Philippe C. 3, 6, 15, 203, 208–9, 217, 219
Schöpflin, George 41, 55, 56, 58, 62, 64
Scott, W. Richard 16, 84
security issues *see* military issues
self-censorship 39
see also censorship
Selznick, Philip 16–19, 24, 40, 58, 71
Shafir, Michael 46, 48
Shain, Yossi 3–4, 209
Shawcross, William 37, 74

Shepsle, Kenneth 14
Shils, Edward 84
Simon, János 51, 65–6, 103, 126, 146, 191, 192, 193
Simonfi, Zsusza 68
Skilling, H. Gordon 23
Skocpol, Theda 12, 13
social forces 29, 62, 66–7, 74, 84–5, 105–6
in transition process 5, 129
social mobility 73
Social Science Institute *see* Tarsadolomtudományi Intézet (TTI)
socialism *see* state socialism
Solidarity (Poland) 48, 85, 116, 135
solidarity groups 83
see also reform circles
Solidarity for the Renewal of the MSZMP *see* Összefogás az MSZMP Megújitásért
Solt, Ottilia 59
Soviet Union
Eastern Europe and 63, 116, 205–7
Hungary and 27–41, 57, 62–3, 109, 110, 160
reformist movements in 57, 58, 62–3
Spain 102
stability
of institutions xvi, 18
Stalin, Joseph 20–21, 22, 27, 29, 73, 75
de-Stalinization 27, 29, 46
neo-Stalinist politics 64
Staniszkis, Jadwiga 6
Stark, David 8, 14, 15, 217, 218
state socialism 72–7
characteristics of 202–3
collapse of xi, xvi
in Eastern Europe 22–4, 41, 77, 79
in Hungary 27–70
institutional structure of xvi–xviii, 13–15, 19–24, 27, 43–7, 80–81, 201–19
military issues and xi
reformist movements and 43–6, 47, 49–52, 55–70, 138–42
in Soviet Union 20–24
strengthening of 8
see also communist parties
intelligentsia class
transition process
statist theory 13
Stepan, Alfred 3, 4, 9, 204
structuralist approach
to transition process 4–7, 9–10, 203
students and young people 29, 47, 65, 73–4, 83, 90, 116, 174, 193
see also educational standards
Stumpf, István xv
Sulyok, Erzsébet 185
surveillance activities 88, 100–101, 191
Swain, Nigel 38, 77
Szabad Demokraták Szövetsége (SZDSZ) 62, 67, 94, 103, 140, 158, 189–91, 192–3, 197–8
Szabó, Béla 119
Szabó, Gábor 216, 217
Szabó, László 110
Szabó, Zoltán 113, 130
Szajkowski, Bogdan 48
Szakadát, István 51, 80
Szakolczai, Árpád 81
Szalia, Erzsébet 65, 215
Szalai, Júlia 37
Szalai, László 161–2
Szántó, Miklós 152
Szeged conference (1989) 117, 118–19, 123, 125–6, 127–32, 133, 137, 138, 141
see also Csongrad (county)
Székely, Sándor 92
Szelényi, Iván 8, 39, 40, 41, 42, 46, 49, 59, 76, 77, 82, 141, 191
Szelényi, Szonja 50, 54, 191
Szenes, Iván 35
Szépesi, Ágnes 163
Szigeti, Péter 139, 187
Szoboszlai, György 78, 192
Szoboszlai, Zsolt 82–3, 96, 138
Szücs, Attila 125
Szűrös, Mátyás 144, 167, 172, 193

Tabajdi, Csaba 142
Takacs, Imre 107
Tamás, Ervin 188

Tamás, Gáspár Miklós 51
Tanács, István 88, 92, 127, 128, 129, 146, 188
Tarrow, Sidney 84
Társadolomtudományi Intézet (TTI) 40, 42, 56–7, 59, 78
TDDSZ 94
technical intelligentsia 24, 41–2, 43, 47, 53, 57–8, 60, 65, 66, 67, 75–6, 116
see also intelligentsia class
Telekes, Annamária xv, 86, 91
Terényi, Éva 115, 127, 128, 129, 163–4
Thoma, László 56
Tivadar, Bernat 105
Tőkés, Rudolf L. xiii, 8, 28, 36, 49, 54–5, 56, 58, 59, 64, 109, 170, 176, 178, 182, 191, 215, 216
Toma, Peter 37, 39, 77, 89
Toonen, Theo A.J. 215, 216
Torkos, Veronika 105
transition process xi–xv, 3–10, 14, 129, 191
economic forces in 5, 8, 55–6, 66, 214
by extrication 211–13
institutional theory of 201–19
integration issues 9–10
mode of transition 5, 201–19
models of 203
post transition consolidation 207–9, 216–19
political elites and 6–8
process argument 4, 6–10, 203
reform circles in xii–xv, xvi, xviii, 7–8, 158–78
social forces in 5, 129
structuralist argument on 4–7, 9–10, 203
see also modernization process
travel and tourism 39, 40
Troxel, Luan 207

Újszász, Ilona 93
unemployment 129
Union of Writers 34
unions 94, 118
urban areas 28
opposition politics in 49, 61–2, 125

Vágvölgyi, András 105
Vajda, Ágnes 193
Vajda, Mihály 49
Valkó, Béla 149
Varga, György T. 51
Varga, Zoltán 83
Vári, László 148, 188
Varjú, Frigyes 160
Varsádi, Zsuzsa 151, 152, 154, 155, 156
Vass, Csaba 186
Vass, László 65, 67, 112, 125, 130, 135, 143, 146, 160, 186, 191, 196
Vastagh, Pál 96, 97, 101, 111, 127, 129, 148, 184
Verdery, Katherine 206
Vitányi, Iván 51, 183, 195
Vitray, Tamás 135
Vödrös, Attila 135
Völgyes, Iván 37, 55, 56, 57, 58, 64, 65, 73
Vörös, László 90

Weber, Max 20, 42–4
the West
contacts with 39, 40, 76
influence of 73–4
Western, Bruce 141, 191
de Weydenthal, Jan B. 47
Whitehead, Laurence 3
Wiarda, Howard J. 4
Wightman, Gordon 46
Woodall, Jean 85, 205
Workers' Councils 32
the Workers' Guard 33, 68, 98–9, 107, 122–3, 149, 156, 175, 180, 185, 189–90
the working class 129

Yakovlev, Alexander 110
young people *see* students and young people
youth organizations 62
Youth Platform *see* Ifjúságért Platform
Yugoslavia 29, 32, 33, 39

Zald, Mayer N. 107
Zucker, Lynne G. 11

DUE	RETURNED	DUE	RETURNED
1.		13.	
2.		14.	
3.		15.	
4.		16.	
5.		17.	
6.		18.	
7.		19.	
8.		20.	
9.		21.	
10.		22.	
11.		23.	
12.		24.